THE VAMPIRE STATE

THE

VAMPIRE

STATE

And Other Myths and Fallacies about the U.S. Economy

FRED L. BLOCK

THE NEW PRESS — NEW YORK

© 1996 BY FRED L. BLOCK

ALL RIGHTS RESERVED. NO PART OF THIS BOOK MAY BE REPRODUCED IN ANY FORM
WITHOUT WRITTEN PERMISSION FROM THE PUBLISHER.

LIBRARY OF CONGRESS CATALOGING-IN-PUBLICATION DATA

Block, Fred L. The vampire state: and other myths and fallacies
about the U.S. economy / Fred Block.
    p.   cm. Includes index.
ISBN 1-56584-193-X (hc)
1. United States — Economic conditions — 1981- . 2. Free
enterprise — United States. 3. Budget — United States.
4. Competition — United States. I. Title.
HC106.8.B6   1996
303.973 — dc2096-4400 CIP

PUBLISHED IN THE UNITED STATES BY THE NEW PRESS, NEW YORK
DISTRIBUTED BY W. W. NORTON & COMPANY, INC., NEW YORK

Established in 1990 as a major alternative to the large, commercial
publishing houses, The New Press is a full-scale nonprofit American book
publisher outside of the university presses. The Press is operated editorially
in the public interest, rather than for private gain; it is committed
to publishing in innovative ways works of educational, cultural, and
community value that, despite their intellectual merits, might not normally
be commercially viable. The New Press's editorial offices are located
at the City University of New York.

BOOK DESIGN BY HALL SMYTH AND GORDON WHITESIDE OF BAD
PRINTED IN THE UNITED STATES OF AMERICA

9 8 7 6 5 4 3 2 1

—·— Contents

—— Acknowledgments

While writing this book, I have drawn intellectual and emotional sustenance from family, friends, and colleagues. Without their ideas, support, and help, this book would not exist. Perhaps writers are also vampires — extracting vital materials from others for their own questionable purposes. But vampires rarely write thank you notes.

My greatest debt is to the colleagues and friends who read parts or all of the various drafts of this manuscript. Peter Evans, Robert Heilbroner, Larry Hirschhorn, Carole Joffe, Karl Klare, Magali Sarfatti Larson, Jeff Manza, Frances Fox Piven, John Roemer, André Schiffrin, and Margaret Somers saved me from many errors of logic, fact, and style and enriched the book with their insights. There are also many other colleagues — too numerous to mention — who have loaned me valuable ideas that appear in these pages.

Paul Davis and Karl Beitel made numerous important contributions to this project while working for me as research assistants. Michael Winter helped me in tracking down several key references. I am also grateful to the Davis Humanities Institute for both financial and intellectual support and to the Davis Research Foundation for research funds. Since I was serving as sociology department chair while writing this book, I have incurred a huge debt to Tracy Ligtenberg, the department's administrator. The book would not have been finished were it not for her managerial skills. I am also deeply grateful to André Schiffrin and the staff of The New Press for their patience and support while the book was evolving.

I have thanked Carole Joffe in similar venues before, and the sentiment remains the same. I am still hard pressed to convey the extent of my gratitude and appreciation. My daughters,

Miriam and Judith, have enriched my life with their love, wit, and intelligence. I hope they can see something of themselves in these pages.

Finally, as a sociologist who is trespassing into the territory of economists, I have sought inspiration from the examples of other intellectual trespassers. Tibor Scitovsky and Albert Hirschman have not been directly involved in this project, but I am grateful to both of them for their encouragement and their insights.

Part One

THE VAMPIRE STATE

1 —·— Introduction

Practical men[sic], who believe themselves to be quite exempt from any intellectual influences, are usually the slaves of some defunct economist. Madmen in authority, who hear voices in the air, are distilling their frenzy from some academic scribbler of a few years back.

— John Maynard Keynes, 1936

In some measure, the articulation of the conventional wisdom is a religious rite. It is an act of affirmation like reading aloud from the Scriptures or going to church. The business executive listening to a luncheon address on the immutable virtues of free enterprise is already persuaded, and so are his [sic] fellow listeners, and all are secure in their convictions. Indeed, although a display of rapt attention is required, the executive may not feel it necessary to listen. But he does placate the gods by participating in the ritual.

— John Kenneth Galbraith, 1971[1]

For close to a generation, politics in the United States has been dominated by a frenzy of antistatism — systematic efforts to reduce the role of government in society fueled by an ideology that sees government as inherently wasteful and ineffective. Budget balancing, tax cutting, and deregulation have repeatedly been proposed as the solution to all of our social and economic ills.

This frenzy began in the mid-1970s as a response to an economy that was battered by both the deep recession of 1974-75 and a period of rapid price increases. It culminated in Ronald Reagan's election as president in 1980, which began a veritable orgy of tax cutting and deregulation. While the "Reagan Revolution" lost its radical edge after the first few years, the twelve Republican years from 1981 to 1993 marked a sharp break from the political assumptions that had dominated American politics since Franklin Delano Roosevelt. No longer was the federal government seen as an instrument that could solve the country's domestic problems; for twelve long years, no new

3

government initiatives were taken to rebuild decaying cities, protect the environment, revitalize industry, or attack poverty.

The election of Bill Clinton in 1992 at first seemed to mark an end to this Republican epoch, since Clinton promised bold new domestic initiatives designed to produce real change. However, Clinton quickly retreated on these promises and placed the emphasis in his first months in office on reducing the federal budget deficit rather than on funding new government programs. The one initiative that he pressed — health care reform — suffered a humiliating defeat. With the Republican congressional victory in November 1994, the attack on government spending and government regulation became even more radical than in the early Reagan years. In June 1995, both houses of Congress agreed on a plan that is supposed to balance the federal budget over seven years while also providing substantial tax cuts. Such plans will mean deep and painful cuts in a wide range of government programs. At the same time, the Republican-controlled Congress has tried to dismantle even more of the federal government's regulatory apparatus.

One indication of the power of this antistatist craze is that it has now become simple common sense to believe that the U.S. must take bold and painful action to balance the federal budget. Twenty years ago, many people saw government deficits as a legitimate tool to stimulate a weak economy, but such a view has become completely illegitimate. President Clinton's only alternative to drastic Republican budget cuts was a now-abandoned proposal to balance the budget over ten years rather than seven years. And anyone foolish enough to question the desirability and urgency of balancing the federal budget is treated like a child who has not yet learned the ABC's of living in a civilized society.

But when one steps back and looks at the U.S. in comparison to other countries, this "common sense" seems strange indeed. With the exception of Great Britain, none of the other developed market economies has experienced a comparable wave of antistatism. Moreover, in such countries as Japan, Germany, France, and Italy, the national government plays a far larger role in the economy than in the U.S.; tax rates are considerably higher, government spending is a higher percentage of total output, and regulation of the economy is more substantial. Further, in many of these countries, government deficits have been even larger than in the U.S. as a percentage of gross domestic product (GDP)[2]. Yet, the kind of antistatist frenzy that has dominated U.S. politics plays only a minor role in these countries.

Even if one looks at the U.S. alone, there is something strange going on. The Reagan-Bush years from 1981 to 1993 provide a kind of natural experiment. During this period, there were dramatic tax cuts, the civilian side of the federal government shrank, and greater reliance was placed on market forces to solve social and economic problems. Yet, there are very few Americans who believe that this experiment was a success; the broad perception is that many of our social and economic problems only worsened over those twelve years.

For antistatist theorists, the point is obvious: the Reagan-Bush experiments were simply not radical and far-reaching enough. What is needed are *far* deeper tax cuts, more drastic reductions in government spending, more dismantling of regulation, and even greater reliance on market forces. These steps will surely begin to solve all of our pressing problems. In a word, if a medium dose of antistate medicine made the patient sicker, then it is obvious that the proper prescription is a huge dose of antistate medication.

THE POWER OF IDEAS

Keynes was partially correct when he argued that politicians are often the "slaves of some defunct economist." It is true that politicians who speak eloquently of the benefits of dismantling much of the federal government draw some of their inspiration from Friedrich Hayek, the libertarian economic theorist, and other more obscure economic thinkers. Moreover, it is not a stretch to describe these thinkers as "defunct economists" because their work has been subject to withering critique from other economists and social scientists for sixty years. Among academic economists in the U.S., only a small fraction today endorse the antistatist views of the Hayekian tradition. One can hardly say that these ideas dominate political debate because of their intellectual persuasiveness.

But Keynes failed to appreciate that there is something even more important than such distant academic influences. Many of the most politically powerful ideas about the economy are inspired by a subterranean level of economic understanding that consists not of formal arguments but of images and stories. This subterranean level exists because modern economies are so complex that they can only be understood through analogies, metaphors, and stories. Donald McCloskey, an influential economic historian, has argued that while economists purport to be rigorously scientific, they cannot avoid the systematic use of metaphors and other literary devices.[3] In fact, many of our key economic concepts, such as inflation and deflation, are based on analogies with physical processes.

But even though this resort to literary devices is unavoidable, the problem is that the subterranean level can develop a life of its own. A certain economic metaphor can easily become fixed in our minds and continue to influence our thinking even if changes in the economy have long since emptied it of its original conceptual value.[4] Moreover, such metaphors are basically immune to empirical disproof; once they become established, they are extremely difficult to dislodge. And like the ideas of defunct economists, some of these images might lie dormant for as long as a generation, only to reemerge suddenly to exert extraordinary influence over political debate.

This power of the subterranean level means that many economic beliefs are not easily influenced by rational argument. The most sophisticated economist might provide a cogent argument and illustration showing that state action in the economy can be beneficial and productive, but if the underlying image that people carry in their minds is of a vampire state that is compelled to suck the blood out of the economy, the arguments will have no real effect. People will continue to believe that state action inevitably produces wasteful and harmful results.

But this focus on the subterranean level also contains a hope. The analogy is to Freud's argument about the therapeutic value of uncovering the subconscious forces that shape our behavior. If this subterranean level of economic understanding can be brought into the light of day and the ways in which it distorts and limits our understanding of the economy are exposed, we might be able to free ourselves of its hold on our imaginations. Moreover, since it is almost impossible to think about the economy nonmetaphorically, this task of exposure can be facilitated by suggesting alternative images that are more useful for making sense of contemporary economic processes. This, in short, is the goal of this book—to excavate the subterranean economic understandings that fuel the current antistatist frenzy in the U.S. and to propose alternative metaphors that could actually help us address our most pressing problems.

CLARIFICATIONS

Since extreme antistatism has been particular to the U.S. and Great Britain, it follows that these two societies share a special set of subterranean economic images. If one were to do the same kind of analysis in France, Japan, or other societies, one would expect to find a very different set of guiding metaphors and images. But where do these images come from, and how do they become embedded in popular understandings? These are important questions, but attempting to answer them would take us too far afield. The goal here is simply to bring these ideas to the surface, and the task of explaining where they came from will be left for another day. However, my intuition is that religious traditions play an extremely important role in establishing these images.[5] Great Britain and the U.S. share a common Protestant heritage, and ideas drawn from that heritage play a central role in organizing the images of our subterranean economic understandings. To be sure, there are other societies with a Protestant religious heritage that do not share Anglo-American antistatism. This suggests that it is not Protestantism alone but the particularities of the Anglo-American Protestant tradition that are relevant. But futher exploration of the links between religion and economic imagery will be left for another time.

It is also important to explain the relationship between these subterranean images and the ideas of professional economists. Economists go through an intense period of reorientation in graduate school, during which they learn to abandon many common sense views about the economy. Nevertheless, many of the subterranean images have—over the past century or two—worked their way into the manner in which professional economists think. Hence, academic economics is hardly immune to the power of these subterranean currents. So it is not uncommon for professional economists to formulate issues in ways that ultimately reinforce the power of these subterranean images.

Hence, there is a complex interaction between popular economics—the way that most people think about the economy—and academic economics. While popular economics is almost entirely shaped by these subterranean images, academic economics has some greater degree of independence. Precisely because of the discipline's intellectual rigor, professional economists are sometimes able to work themselves free of the unconscious assumptions dictated by the subterranean metaphors. Yet, academic economics is continually pulled back in the direction of popular economics because of the power of the underground currents. And it is not uncommon that the pronouncements of professional economists serve to give greater legitimacy to popular economic beliefs.

This complex relationship makes it easier to understand the process by which certain unorthodox or radical economic ideas can end up being neutralized over time. At the time that he wrote *The General Theory*, for example, Keynes thought he was making a fundamental assault on the economic common sense of the day. But almost immediately, an effort began to reabsorb Keynes' ideas into the mainstream tradition. In the famous "neo-classical synthesis," Keynes' General Theory became simply a special case of the very theory that he had sought to overturn. Like a powerful underground river, the subterranean currents draw everything back toward the mainstream of the tradition.

Yet, there is also hope here as well. In recent years, economists have become aware of the power that metaphors exert over economic thought.[6] With this newfound awareness and a systematic effort to bring these subterranean metaphors to the surface, it should be possible to reconstruct the metaphoric underpinnings of the discipline. The result could be a revitalized economics that is no longer compelled to minimize the major insights of its most gifted practitioners.

METAPHORS AND INTERESTS

Debates over economics and economic policy are inevitably intertwined with political battles over who benefits and who loses. For example, each time corporations gain certain kinds of tax relief, it means that another group of taxpayers will have to make up the difference. Or when a particular government program is cut, legislators decide which group will bear the burden of the reduced public spending. While some economists speak about optimal tax policies or optimal spending policies, the reality is that there are always winners and losers. Yet, when these battles occur, the different parties do not simply argue on the basis of self-interest, rather they argue that what benefits them will also benefit society as a whole. Hence, business interests invariably argue not only that lower corporate taxes and less regulation are good for business, but that everyone in society will benefit from greater business prosperity.

In these ongoing struggles for advantage in shaping government policies, the metaphors and other rhetorical devices analyzed here are powerful weapons. They have been used effectively by certain interest groups to define their interests as identical to the general interests of society. It is highly doubtful that without these powerful tools, those interest groups would have been so successful. Yet, of course, these special interests did not invent these metaphors; they made use of materials that were already there.[7] Similarly, many of those who employ the metaphors do not have a special-interest agenda; they genuinely believe that the metaphors help us to understand what the whole society needs to do to prosper.

In challenging the use of these particular literary devices, I am trying to show that the special interests who have been winning in the political arena for most of the last twenty years have been advancing policies that are not in the interests of the whole society. Despite all their claims, the performance of the economy has been deteriorating. But by moving beyond the Conventional Wisdom—those widely shared beliefs about the economy—it is possible to identify alternative policies that would improve the situation of those who have been losing in recent years *and* that would simultaneously make our economy work more effectively.

In short, it is easy to imagine different interest groups entering the terrain of political battle armed with competing sets of metaphors designed to show that each one's particular interest coincide with the needs of society as a whole. Citizens, however, cannot afford to accept one or another set of metaphors uncritically. We all must face the hard task of figuring out what is really in the interest of society as a whole.

A NOTE FOR THE MEGOS

The difficulty, of course, is that there are many intelligent people who say, "my eyes glaze over (MEGO) as soon as any economic topic is introduced." In part, this reaction is understandable since economic arguments—whether of the Left, the Right, or the center—are often mobilized more to intimidate than to enlighten. When one routinely experiences other people trying to badger one into agreement by using convoluted and confusing economic arguments, glazing over can be a good defense.

But just as war is too important to leave to the generals, the economy is too important to leave to the nonglazed minority. The economy sets the limit of what is possible in any particular historical period. If we want to find a cure for AIDS, protect the environment from degradation, or simply lead lives with lower levels of insecurity, there are economic constraints. Some people will always insist that we cannot afford more funds for AIDS research, for environmental protection, or for expanding social programs. Without some knowledge of economic issues, it is impossible to tell whether the "can't afforders" have a real argument or are simply justifying their own preferences with economic arguments.

In fact, this "can't afford" rhetoric has dominated and will continue to dominate U.S. domestic politics. Proposals by Congress and the president to balance the federal budget over seven years while reducing taxes would mean *drastic* cutbacks in a wide variety of government programs. Scientific and medical research, Medicare, mass transit, tuition assistance for students, aid to poor children, and a host of other programs will all suffer large cuts. The result will surely be an even further deterioration in the quality of life for millions of Americans. But in every case the argument will be that we can no longer afford these expenditures because of the absolute necessity to balance the federal budget.

All efforts to defend the current — often inadequate — quality of life in this society immediately leads one to battle a whole series of economic arguments. Hence, to glaze over is, in effect, to surrender in advance to those who are currently controlling the debate. Glazing over makes one powerless to influence the direction in which this society is headed.

But there is nothing inherent in economic debates that make them any more difficult than arguments about whether O.J. Simpson deserved to be acquitted or convicted. Economic issues can be discussed fully and carefully in standard, jargon-free English. Moreover, each of us has cultivated our own personal lie detectors that we use to identify statements that we think are flawed, stupid, or illogical. Most of the time, these detectors work pretty well to protect us from people who want to put something over on us. It takes only a little bit of practice to adjust these inbuilt lie detectors to identify fraudulent or deceptive economic arguments.

PREVIEWING THE ARGUMENT

The first part of this book is designed to arm the reader's lie detector by uncovering some of the subterranean images that dominate our economic debates. It argues that a Christian allegory and a series of biological metaphors provide a plausible structure for what is generally believed about the economy. John Kenneth Galbraith invented the useful phrase "Conventional Wisdom" to describe those widely shared beliefs about the economy.[8] Following him, I will also use this term for ideas that are common to both popular economics and much of academic economics.

The second part continues this critique of the Conventional Wisdom by reviewing the standard accounts of what is wrong with the U.S. economy. Once one strips away the subterranean images, many of the familiar arguments about the government's deficit, inadequate household saving, and the need for austerity fall apart. The third and fourth parts are a critique of what the Conventional Wisdom prescribes for the organization of finance and the international economy. In both cases, we have unnecessarily made our economic livelihoods vulnerable to irrational forces that can never deliver what they have promised. The fifth part moves beyond critique to suggest an alternative wisdom about how we should reorganize and restructure the economy to serve human purposes. It is not intended as a political pamphlet for the next election cycle, but as a vision of where we should be headed in the next millenium.

2 —·— The Subterranean Underpinnings of the Conventional Wisdom

Amazing Grace, How sweet the sound
That saved a wretch like me.
I once was lost, but now I am found
Was blind, but now I see.

—John Newton, 1779[1]

When I shut up the heavens so that there is no rain, or command the
locust to devour the land, or send pestilence among my people, if my peo-
ple who are called by my name humble themselves, and pray and seek
my face, and turn from their wicked ways, then I will hear from heaven,
and will forgive their sin and heal their land."

— 2 Chronicles 7:14

The antistatism that has dominated U.S. politics for the past generation draws its inspiration from a series of images or metaphors that often lie buried under the surface of political and economic debate. The chapters that follow examine some of these metaphors, such as the view of money as the lifeblood of the economy and the image of the "vampire state." But prior to the metaphors, there is an allegory that plays a key role in giving structure and coherence to the Conventional Wisdom and its underlying metaphors. An allegory is a metaphor that has been tied to a narrative or storyline.[2] When we say that an economy is like a balloon that can be inflated or deflated, all we have is a metaphor. But if we add the story that if the economy is inflated too much it will explode, then we have an allegory. The allegory adds an implicit assertion about cause and effect. In this case, the causal claim is that overinflated economies will suffer a disastrous crash. The most familiar allegories are those medieval morality plays in which a figure representing Good literally does battle with a figure representing Evil and usually Evil's initial advantage is linked to one or another moral failing of the forces of Good.[3]

Allegories represent a double threat to our efforts to make sense of the society around us. While metaphors are unavoidable in analyzing complex structures such as economies and societies, allegories have an even stronger tendency than metaphors to take on a life of their own. Once an allegory is established, it is common to forget the causal theory that is embedded in it. Yet, as long as we think within the allegory, we have embraced that causal theory. Allegories also dull our ability to think critically. Effective allegories, such as morality tales, work by tapping into powerful mythic and unconscious themes. Just as little children often enjoy endless repetitions of a favorite story, so, too, are adults comforted by the frequent rendition of a familiar allegory. Such often-told allegories can be extremely powerful, and they can effectively block out any alternative way of thinking about a particular reality.

Few allegories are more powerful than the central Christian story of the person who begins on the righteous path but then falls into sin and error from which he or she can only be redeemed by redoubled self-discipline and repentance. This story is the basis of the asceticism—the ethic of self-denial—that the great German sociologist Max Weber identified as central to the rise of modern capitalism.[4] The followers of Calvin believed that only by the most extreme self-discipline and self-denial could they be worthy of salvation. A very similar ethic lay at the heart of the religious revivals that swept through England and the U.S. in the early nineteenth century.[5]

But one hardly needs to be Christian to be deeply affected by the haunting words of "Amazing Grace." The idea of being spiritually lost, and then finding a path to redemption taps into universal themes. In fact, to move from the sublime to the mundane, many of us experience an analogous drama in that most material aspect of our lives — our bodies. If we eat too much rich food and fail to exercise, we enter that state of sinfulness called obesity. The only way to return to the path of righteousness is to repent and work harder at eating more wisely and exercising more diligently. Through exercising greater personal discipline, we can "find" once again our true bodies.

The Conventional Wisdom takes this familiar allegory about the individual and applies it to the national economy. The whole economy becomes like the individual who is lost and then potentially found. The allegory begins at some point in the past when the economy was still on the right path, but then — either gradually or abruptly — there was a loss of discipline and moral direction. As a result, the economy becomes lost; it is no longer on the right path. The consequences of being lost are all kinds of bad economic results — too much inflation or unemployment or too little economic growth. For the economy to be "found" — to return to the righteous road of good economic results — requires a period of renewed discipline and repentance. Only after such a period of greater discipline and belt-tightening can there be any assurance that good economic results will return.

Many popular books on the economy and many political speeches tell this story. At some time in the past — in the good old days — the economy was strong, but then people fell into temptation and prosperity disappeared. Only a renewal of discipline and collective sacrifice will bring us out of these difficulties and restore the better times that we enjoyed during the past. Ronald Reagan presented a version of this allegory during his election campaign in 1980. He described the primary sin as the abandonment of the traditional American ethic of self-reliance. The collective individual had prospered for many years through hard work and self-discipline, but at a certain point this person had become lazy and looked to government to solve problems through regulations and benefit programs. This created an opening for an expansion of state activity, which produced higher taxes, wasteful and unproductive programs, and the draining of the lifeblood from the economy. With insufficient new investment and excessive taxes, the economy was vulnerable to both slow growth and high inflation. The only solution was for the body politic to return to the path of the straight and narrow by dramatically reducing its dependence on the state. Cutting taxes and government programs would assure that the state could again be controlled, and economic prosperity would soon return through higher levels of investment in the economy.

While some people have come to recognize the Reaganite story to be a fairy tale, the failures of the Reagan administration have led not to the rejection of the allegory, but to its refinement. In one popular version, Reagan himself is added to the story as a false prophet. While he preached righteousness, he actually offered people something for nothing—lower taxes and more government spending. As a result, our wayward friend was led even further into sin and dissolution, so that even greater exertions will now be necessary to return to the path of righteousness.

This was the version of the allegory that Paul Tsongas and Ross Perot advanced in the 1992 presidential election and which has also received considerable support from the ranks of professional economists.[6] In this version, the U.S. economy was seen as functioning effectively in the 1950s and 1960s because government budgets were close to balanced and adequate household saving sustained strong levels of new investment. However, beginning sometime in the 1970s, governmental budgetary restraint diminished and, simultaneously, rates of household savings declined. The result was a diminishing pool of capital available for productive investment and this meant slower growth and the continuing danger of a revival of inflation. In a word, the federal budget deficit was proof that state spending was totally out of control, while low rates of household savings reflected a parallel lack of self-discipline in the populace. The religious fervor of those who have made this argument is hardly surprising; they are asking for nothing less than moral renewal to solve our fundamental economic problems.

It is, of course, this allegory that lies behind congressional plans to balance the U.S. budget over the next seven years. While proponents acknowledge that this process will be very painful, the point is that the pain will be redemptive. It is only through this period of pain and sacrifice that those who have been lost can again be found.

THE LIMITATIONS OF THE ALLEGORY

This allegory draws its force from centuries of preaching and sermonizing in Christian churches. It also resonates with the mundane everyday experience of struggle with an expanding waistline. Either way, the allegory works by connecting the virtue or vice of individuals with virtuous or vicious economic outcomes. If the economy has fallen on hard times, then it is clearly because millions of individuals are making bad or wrong choices, such as the choice to consume rather than to save. As Walt Kelly's Pogo said, "We have met the enemy and he is us." Instead of placing responsibility on particular institutional structures or the poor choices made by the powerful, blame is clearly directed at the mass of individuals. In this way, the allegory also resonates with well-established beliefs in American culture about how each individual is responsible for his or her own fate.

But economists have known for hundreds of years that things are not so simple. Individual actions motivated by vicious motives can have benign effects for the whole economy, and vice versa. This paradox was stated most beautifully at the beginning of the eighteenth century by Bernard de Mandeville in his *Fable of the Bees*.[7] The fable is about a hive of bees whose prosperity and military strength is rooted in the greed and vanity of the individual bees:

> *Thus every Part was full of Vice,*
> *Yet the whole Mass a Paradise;*
> *Flatter'd in Peace, and fear'd in Wars,*
> *They were th' Esteem of Foreigners,*
> *And lavish of their Wealth and Lives,*
> *The Balance of all other Hives.*
> *Such were the Blessings of that State;*
> *Their Crimes conspir'd to make them Great.*

In Mandeville's fable, when the bees reform their evil ways, the result is economic disaster followed by military defeat. The same idea was elaborated by Adam Smith when he said that, "It is not from the benevolence of the butcher, the baker, or the brewer that we expect our dinner, but from their regard to their own interest."[8]

One obvious manifestation of this gap between individual intentions and outcomes are periodic crises of agricultural overproduction. Each farmer works with the utmost discipline to bring in a bumper crop, but the resulting surfeit brings a disastrous fall in price. Virtuous action brings bad consequences, and it is precisely to protect against those consequences that societies develop agricultural policies to protect farmers. It hardly would make sense to blame such crises of overproduction on the moral failures of farmers.

But the point is more general. In a complex economy, it rarely makes sense to blame bad economic outcomes on the moral shortcomings of individuals. Factory workers in the former Soviet Union had very low rates of productivity, but few of us would blame that on the poor moral character of the Soviet people. It is more persuasive to blame the Soviet system for providing inadequate rewards for effort and insufficient punishments for lack of effort. As the old joke went, "They pretend to pay us, and we pretend to work." But the allegory about the U.S. economy skips over the entire institutional structure of the society and the specific incentives and disincentives that individuals face. It deflects attention from institutions, while focusing attention on the failings of individuals. This always leads to the same default policy recommendation—a period of belt-tightening in order to restore the economy to the path of righteousness.

THE UNDERLYING METAPHORS

But this powerful allegory does not stand on its own; it helps to organize a whole family of economic metaphors that are critical ingredients of the Conventional Wisdom. The sections that follow will explore three of these metaphors in some detail: capital as blood, the state as vampire, and the economy as an arena for natural selection. The connections between the religious allegory and these biological metaphors are subtle and complex, but the two share the idea of a natural order that has been disturbed.

On the allegorical side, the natural order was disrupted by human sin as represented in the banishment of Adam and Eve from the Garden of Eden. That disruptive sinfulness is precisely the reason why the need for moral discipline and repentance is so urgent. But each of the biological metaphors also suggests a natural order that has been breached. In a healthy economy, capital is supposed to flow through the economy's veins and arteries vigorously and in ample supply. But when government grows too large and too intrusive, this healthy flow is disrupted. The monstrous and parasitical state destroys the harmony of nature. Similarly, when economic competition is allowed to proceed freely, the discipline of the market produces a natural harmony that rewards the fittest firms and the most self-disciplined individuals. But when government interferes with those market mechanisms, there is a proliferation of dysfunctional behaviors by both firms and individuals. The biological metaphors reinforce the urgency of a moral and political reawakening that will allow the lost harmony of nature to be refound.

The obvious problem with these images is precisely that there is nothing natural about a modern complex economy. Much as we might wish that the laws of nature would regulate our economy, they do not and cannot. It requires human action and human decisions to make a modern complex economy work, but the allegory and the metaphors blind us to the choices that we have to make.

3 —·— Capital As Blood: The Macro Level

Money is the life blood of the nation.

—Jonathan Swift, 1706

"The naïve imagery of the social body which underlies the political economy of a Canard (1801) may prompt the modern reader to giggle. In the giant organism of society, merchants occupy the center of the circulatory system, where the shop and the cash desk form the two ventricles. Labor and its products are represented by the arterial system, whilst monetary circulation is associated with the venous system. Equilibrium is simply the state of the mature social body; the circulation of the blood pulses in the active rhythm of procreation..."

—Claude Menard, 1983

Capital, as we know, is the lifeblood of the economy. Without capital, workers cannot enhance their productivity and their wages stagnate. Today's double, even triple taxation of income discourages saving, reduces the pool of capital available to entrepreneurs and workers, slows productivity and wage growth.

—Representative Jon Fox, 1995[1]

Several of the core metaphors that underlie the Conventional Wisdom are linked to blood.[2] This is hardly surprising in that the imagery of blood is powerful in many cultural traditions and the blood of Christ looms large in the same religious tradition that provides the core allegory of sin and repentance. In the sacrament, the wine represents the blood of Christ, and by drinking the wine, the sinner absorbs His suffering and is purified.

In economic discourse, money capital is often described as the lifeblood of the economy.[3] The flow of this powerful and almost magical liquid makes possible a vigorous and expanding economy. Moreover, when the economy is weak, the image is often evoked of a sick economy being like a patient lying on a hospital bed. The patient's vital signs are weak, the flow of blood through his or her veins is not sufficient, and he or she requires transfusions of new blood to return to health. This is a generic diagnosis; almost any economic illness can be cured by increasing the flow of private capital.

Many of our basic institutional arrangements derive from this belief in money capital as the life-giving fluid of the economy. While it is widely acknowledged that many different groups — employees, managers, creditors, customers, suppliers, and so on — are significant stakeholders in the modern corporation, our legal rules give sovereignty over the firm to only one group — those who hold equity shares — investors who have provided capital with no promise of repayment.

But when one questions the metaphor, it is apparent that arguments can easily be made that other things are the single most potent factor in making the economy work. One obvious claimant is the flow of scientific and technological ideas. After all, the economic progress of the last two centuries has depended enormously on a continuing series of technological advances. It is hardly persuasive to say that the process of technological advance has depended entirely on private capital flows. Many of the important technological advances have been made by self-funded inventors or tinkerers on the one hand or by scientists and engineers hired by the government or the nonprofit sector on the other. Moreover, some of the most important technological advances have diminished the importance of money capital by significantly reducing production costs. To use a familiar example, the continuous improvements in microchip technologies have made possible a spectacular advance in the amount of computing power that can be purchased with a given amount of money.[4]

This makes an awkward metaphor, but it can also be argued

that organizations and organizational innovations are the lifeblood of the economy. Through their roles in coordinating the activities of different economic agents and facilitating the flow of information — including scientific and technological information — organizations have increased human productivity enormously. Just as the organization of the ant colony vastly multiplies the effectiveness of individual ants, our development of more sophisticated organizational forms has made possible the great advances over the yeomen farmers and independent artisans of our past. The sociologist Max Weber insisted that the invention of bureaucratic forms of organization was one of the great turning points of history that made possible vast productive advances, and it can similarly be argued that contemporary efforts to develop post-bureaucratic forms of organization are the key to further productive advances in the future.[5]

While even other candidates for the category of privileged contributor to economic progress could be suggested, the point is that the lifeblood metaphor overstates the importance of money capital. Conservatives habitually argue that throwing money at social problems is usually a bad idea, and there is substantial truth in that argument. It is not automatic that more spending will improve educational outcomes in public schools; the money can easily be wasted on excessive administration or ineffective experiments. But the same point can be made about capital spending — throwing money at production problems does not automatically assure greater productivity. In the 1980s, for example, General Motors (GM) spent hundreds of millions of dollars on new sophisticated manufacturing technologies that did not deliver the expected results because the firm failed to change the organizational framework within which those technologies were being deployed.[6] In fact, the capital-as-blood metaphor was part of what misled GM's managers into imagining that money alone would provide a quick fix to their deep organizational problems.

The risks of throwing money away by throwing resources at production problems has increased. Technological decision making has become difficult. Firms are afraid of missing out on technological innovations that could cut costs significantly, so they are vulnerable to being swayed by the exaggerated claims made on behalf of new products. Moreover, it is easy for a firm to invest in a new technology that is incompatible with its patterns of work organization.[7] Without a concerted effort to change those patterns, the new technology is likely to fail. While estimates are hard to come by, it would seem that annual expenditures in the U.S. economy on capital equipment—both hardware and software—that are relatively quickly junked amount to billions of dollars a year.

There is still another reason for doubting that private capital is the lifeblood of the economy: it has simply ceased to be as scarce a resource as it once was. Large sectors of the economy have experienced dramatic reductions in the costs of physical capital. The cost of computer power has been dropping at 20% or more per year. Moreover, smaller price reductions have been occurring within a broad range of capital goods that incorporate computer technologies. Hence, computer-controlled machine tools, communications equipment, and scientific and medical instruments have all seen dramatic improvements in effectiveness without comparable increases in cost. This means, in short, that a million dollars in 1994 can purchase capital equipment that is substantially more powerful than that which could have been purchased with a million 1989 dollars. Hence, dollars set aside for capital investment now go further than they did in the past.

MORE METAPHORIC PROBLEMS: POOLS OF BLOOD AND SAVINGS

Another difficulty created by thinking of capital as blood is the tendency to imagine that the supply of financial capital available in the economy at any given time is a relatively fixed or inelastic quantity. According to this view, the size of the blood/savings supply is imagined to be the sum of the individual savings decisions of households and firms. If, for example, people prefer to spend rather than to save, the pool of financial capital will be limited, and many worthy investment projects will not be pursued for want of available finance. In this view, the failure to save is comparable to a dietary deficiency—such as too little iron—that prevents the body from producing new blood cells. This dietary deficiency leads inevitably to sluggishness and ill health.

This is another example of how a metaphor can help perpetuate previously discredited ideas. The idea that savings represent a fixed pool of resources was a standard feature of much economic thought through the 1930s. However, one of Keynes' central contributions was to overthrow that view, and to show on the contrary that the supply of savings varies significantly with the level of economic activity. Yet, the capital-as-blood metaphor has allowed the idea of a fixed supply of blood/savings to survive Keynes' attack. Even many economists who describe themselves as Keynesians openly embrace the idea of a fixed pool of savings.

These arguments are often used to explain the problems of the U.S. economy. Low savings rates by households have led to a diminished pool of savings. Huge federal budget deficits have further depleted the available savings. The result is that the savings needed to finance new investment are in short supply so that investment levels have fallen. By this line of argument, the only thing that will make possible an increase in investment is an expansion in the pool of savings. Such an expansion could occur through greater frugality by households, a sharp reduction in the federal budget deficit, or ideally by a combination of the two.

Keynes argued instead that the key limit on an economy are the supplies of labor and fixed capital—the stock of machines and buildings.[8] Since a society's capital stock and labor force are often not fully utilized, there is a gap between actual output and the potential output that could be realized if the capital stock and labor force were fully mobilized. In his view, this lost output of both consumer goods and capital goods is far more consequential than individual savings decisions. If, for example, an economy were suddenly able to increase capacity utilization from 80% to 90%, there would be a proportionate increase in total output and incomes, resulting also in increased savings. Putting the unused capacity to work will mean increased production of machine tools and other capital goods, and with the corresponding increase in incomes, firms will be able to find the financing required to purchase those machine tools.

In other words, Keynes saw unused capacity as a kind of latent savings—a hidden treasure trove—that a society could utilize regardless of the availability or unavailability of money capital. Those who subscribe to the fixed pool of savings argument would insist that a shortage of finance represents an absolute constraint on an economy. If banks do not have sufficient deposits, then bankers will be unable to provide businesses with the loans that are needed to finance new investment. Hence, the level of economic activity will remain depressed. But Keynes insisted that so long as there is unused capacity, the availability of finance is not a real constraint. The correctness of his approach can be seen from a financing mechanism that has become widespread in contemporary Taiwan.

In the Taiwanese economy, there are literally thousands of small export-oriented firms that have been largely responsible for that country's successes in the world market. However, those small firms have generally been unable to borrow money from Taiwan's banks because those banks prefer to lend to the small number of large corporations. As a result, the small entrepreneurs have developed a number of alternative financing mechanisms. One of these is the widespread use of the post-dated check. For example, Firm *A* needs to buy raw materials and machines in order to get its production going. The firm simply writes checks to Firms B and C dated two weeks in the future, and receives its raw materials and machinery right away. By the time the checks come due, Firm A has produced and sold a quantity of output, so that it has been able to deposit enough money to cover the checks. Firms B and C have simply extended credit to Firm A and by doing so, they allow the economy to realize some of the output that would otherwise not have been produced.[9]

Keynes insisted that government deficits can play the same role of helping a society to realize more of its potential output. He noted that when an economy was experiencing high rates of unemployment and unutilized capital, deficit spending by the government would put people to work and those people would, in turn, increase their consumption, leading to further employment gains, so that the economy would move closer to the full use of its capital and labor force.

A final twist in Keynes' argument was his recognition that private savings are not always a good thing. This is an obvious heresy for anyone who believes that money capital is the lifeblood of the economy, since private savings generate that lifeblood. Keynes argued that when an economy is weak, there is absolutely no guarantee that money put aside for savings by individuals will actually be translated into private sector investments. Individuals might put money in the bank, but because of the weak economy, the bank might be extremely reluctant to make business loans and businesses might have little interest in borrowing even though interest rates are low. The bank instead is likely to put the money into government bonds, which can be relied on to produce a predictable return. Keynes' heresy was to argue that had those same individuals spent the money that they put in the bank, the effect on the economy would be more positive; demand would increase and some productive capacity would be put to use.

In short, the relationship between savings and investment is quite different than the lifeblood metaphor suggests. The supply of financial savings need not be a constraint on the level of investment activity. When unused capacity exists, deficit-financed investment can create its own savings out of the treasure trove of previously unrealized output. Moreover, low rates of investment can result from other sources than inadequate private savings. Finally, too much private frugality can make a weak economy even worse.

4 —— Capital As Blood: The Micro Level

> *Capital is the lifeblood of every small company, spreading nutrients throughout its operations, and without sufficient capital, an otherwise healthy small company with a great product line will be doomed to wither away.*
>
> —Representative Ron Wyden, 1995[1]

In addition to being used to envision the economy, the capital-as-blood metaphor is employed in conceptualizing the process of production within firms. Production is usually thought of as a process of combining a series of ingredients —money capital, machinery, labor, and raw materials—in fixed proportions to produce a certain quantity of output. But the ingredients are hardly equal; the money capital— or blood— is the most powerful ingredient, the one that really makes the production process work. This is because money capital is the universal ingredient: it can be used to purchase all of the others. The consequence is the kind of transfusion version of the firm that is suggested in Congressman Ron Wyden's language —add money capital to an otherwise healthy small company and there will be vigorous growth.

In academic economics, this same conception is expressed in the idea of the production function. A production function predicts that with the input of certain quantities of physical capital, labor, and raw materials, there will be a fixed quantity of economic output. For example, to produce a certain product, say a thousand widgets (an imaginary manufactured item that economists often use for illustrative purposes), one must take 300 hours of labor costing $15 per hour, two machine tools that cost $10,000, 400 pounds of steel, and twenty gallons of paint.

If one wants to vary the output, one simply adjusts the formula to retain the same proportions. But the fundamental idea is that a certain input of money produces a predictable output of goods.

This view sees production as exactly analogous to the chemical reactions that can be produced with a child's chemistry set—a certain amount of this, a certain amount of that, a teaspoon of catalyst, heated to a certain number of degrees, and bingo! One gets a fixed amount of a new chemical. But unlike chemistry, all of the ingredients can be expressed in terms of one variable—their cost. While most economists recognize that actual production is more complicated and variable than this, the idea of a stable production function remains one of the central tools of economic analysis.

This way of thinking about production is mistaken for two interrelated reasons. First, there are tremendous variations in the efficiency by which labor, physical capital, and raw materials are combined. There is no fixed production function; rather, there are many possible recipes and some work far better than others. Moreover, actual firms are constantly experimenting with different recipes so that last week's production function is unlikely to be accurate this week. Second, the idea that all of the ingredients can be expressed in terms of money ignores this incredible variety of recipes. And the fact is that firms can sometimes find better recipes that cost nothing at all.

It often happens in workplaces that a different way of organizing the flow of work and the tasks of employees can produce dramatic increases in output. Sometimes these changes in production recipes involve no additional cost in new equipment or in increasing worker skills. The same dollar value of inputs suddenly produces greater outputs.[2] But this common possibility is completely ignored when one thinks of production in terms of money capital as the key input.

31

The central problem is that the metaphor thoroughly ignores the human context in which production takes place; human beings actually disappear from the picture and production is reduced to a totally formulaic and predictable process of combining ingredients. But two workplaces might have quite similar labor forces and equally expensive capital equipment and yet have vastly different rates of output. The differences can be the result of different levels of labor-management conflict, differences in the quality of communication within the organization, differences in the quality of the hardware or software being used in production, differences in the ease of manufacture of the product, or a host of other factors. The central point, however, is that all of these organizational factors are excluded from the production function. The capital-as-blood metaphor assumes that production is simply a natural process of combining capital, labor, and raw materials, but this naturalistic view obscures the millions of ways to combine the ingredients.

It is actually quite revealing that when economists teach students the concept of the production function, they often do so by making reference to mythical widgets—a commodity that is far simpler than the goods or services that most workers labor to produce today. Widgets are standardized goods that have no qualitative dimension; one widget is just as good as another. But in the contemporary world, whether one is producing consumer goods, capital goods, standardized services, or specialized services, not only the quantity but the actual quality of the output matters a great deal. Whether the product is an automobile, a machine tool, a fast-food hamburger, or a medical procedure, the level of attention and concern for quality by the producers usually makes a difference to the consumer. Further, it is obvious that different types of workplace organizations differ dramatically in their ability to achieve or maintain high-quality production. Yet, this increasingly central qualitative dimension of output is neglected in the capital-as-blood approach to production.[3]

But there is even more at stake than the vital issue of quality. In both goods and service production, firms face a dizzying array of technological choices in deciding what tools should be used for a particular process. The experience of a consumer who goes out to purchase a new computer is increasingly typical of the choices that capital goods purchasers face. The purchaser is faced with an incredible array of choices as to the type of hardware, the type of software, and the various bells and whistles one may or may not need. Moreover, choosing among the alternatives involves complicated calculations as to which products are likely to become obsolete and which are likely to become the technology of the future. Making these choices is far more complicated than a simple calculus of the relative costs and benefits of different options.

The choice among varied types of physical capital raises all kinds of complex questions. One of these centers on a firm's production goals. Contemporary workplaces usually produce a wide range of products. Few factories produce only one product; generally, a variety of models and product lines are being produced at any given time. This is even more true in service organizations; hospitals, universities, banks, entertainment companies, and retail firms provide a continuously changing stream of diverse products. This means that managers are almost universally dealing with the issue of how best to deploy their labor force to produce the optimal mix among different products. But this raises a whole other series of problems that are generally left out of the capital-as-blood framework. How flexible is the production unit in its ability to shift from one type of good to another? How quickly can the production unit adapt to producing an entirely new product? How effective is the organization in managing inventories of raw materials and finished goods to reduce costs? How effective is it in maintaining a high level of utilization of its productive capacity?

In short, managers who have mastered the economics of the

production function and think of their task as mixing together so many parts of labor with so many parts of capital will have trouble mastering the human and organizational dimensions of production, which are absolutely vital in determining the quality of output and the flexibility of the production unit. But this is precisely the mind-set of the increasingly influential field of corporate finance, which has built an entire intellectual edifice on the shaky foundation of the production function.

Scholars of corporate finance have developed a set of sophisticated mathematical tools that are designed to make the most effective use of a firm's assets. These tools are the equivalent of a computer program that examines a particular set of recipes and precise information on the costs of different ingredients and informs the user that to receive the greatest value for his or her money, lasagna should be made for dinner tonight. But such tools treat the production function—the specific recipes for producing particular goods—as a given. People who use these tools then have the illusion that they are using the firm's resources optimally. The reality, however, is that there may be much better lasagna recipes out there and better ways to structure the factory to increase its ability to produce a range of different products.

As a result, the imagery of capital as blood does not encourage a self-conscious search for better ways to organize production.

MACROECONOMIC PROBLEMS AND THE CAPITAL-AS-BLOOD METAPHOR

The production function mentality creates even more problems when it is used to envision the economy as a whole. The formulas for all different products are aggregated together to produce a formula for the entire economic product—so many hours of labor combined with a certain quantity of capital and various amounts of raw materials equals total output. It would be relatively harmless if this exercise were limited to an attempt to describe the whole economy, but economists use these aggregate production functions as policy tools. The general belief among economists is that since total economic output is a function of total inputs of labor, capital, and raw materials, then we can expect that an x% increase in the amount of capital investment will produce a y% rate of growth in total output.

Making deductions based on fixed recipes or production functions is misleading at the level of the individual production unit. Maximizing the output of a particular factory is much more complicated than simply sprinkling in the right proportions of capital and labor. But the idea is even more misleading for the economy as a whole. This is not one of those cases where errors at the unit level wash out when one adds up all of the units; it is exactly the opposite—the aggregate results are even more distorted than the unit results. There are several reasons for this.

First, all of the unit recipes or production functions ignore the role of the organizational context in making it possible for certain amounts of labor and capital to combine to produce a fixed amount of output. To be sure, in better managed workplaces, the organizational context makes an even larger contribution by producing highly motivated employees and enhanced communication and coordination. But the aggregate production function compounds all of these omissions by creating an abstract model of the economy in which organizations disappear. The result is the theoretical equivalent of the joke about the drunk who looks for his lost key in the wrong place because the light is better. Since it is hard to measure the impact of organizational contexts, economists have generally ignored them. But they then rely on the resulting incomplete models to produce policy conclusions that always concentrate on the variables that are easily measured.

Second, in thinking about the economy as a whole, it quickly becomes apparent that maximizing output is far more complicated than producing an increased volume of widgets. It is like the problem of managing a factory with dozens of different products, but more so. The trick is to get the optimal mix among different products in a given time period so that producers get the input they need and consumers are able to acquire what they want without stores and producers accumulating costly inventories. To be sure, this is the coordination task that market signals are designed to solve—if a particular product is being overproduced, prices will fall and producers will cut back production plans.

But market signals work imperfectly for a variety of reasons. Some products, such as office buildings and agricultural products, take so long to produce that the appropriate market signals come too late to influence investment decisions. Other products, such as public goods, will not be produced in adequate quantities by the market alone. Still other markets work imperfectly because buyers and sellers have different amounts of information. To overcome these problems, societies develop special arrangements to improve the functioning of markets and to provide additional coordination.[4] These arrangements include government provision of public goods, government regulation, and various types of formal and informal associations among producers. Taken as a whole, these special arrangements might work well or poorly to maximize the efficiency with which an economy turns inputs into outputs. To use extreme examples, one country might experience long periods of slow growth because there are chronic shortages of skilled labor due to the inadequate educational system, while another country might experience rapid growth because its educational and vocational training systems work well. One country might find its rate of growth diminished because of frequent crises of overproduction, while another country is able to adjust supply to demand far more effectively.

These nonmarket arrangements are another key ingredient

in determining how much output results from inputs of capital and labor. But these structures are also ignored in the aggregate production functions that economists develop. Since their impact is difficult to measure, they are simply left out of the calculations. The result of this myopia is that policy prescriptions almost always emphasize that a weak economy needs new infusions of private capital investment when what is really needed is more public sector investment or more effective institutional structures. In short, the capital-as-blood metaphor of economic production leaves out some of the most important ingredients in the production process.

5 —— The State As Vampire

These are the Vampires of the Publick, and Riflers of the Kingdom: They lessen the Publick Stock of what Merchants have continual occasion for to carry on Trade with...

— Charles Forman, 1741

If this bill is signed into law, it will be like Count Dracula to the entrepreneurs of this land. This bill will suck the life blood out of small businesses. It will increase the effective small business tax rate by more than 30 percent. It will cut capital expenses. It will increase the capital gains tax by 10 percent. Mr. Speaker, we need to put a stake in the heart of this Count Dracula tax bill before it sucks the blood out of our small business sector.

— Representative Thomas Craig, 1993

I have never understood how you make people better off by taking more of their hard-earned tax dollars. It is like the old practice of bleeding a patient with leeches in order to make the patient healthy. They figured out after a while that taking a patient's blood did not make him [sic] more healthy. The same thing is true with extracting tax dollars. If you leave these dollars in people's pockets, they invest them, they spend them on things that are important in their lives, they will send their kids to college, they will put some money in a savings account.

— Senator Jon Kyl, 1995[1]

I f capital is seen as the lifeblood of the economy, then the Conventional Wisdom treats the state as a vampire who is regularly sapping the economy's strength. The underlying idea is that economic processes are natural, but that the state is unnatural and hence monstrous. It is true by definition that state action will be destructive and will undermine the natural workings of the economy.

This imagery of a parasitical state is centuries old. It dates from the long struggle of liberalism against absolute monarchies that were depicted as parasitical monsters preying on their societies. Ironically, those governments that were created as a consequence of democratic antimonarchical revolutions inherited the same set of images. Like their monarchical predecessors, democratically elected governments are sometimes accused of sucking the lifeblood out of their societies.[2]

This image of the wasteful, predatory vampire state is continuously invoked in American politics; it is the central image that has fueled the current antistatist frenzy.[3] Most discussions of the evils of the federal budget deficit rely on this imagery to make their case; the federal government is seen as little more than a pickpocket stealing money from the average citizen and using the proceeds in wasteful and destructive ways. But even sophisticated economic arguments often come down to the assertion that an inherently predatory state simply cannot be trusted to carry out certain tasks effectively.

The vampire state metaphor is a powerful means to make several important claims. The first is that the production of goods and services by the state will tend to be less efficient than production by private firms because the state is not subject to the discipline of the market.[4] A state agency that is funded by tax revenues can simply add additional employees when a comparable private firm would be forced by competition to extract higher productivity. This inherent inefficiency of state agencies means, in turn, that state regulation of the economy will generally be carried out badly. If, for example, the intention of legislation is to reduce pollution, the inefficiency of state agencies means that they are likely to impose large costs on private firms without producing corresponding benefits. The second claim is that the inefficiency of government results inevitably in increases in the government's share of total output, which will undermine the private economy.

When one explores these claims on their own terms — stripped of the powerful imagery of bloodsucking monsters —

they are not terribly persuasive.[5] Certainly, it is easy to provide examples of predatory regimes such as Marcos in the Phillipines, who stole hundreds of millions of dollars and hid the funds in Swiss bank accounts. There are also many examples of inefficient government agencies, such as the Pentagon purchasing $50 hammers. Yet, there are also abundant examples of the opposite — governments that are quite restrained in their efforts to raise revenue and public agencies that are extraordinarily efficient in providing goods and services. The interesting question is what determines the variations. What are the conditions under which government spending appears to be disciplined? What are the conditions under which government agencies tend to be more efficient in using resources? These questions, however, are rarely asked by those who invoke the metaphor of the vampire state.[6]

These claims also rest on the highly problematic belief that market competition is natural and automatically results in the optimal use of resources. But, as will be argued at greater length later, this is simply not the case — highly inefficient practices can persist in private firms for decades or even centuries. If one establishes by definition that private production of goods and services will automatically result in the most efficient production possible, then it follows logically that government production will always be less efficient. But this is simply arguing by definition.

In the real world, privately owned U.S. automobile firms were terribly inefficient and slow to respond to Japanese competition during the 1970s and much of the 1980s. There was no automatic process of adjustment that led these firms to adopt more efficient ways of making cars. At the same time, some state-owned European firms, such as the aircraft manufacturer Airbus, have been quite successful in recent years in increasing their efficiency of production and staying competitive relative to private corporations.

The point is that the relative efficiency of public agencies and private firms is very much an empirical question. Under some circumstances, public agencies will be overstaffed, waste a great deal of money, and extract relatively little work effort from their employees. But the same is true of some private firms. Similarly, both types of institutions can also be managed extremely effectively, so that resources are continually stretched further and quality is continuously improved. Where a particular firm or agency falls on this continuum depends on a series of different factors: the quality and effectiveness with which managerial performance is evaluated, the intensity of competition within a certain market, and the ability of consumers to influence the quality of production.

Unfortunately, surprisingly little work has been done on this empirical question. It is a difficult question to investigate because most types of production are not overlapping. In the U.S., for example, public agencies rarely compete directly with private firms in producing specific goods and services. Hence, it is not possible simply to evaluate whether a government firm produces automobiles more efficiently than General Motors, or whether a private agency could dispense justice more efficiently than the court system. Most of the circumstances under which there are direct overlaps are basically monopoly situations, such as garbage collection, public utilities, or community hospitals. The choice is generally between a public agency providing the service directly or local governments contracting with a private agency to provide service for a certain geographical area. Research on these situations suggests that there is no clear-cut superiority of one pattern or the other. The relative costs and benefits of each depend upon local circumstances and the specific measures that different analysts use. For example, a private firm collecting garbage might put speed ahead of neatness, so that costs are shifted to streetcleaning services. The evaluation of the relative efficiency of public or private provision of the service will often depend on whether or not analysts attempt to measure this kind of cost shifting.[7]

But if the argument that the public sector is inherently wasteful is flawed, what happens to the claim that government spending has a natural tendency to absorb a growing share of total output? Some political scientists and economists have argued that legislators know that they can increase their chances of reelection by providing more goodies to their constituencies as long as they do not increase taxes. The result is that rising government deficits are inevitable and the growing deficits are likely to produce strong inflationary pressures that will weaken the overall economy. This argument became famous in the 1970s when various analysts insisted that Western societies were suffering from an excess of democracy.

Each link in this causal chain is, however, problematic. Situations in which rival political parties get into bidding wars to provide more benefits to constituents are actually quite exceptional. Between 1973 and 1985, there has been a trend toward rising government deficits in most of the developed market economies, but this had less to do with adding new programs and more to do with the difficulty of financing established programs in a period of slower economic growth. Moreover, it is clear that rising deficits do not automatically produce higher levels of inflation. The case of the U.S. is striking here; the 1980s were marked by huge federal budget deficits, but rates of inflation were low relative to those of the 1970s.

THAT KINDLY COUNT DRACULA

The vampire metaphor has been a powerful political tool because it obscures the actual and necessary roles of governmental activity in the economy. Our basic understanding of how things work has been distorted because of the futility of saying, "Just think of all of the good things that Count Dracula does for Transylvania."[8] But the idea of condemning the state because political power is sometimes abused is comparable to condemning markets in general because human greed sometimes produces horrible consequences. The reality is that both markets and political power are necessary components of any complex human society, and that these societies have to find ways to protect themselves from the excesses caused by those who recklessly pursue both political power and economic wealth.

But the vampire imagery works because the tendency to see the market as natural and the state as unnatural and monstrous is so deeply ingrained. One way to get beyond this way of thinking is to recognize that our model of market competition is actually artificial and brittle. Recent experiences of the transformation of the former Soviet Union provides powerful evidence of this artificiality and brittleness. Western economists with their deep faith in the naturalness of markets argued that if the state's control over the economy could be quickly dismantled, capitalism would spring up almost instantly in the former Soviet Union. But one thing the economists forgot is the difference between the systematic pursuit of wealth and our notions of market competition. When people were freed to pursue wealth systematically, but without the elaborate rules and enforcement mechanisms that exist in the West, the result was a sudden explosion of gangsterism and financial fraud.[9] After all, building a better mousetrap is always a risky and uncertain way of getting wealthy as compared to stealing things of value. When you try to develop a new product, you might fail for thousands of reasons; but when steal, the only risks are being caught or losing out to a bigger thief. And if the government is weak, it is only the bigger thieves who represent a genuine threat.

In short, market competition requires an active government that is able to enforce property rights and the contracts made between economic actors, or economic competition will quickly degenerate into gangsterism. Moreover, the task of developing these rules is more complicated than simply saying, "Thou shall not steal." There are many ways of defining property rights and the nature of valid contracts. Can human beings be owned as property? Is a contract valid in which an employee waives his or her right to join a union? Can intangible things like ideas be a form of property, and, if so, how can their owners be protected against a violation of their property rights? While it is easy to argue that one set of legal answers to these questions might be better for economic production than another, the fact is that there are no "natural" answers.[10]

But even when these issues of contract and property rights have been solved, there is still another source of fragility of market competition. The benign competition of economic theory requires that there be multiple buyers and sellers, with no firm being large enough to influence the market by itself. Since the rise of the modern corporation, however, there are many markets in which a small number of firms play a dominant role. If government plays no role, what is likely to happen when three giant firms together provide for 90% of the domestic consumption of a particular product? One scenario is that the three firms will reach some kind of market-sharing arrangement that minimizes the role of price or product competition. Another is that the three firms will engage in an extended process of intense competition that ultimately leaves one firm completely dominant and the other two either bankrupt or forced to accept a small corner of the market. In such episodes of cutthroat competition, the firm with more financial resources pushes product price levels so low that nobody can make a profit, and then simply waits for its competitors to fold. (Precisely because of antitrust rules, such knockdown competition among giant competitors is comparatively rare. It has, however, occurred in recent years in the warehouse store industry where Wal-Mart and Costco have been going head to head. The two chains knowingly establish new stores near their competitors even when it is obvious that the market is not large enough to support two stores.[11] In such all-out wars, one competitor is likely to fail.) Each of these scenarios means that the society will not gain any of the promised benefits of market competition.

In short, the "natural" tendency of market competition among a small number of firms is degeneration into either monopolies or cartels. It is only the "artificial" action of governments in restraining cutthroat competition and antitrust violations that produces relatively stable competition among a small number of large competitors. Hence, even at the most fundamental level of gaining the benefits of competition, market societies depend upon sustained governmental action.

Beyond these important basics—property rights, contracts, and maintaining competition—there are still many other critical roles that governments play in making market economies work more effectively. But before discussing these, it is essential to show the limits of another of the core metaphors of conventional economic thinking.

6 —— Survival of the Fittest through Market Competition: The Firm

The free-enterprise system — which is evolution in action — always improving — basically is a system of survival of the fittest.
> —James E. Perrella, Executive Vice President,
> Ingersoll Rand Company, 1990

Unless the behavior of businessmen [sic] in some way or other approximated behavior consistent with the maximization of returns, it seems unlikely that they would remain in business for long. Let the apparent immediate determinant of business behavior be anything at all — habitual reaction, random choice or whatnot. Whenever this determinant happens to lead to behavior consistent with rational and informed maximization of returns, the business will prosper and acquire resources with which to expand; whenever it does not, the business will tend to lose resources and can be kept in existence only by the addition of resources from outside. The process of "natural selection" thus helps to validate the hypothesis — or, rather, given natural selection, acceptance of the hypothesis can be based largely on the judgment that it summarizes appropriately the conditions for survival.
> —Milton Friedman, 1953[1]

The metaphor of market competition producing the survival of the fittest is drawn from evolutionary theory. It is often deployed both to describe the relationship among firms and the dilemmas of individuals in society. This chapter focuses on the firm while the next chapter addresses individuals. In the survival-of-the-fittest metaphor, the competition among business firms is viewed as comparable to the struggle for survival among competing species. The process of "natural selection" means that firms that are slow to adapt to changing circumstances will "die," while the survivors will be firms that have successfully adapted. As in nature, the competition for business survival encourages successful adaptation.

When stated this way, the metaphor sounds obvious and unobjectionable. But the Conventional Wisdom adds a special twist to the metaphor. Evolutionary theory is interpreted to suggest that every trait of every surviving species must be the best possible adaptation to the species' environment because the process of natural selection is so extremely demanding that anything short of optimal adaptation will be punished. This view can be called "extreme evolutionary functionalism," but such a view of biological evolution has been largely discredited. The dominant biological view now emphasizes the randomness and imperfectness of species' adaptations. Natural selection is not some goal-driven process that forces species to perfect themselves. On the contrary, some quite imperfect modes of adaptation have proven extremely durable. In describing natural selection, one analyst writes:

> In selecting variants for differential survival, nature works with what variation presents itself and shapes available properties. Thus, it has the appearance of seeking the quick and dirty solution to an adaptive problem, not the optimally adaptive one.[2]

Nevertheless, in both popular and academic economics, this extreme evolutionary functionalism continues to be influential. The argument is often made that market competition is such a rigorous and demanding process that firms must either follow the best possible business practices available at the moment or die. Market competition is seen as an almost perfect mechanism that punishes any deviation from the best possible business practices. Hence, one can reasonably assume that those firms that have survived market competition used their resources in the best possible manner.

This argument is at the core of the Chicago economist Gary Becker's famous explanation of why market competition should quickly eliminate any forms of racial discrimination.[3] Since discrimination artificially limits a firm's potential labor force, its "taste" for discrimination will mean that a firm is not able to hire the best workers for a given amount of wages. The lower quality of its labor force will then mean that the firm will be less profitable than its nondiscriminatory competitors. Being less profitable will produce cumulative disadvantages as the firm faces greater difficulties in raising the capital that it needs, so that eventually the firm will either have to abandon its taste for discrimination or go under.

This belief in the market as a nearly perfect selection mechanism was once widely accepted by economists. It was thought that if one firm developed a better way to organize job skills or to lay out the machinery on the factory floor, then it could be assumed that the pressures of competition would quickly guarantee that improvement would diffuse to the entire industry. This extreme evolutionary functionalism is also closely linked to the idea of capital as the lifeblood of the economy. Once it is assumed that inefficient firms are automatically driven out of business and that profitable firms are performing at close to optimal levels, then the main economic problem is to assure that more capital is put in the hands of those profitable and efficient firms. Hence, the Conventional Wisdom emphasizes increasing the supply of savings and developing more efficient capital markets because competition in the product market has already solved the problem of weeding out inefficient producers.

The reality, however, is that firms are not automatically pushed to adopt the best practices. Neither in nature nor in the economy can it be assumed that survival is proof of high-level adaptation. But for many years, the only explanation for the failure of effective market selection that was significantly debated by economists was the existence of oligopolies or monopolies. Some analysts argued that if there were only a handful of major competitors in an industry, they could agree to limit the extent of price competition. If none of the firms were aggressive in pushing down prices, then the pressures on individual firms to find the most efficient ways to use resources would be reduced and there would emerge a significant gap between actual output and potential output. Such a situation could persist as long as there were barriers to entry for other firms that might be more aggressive in their pricing policies. While economists disagreed sharply about the actual extent of this kind of oligopoly distortion of competitive markets, the underlying idea of perfect market discipline remained unquestioned.

PRINCIPALS AND AGENTS

But contemporary economists have developed new arguments that have weakened the idea of a highly discerning natural selection process in the economy. One argument is the recognition of the agency problem in the running of the corporation.[4] Most large corporations are run on a day-to-day basis by managers who are the agents of the actual owners—the shareholders. But whenever a principal hires an agent, it cannot be assumed that the agent will do exactly what the principal wants. While the principal might want the firm run to maximize profit, the agent might well have other ideas. It might be substantially easier and more attractive for the agent to focus his or her energies on increasing the firm's number of employees. That kind of expansion in the size of the firm might justify a higher salary for the top manager and it might make it easier for him or her to motivate other managers because continuing expansion will open up new opportunities for other managers. To be sure, growth will require profits, but it does not require the aggressive discipline suggested by the model of pure competition. For example, one division of a firm might be tooling along producing reasonable profits with no efforts at developing new products for the future. An agent who totally accepted the principal's agenda would force that division to shift resources to new product development to assure that profits were sustained into the future. But the agent who is oriented toward maximizing growth might be content to let the division continue with its suboptimal performance while putting most of his or her managerial energies into expansion through buying up other firms.

After locating the likelihood of these conflicting interests, the principal-agent framework emphasizes the importance of monitoring. The more closely the principal monitors the behavior of the agent, the more likely the agent will pursue the principal's objectives. However, monitoring is costly, difficult, and time consuming, and certain rules of corporate governance can further diminish the likelihood of effective monitoring. For example, figuring out whether top managers are doing a good job running the firm is usually much more complicated than simply looking at a few quantitative indicators. Even a very badly managed firm might get very lucky and have a few years of spectacular profits. It often takes very close scrutiny to evaluate the performance of these managers, and corporate boards of directors might be too lazy or too busy to devote the necessary energy.

But in an economy where the level of monitoring of top managers is relatively low, agents are freer to pursue their own agendas. This can create a situation where most of the key firms involved in an industry in a particular country have growth-oriented top managers who are not strongly oriented toward innovation and efficiency. Under such circumstances, inefficient work practices or a failure to adopt the most up-to-date techniques could persist. As long as there are steep barriers to entry for domestic competitors, only competition from more tightly monitored foreign firms will work to shake up the industry.

In short, principal-agent problems between managers and owners provide a powerful explanation for why markets might be an imperfect mechanism for enforcing efficient business practices. In fact, the basic assumption that firms are run strictly to maximize profits can be mistaken when managers and owners are different people.

A second line of argument focuses on the way that firms develop their employment practices—something that also has important implications for how a firm uses physical capital. Here again, there is a principal-agent problem. In this case, the principals are the firm's managers and the agents are the employees who are hired to carry out certain tasks. While the principal wants the agent to work at the highest sustainable level of intensity possible—not just physical effort, but mental effort as well—the agent's interests are often quite different. The principal can invest resources in monitoring the intensity with which the agent works, but monitoring can be costly, especially in circumstances where it is not possible to identify easily the output of the agent's labor. It is easy to get to a situation where the costs of additional monitoring exceed the benefits that they produce. In this circumstance, it makes sense for the principal and the agent to cut a deal.

Generally, the nature of the deal is that employees agree to work harder than the minimum effort that they could get away with at a given level of monitoring.[5] This allows managers to economize on the expense of monitoring. In exchange, managers generally offer several inducements. First, wages are set higher than the pure replacement wage—the wage needed to hire a new employee off the street. Second, employees are offered the possibility of movement up a job ladder in the future. Third, managers agree to treat employees with a certain level of respect, which might mean, for example, taking employee preferences into account in deciding on the deployment of new technologies.

The precise nature of the tacit or open bargain that is established at a particular workplace will vary considerably because of local conditions. If the previous distrust between employee and employer was high, for example, a given bargain might produce a level of work intensity that is not particularly high. Whereas in another work setting where trust is higher, the bargain might establish high levels of work intensity and substantially larger wage premiums.

The point, simply, is that there is nothing automatic about reaching the most productive wage-work intensity bargain.[6] Managers and employees might find that a second best bargain makes them both better off than they would be without any understanding at all. Either because of habit, lack of information, or lack of effort, they might never move toward a better bargain. For such a firm, even if competitive pressures were to intensify, it might very well continue to take the established level of work intensity as a given and try to find other ways to cut costs or raise output.

Moreover, these bargains also can have important implications for a firm's decisions about deploying physical capital. A firm might resist adopting a new technology because of fears that this technology would disrupt the existing understandings between employees and managers on the shop floor. Or the firm might adopt the new technology, but avoid carrying out a radical reorganization of the work-flow, and that could have the consequence that the productive potential of the new equipment is not fully realized.

In short, the recognition of these agency problems makes it possible to understand how even in a highly competitive economy it does not follow that employers will adopt the best available practices in their industry. For smaller firms, there is also another set of factors. Small firms are often resource constrained; they cannot afford to purchase the most up-to-date capital equipment or pay for the best management consultants. Managers of small firms might simply be unaware of the best practices in the industry and unwilling to devote the precious time necessary to acquire that information.

But if market competition does not automatically produce

optimal use of labor and capital, then the gap between actual output and what would be produced if firms moved closer to the best practices might be substantial. This gap represents the second treasure trove — resources that could be effectively released by accelerating the diffusion of more optimal ways of combining labor and capital.

THE CONCEPT OF
COORDINATION EFFICIENCY

Recent studies of the international automobile industry highlight large productivity differences between comparable factories. Even when one compares plants with the same level of automation, the differences in productivity are huge. Among plants where 34% of the production steps are automated, the average hours of labor required to produce a car vary from eighteen to fifty-four between the most efficient Japanese plant and the least efficient European plant. Moreover, when GM compared the productivity of one of its U.S. plants to a comparable but less automated Ford plant, it found that its plant was substantially less efficient. GM estimated that 41% of the gap was explained by differences in the ease of manufacturing the two cars. The Ford car had fewer parts that fit together more easily. Another 48% of the productivity gap was explained by differences in factory practices — the organization of the work on the shop floor.[7]

The more productive plants were taking advantage of what can be called "coordination efficiencies," such as better coordination among production workers and between production workers and the people in charge of design. This concept of coordination efficiency was first suggested by Harvey Leibenstein, a Harvard economist who distinguished between two types of efficiency — allocative efficiency and X-efficiency.[8] Allocative efficiency is the kind that the Conventional Wisdom is obsessed with; it is the efficiency that results from allocating capital and labor to their most productive uses. When flows of money capital are directed to high-profit firms and away from low-profit firms, that is allocative efficiency. Leibenstein used X-efficiency, in contrast, to refer to the efficiency with which physical capital and labor are combined in a given enterprise. Since the coordination of effort is central to what Leibenstein meant by X-efficiency, I prefer to use the term coordination efficiency.

But coordination efficiencies are invisible as long as we think about production from the capital-as-blood perspective. The production function specifies that a certain amount of inputs must give you a certain amount of output. However, firms that are able to take advantage of substantial coordination efficiencies will get substantially more output from those same inputs.

For example, a firm that is able to mobilize the intelligence and energy of its employees will be able to find numerous ways to diminish waste and increase both the efficiency and quality of production for any particular product. But the greatest gains in coordination efficiency come in mobilizing the firm's energies across a range of different products. If a particular firm produces five distinctly different products, it faces complex decisions about which resources to use to produce each of those products. High coordination efficiency means both that resources are used optimally across the five products and that there are positive spillovers. Things that are learned in producing one product are quickly transferred to make the production of other products more efficient.

For firms and the whole economy, the potential gains from improving coordination efficiency are far greater than the potential gains from improving allocative efficiency. When one factors in all of the difficult to measure variables such as product quality, ability to shift production quickly, safety, waste of energy and raw materials, and so on, it is not uncommon for the best practice firms in an industry to have double the productivity of other plants.[9]

Hence, the potential gains in aggregate productivity that

can come by improving coordination efficiencies are huge. Even if all of the less productive plants cannot be brought up to the level of output of the best plants, improvements of 20% to 40% are perfectly feasible. Moreover, these are not simply one-shot gains, because today's improvements in coordination efficiency make it more likely that the firm will be able to utilize effectively new and more sophisticated generations of capital equipment. Most studies of allocative efficiency, on the other hand, suggest that the differences between more and less effective mechanisms for allocating capital are likely to shift total output by 5% or less.

In a word, our society has focused its energies on increasing allocative efficiency through the development of highly sophisticated capital markets, while it has largely neglected the much larger potential gains that could come from increasing coordination efficiency. Unrealized coordination efficiency is a treasure trove of enormous magnitude that is literally invisible to the Conventional Wisdom.

But the problem is even deeper. There are fundamental conflicts between the pursuit of allocative efficiency and the pursuit of coordination efficiency. The mechanisms that have been created in the name of allocative efficiency actually make it harder to realize coordination efficiency and, in many cases, they actually act to diminish the coordination efficiency of particular firms or of the entire economy.

The most striking illustration of this conflict are the set of problems that are usually discussed under the title, "the short-term time horizons of U.S. managers." A substantial and useful body of work has evolved that contrasts U.S. corporate managers with those in Japan and Western Europe in terms of their decision-making horizons.[10] The general argument is that U.S. managers often make decisions based on improving profitability in the next quarter or the quarter after, while foreign managers are more likely to think in terms of improving profits in three or five years. This difference means that established U.S. firms are less likely to invest in human capital and physical capital that does not produce immediate payoffs, and they are unlikely to carry development projects that might only pay off in five years.

The best of this literature goes on to argue that these differences are not the result of innate cultural differences, but that they flow from the ways that financial markets are organized. In Japan and Germany, for example, stock markets play a minor role in determining control of the corporation, while in the U.S. stock markets play a central role.[11] If a company's stock price slides in the U.S., the firm is vulnerable to a takeover, and the board of directors will likely begin reconsidering the top manager's contract. The result is that corporate managers spend a lot of time worrying about persuading the financial markets not to sell off the stock. The best means of persuasion is to produce good quarterly results, but this can easily lead to neglect of the long-term. Managers in the other countries cannot ignore short-term profitability, but they are more insulated from the effects of week-to-week variations in the stock price.

Those who argue in this vein, however, usually fail to recognize that there is a direct trade-off between allocative efficiency and coordination efficiency. The U.S. capital markets have a higher level of allocative efficiency than do the German and Japanese.[12] The relatively weak role in the U.S. of patient stockholders — those who are committed to holding shares for the long term — means that the price at which shares turn over each day is far closer to the pure market price than are the share prices in Japan and Germany. Similarly, the fact that corporate managers are less insulated from the stock market in the U.S. also enhances allocative efficiency. Managers in Japan and Germany are freer to ignore the daily signals that are being sent by the financial markets. The point, however, is that our allocative efficiency comes at the expense of coordination efficiency. While the foreign systems skimp on allocative efficiency, they have a distinct advantage in pursuing coordination efficiency.

Realizing high levels of coordination efficiency means establishing a bargain between employers and employees in which employees trade high levels of work intensity for management commitments to employment security and employee skill development. The basic glue of these bargains is the understanding that the bargain will extend over time. As has often been noted, these bargains need not be rigid; employees are not promised that one particular job will always be there. The idea, instead, is that the firm will do its best to keep the person employed even if that means extensive retraining. And, in fact, the more emphasis a firm places on training, the less it has to promise by way of employment security since highly skilled employees have less reason to fear the outside labor market.

The difficulty is that the logic of allocative efficiency undercuts these bargains. A firm that is responding rapidly to the signals of the financial markets will close a low-profit division quickly regardless of all of the promises—explicit and implicit—made to the division's employees. The financial markets are not able to effectively evaluate a firm's accumulation of highly skilled and dedicated employees independent of the actual flow of profits that those employees produce. Hence, when profits turn down, even if for reasons that have nothing to do with productivity and product quality, the message is unequivocal— unload those expensive employees. In short, the more that a firm responds to allocative efficiency, the less able it will be to negotiate the bargains that maximize coordination efficiency. This is precisely the reason why less efficient capital markets in our competitors can produce better economic results.

The discussion of coordination efficiency has taken us a long way from the original metaphor of survival of the fittest. But once one rejects the functionalist version of survival of the fittest —that the market automatically forces surviving firms to the best possible use of resources—the problem of actually achieving coordination efficiencies suddenly looms large indeed.

7 —— Survival of the Fittest through Market Competition: The Human Species

To remove the wants of the lower classes of society is indeed an arduous task. The truth is that the pressure of distress on this part of a community is an evil so deeply seated that no human ingenuity can reach it.
— Thomas Robert Malthus, 1798

If you do not have the key ingredients of personal strength, integrity, courage, discipline, perserverence, hard work, if you do not have those characteristics then you cannot survive either in a free market or in a free society, because the individual has to have a considerable amount of personal discipline, personal commitment, personal courage for a free society to operate and for a free market to operate.
— Representative Newt Gingrich, 1993[1]

I n addition to describing interfirm relationships, the Darwinian metaphor also influences our view of individual economic activity. It is most obvious in the classic definition of economics as the science of managing scarce resources. The implicit idea is that human beings — along with other species — are engaged in an ongoing struggle for survival against an unyielding natural environment. Again, this is obviously true as a description of the human predicament through much of history. But it is inadequate as a description of the situation that people face in developed market societies that have successfully mobilized science and technology to produce vast quantities of material goods.

One place where both the metaphor and the distortions that it creates can be seen is in the current debates about "welfare reform." Advocates of "welfare reform" often ask, "Can we as a nation afford to pay millions of people to sit around and do nothing but cash their welfare checks when the rest of us are hard at work trying to make a living?" The fable of the ant and the grasshopper is often suggested in these discussions: the foolish grasshopper played while the ant worked, and as a consequence, the grasshopper starved to death when winter came. While charity or a safety net might have kept the grasshopper alive through one winter, its ultimate survival depends on learning the need for discipline and hard work. The core Christian allegory is also suggested here. When we lose our economic way and become lazy and spendthrift, we have not only fallen into sin, but we also risk the fate of the grasshopper.

To be sure, many human communities throughout history—and in poorer countries today—have faced a direct link between the amount of human labor they can mobilize and their ability to raise enough food for everybody to eat. But this is not a description of contemporary life in advanced market economies. Quite the contrary is true: for most of this century, the developed economies have faced the enormous problem of providing enough jobs for everyone who wants to work. The reality is that neither our survival nor our standard of living requires that welfare recipients earn their bread through the sweat of their brow.

In developed societies and in some developing societies, it now requires only a small percentage of the population working in agriculture to produce more than enough food for everyone. Barring natural or man-made disasters, the basic struggle to grow enough food no longer exists. And as we find that it also takes only a relatively small percentage of the population to produce more than enough goods for everyone, the survivalist metaphor becomes less relevant.

In fact, we face the opposite of the survivalist problem: the danger of technological unemployment. Human productive capacity has become so great that millions of people find it difficult to find any employment at all. Deep anxieties about technological unemployment were stimulated by the industrial revolution and have erupted periodically since. The last such wave of anxiety occurred in the U.S. in the first half of the 1960s when intellectuals argued that factory automation would have a devastating impact on the health of the U.S. economy unless drastic steps were taken.[2]

The Conventional Wisdom treats these eruptions of anxiety about technological unemployment as the blatherings of a bunch of Chicken Littles, persuaded that the sky is falling when everything is actually fine.[3] Advocates of the Conventional Wisdom point out that despite warnings about the sky falling that date back to the industrial revolution, total employment has continued to rise. They argue that the emergence of new needs continually creates new types of employment. Proponents of this view recognize that some economies go through long periods of high unemployment — such as what Europe has been experiencing for more than a decade — but they believe that such problems can be solved by dismantling regulatory barriers that have artificially limited job growth in new areas.

A COUNTERVIEW

John Maynard Keynes was among the Chicken Littles who worried about technological unemployment. In an essay written in 1930, Keynes attributed the economic problems of that time to technological unemployment: "due to our discovery of means of economizing the use of labour outrunning the pace at which we can find new uses for labour."[4] Keynes went on to argue that in another hundred years when the standard of living could be expected to be eight times its 1930 level, humanity would be near to solving its economic problem. The struggle for subsistence that had characterized all of human history and "the whole of the biological kingdom from the beginnings of life in its most primitive forms"[5] would either be ended or on its way to being ended. Keynes went on to speculate as to how society and individuals would adapt to a new world in which the struggle for survival did not dominate. He imagined that society "shall honour those who can teach us how to pluck the hour and the day virtuously and well, the delightful people who are capable of taking direct enjoyment in things, the lilies of the field who toil not, neither do they spin."[6]

Keynes addressed that essay to "our grandchildren"—a generation that would be reaching old age in the year 2030. In this final decade of the twentieth century, that generation is already in its thirties and would likely be puzzled by Keynes' musings. After all, thirtysomething people in the U.S. are far more concerned about being "overworked Americans"[7] than finding a way to "pluck the hour and the day" of expanded leisure. Hence, it is tempting to dismiss Keynes' speculations as a misguided response to the crisis of the interwar years. This has been the position of mainstream economics, which has argued that periodic anxieties about technological unemployment—including those of Keynes—grow out of a failure to recognize both that human needs are unlimited and that an adaptable economy will always find new uses for human labor. Economists are quick to insist that the disasters predicted by theorists of technological unemployment have never come; they have usually been followed by periods of rapid economic growth, including growth in overall employment.

There is, however, a way to recast this old argument in a way that gives us new leverage on our current situation. Mainstream economists are correct that developed societies have generally coped effectively with the dangers of technological unemployment. But the principle way in which they have done this is not by the simple expedient of expanding the total quantity of goods that the average individual consumes. On the contrary, most of the adaptation has come through changing the qualitative dimension of economic output.

Two dimensions of quality change have loomed largest. First, there has been an extraordinary increase in the role of leisure or nonwork activity in individual lives. At the end of the nineteenth century, it was the norm for male workers to enter the labor force at age 14 and work until their deaths. Moreover, an average work year in manufacturing comprised somewhere between 2,700 and 3,200 hours of work. Today, full-time entrance into the workforce for male workers is unlikely to occur before age 20, with retirement coming at age 65, and an average work year in manufacturing of 1,900 hours. In Western Europe, the average work year in manufacturing is significantly shorter, reaching 1,500 hours in France. But even in the U.S., if one assumes a life expectancy of age 70 for male workers in 1900, total expected lifetime hours of work are half of what they were a century ago.[8]

The situation for women is more complex, since their participation in the paid labor force has increased dramatically between 1900 and the present. Nevertheless, if one adds together the housework, the unpaid labor in family businesses, and the paid labor done by the average woman in both 1900 and 1995, one will also see a significant increase in leisure time. While a number of studies have shown that the average number of hours of housework performed by women has remained high, especially in families with small children, the nature of the work has changed dramatically. Labor-saving appliances have dramatically reduced the time devoted to the traditionally arduous tasks of meal preparation.[9]

The reduction of the burden of work during the average individual's lifespan represents a significant improvement in the quality of life. It marks a movement away from a situation in which the struggle for subsistence dominates human existence. Moreover, this increase in leisure represents a qualitative dimension of economic output because society has made a clear trade-off. We could have kept the length of the average work year at the 1900 level with the idea that more hours of work in factories and offices would have given us a greater volume of goods and services. Instead, we have chosen to consume a portion of our greater productive capacity in the form of leisure—a qualitative good.

It must be noted, though, that the relationship between working time and economic output is also more complex than the production function suggests. When the length of the working day has been shortened through legislation, there has generally been substantial increases in productivity.[10] Employees are able to work with a higher level of intensity in an eight-hour day than they were in a twelve-hour day. Hence, these reductions have historically produced a double dividend—increased leisure and increased productivity. Whether or not a further reduction to a four-day week or a six-hour day would produce similar increases in productivity remains a debated issue.

The second important qualitative change has been the vast expansion in categories of employment that barely existed 100 years ago. In many cases, the direct purpose of this employment is precisely to improve some dimension of the quality of life. The most obvious is the health care sector of the economy; these days we are constantly reminded that health costs are threatening to swallow the entire GDP. But if we bracket for the moment all of the questions about inefficiencies and waste in the health care industry, the reality is that we are spending this share of our GDP on health in order to improve our collective quality of life. The evidence is strong that all of our scientific advances and medical expenditures have only slightly increased the lifespan of a healthy individual, but we have been able to save tens of millions of people from early deaths and have made dramatic improvements in the comfort levels of those who suffer from one or another illness or infirmity, including mental illnesses.

While health is the most dramatic example, there are many others. In both the private and the public sectors, we now employ thousands of people whose job is to limit the damage to the environment from industrial processes. Again, all kinds of questions can be raised about whether or not these people are doing a good job, but the fact remains that the expansion of employment in waste management and environmental protection also represents a commitment to the qualitative dimension of output. The categories of employment associated with preserving our culture's past are another example. Museums, libraries, and archives now employ hundreds of thousands of people, whereas a hundred years ago the role of preserving cultural artifacts was generally performed by people whose primary work was something else entirely.

Yet, we have attained a level of economic development where most employment does not focus on satisfying basic human needs. It is useful here to pose the following question: How many people are there in the contemporary U.S. who perform work that is directly necessary for the day-to-day survival of the rest of the population? If, for example, a U.S. city were to come under the kind of siege experienced by Sarajevo in the mid-1990s, what percentage of the labor force would have to get to work to assure that the city could survive? The list of urban occupational groups that are essential is short; it includes some portion of the labor force devoted to processing, distributing, and retailing food and fuel; employees of electrical utility companies; police, sanitation workers, and enough public health workers to prevent the spread of epidemics. The vast bulk of the labor force — in banking, insurance, education, advertising, computers, health care, retail trade, and so forth — could call in sick every day for six months or a year without causing anything more serious than inconvenience for others.

PROBLEMS OF ADAPTATION

The point, quite simply, is that we already live in the world that Keynes anticipated. Not only has the weight of work on the individual life course been dramatically reduced since when our grandparents were young, but most of us do work that is far removed from our ancestors' struggles to subsist. Most of us do not work at producing goods and services that are indispensable for human existence. This is not a reality that we readily acknowledge. Keynes argued that "we have been expressly evolved by nature — with all our impulses and deepest instincts — for the purpose of solving the economic problem."[11] The result is that even when the work we do is far removed from any pressing economic necessity, we still act as though the social consequences of laziness or negligence will be as severe as they were for our less fortunate forebears. In the U.S. particularly, we tend to reinforce that psychological tendency by continually reminding ourselves of those dramas of downward mobility where people who once enjoyed a middle-class existence are reduced to struggling for their day-to-day survival on the streets.

But for society, it is clear that we have adapted to our expanding capacity to produce by devoting more and more resources to qualitative ends — increased leisure and the production of many nonnecessities. But this adaptation has occurred almost unconsciously for the reason that Keynes indicated — that it is such a break with our entire evolutionary history to acknowledge that the struggle for survival against unyielding nature has been won. Our adaptations have been like a form of collective sleepwalking; we make moves in the right direction but we often cannot even remember why we made them. But these partial, piecemeal, and semi-conscious forms of adaptation to this epochal transformation are continually creating new strains since they can be difficult to reconcile with existing institutional structures.

One of the obvious areas of strain is in the relationship among different nations. While each nation attempts to adapt to the problems created by expanding productive capacity in its own way, it is not free to ignore what is going on elsewhere. A country, for example, that sought to increase leisure by mandating a shorter workweek might be placing itself at an international competitive disadvantage by imposing higher costs on its firms that compete in the world market. Recent history provides many examples of similar strains. For example, after World War II, the trilateral relationship among the U.S., Japan, and Germany was stable for some time. The U.S. used huge investments in military production to absorb its excess productive capacity, and it encouraged Japan and Germany to run large export surpluses of manufactured goods with the rest of the world. This strategy kept the U.S. economy strong and facilitated the rebuilding of Japanese and West German industrial strength as an added bulwark against the Soviet Union. But the high levels of military spending in the U.S. gradually undermined the competitiveness of civilian industries, and the Japanese and Germans were suddenly too successful in capturing U.S. markets. In short, forms of adaptation can easily become contradictory in their effects.

A similar problem occurs within societies between the public and the private sectors. Many developed societies have concentrated on collective consumption and the expansion of state employment as the central means to adapt. The most extreme example has been the Scandinavian welfare states that have dramatically expanded public-sector employment for producing such services as child care and care for the aged. But once one embarks on this path, it is extremely difficult to fine-tune the annual rate of growth of the public-sector to the precise level needed to adapt to expanding private-sector productivity. Public-sector spending then takes on a life of its own, leading to severe fiscal pressures and a rising tax burden on the private sector that causes social and economic strains.

All of these resulting conflicts are more difficult to handle precisely because we have sleepwalked our way to adaptation. When we hit a crisis such as severe governmental budget crises or international trade conflicts, it is like a sleepwalker who is suddenly jolted awake by having walked into a wall. When we are awakened, what flashes into our mind is the Conventional Wisdom that is still grounded in the struggle for survival against nature. Instead of moving forward to consciously chosen forms of adaptation, we are offered the usual program of belt-tightening and greater self-discipline.

8 —— The Counternarrative of Conscious Adaptation

We find ourselves stultified by the legacy of a market-economy which bequeathed us oversimplified views of the function and role of the economic system in society. If the crisis is to be overcome, we must recapture a more realistic vision of the human world and shape our common purpose in light of that recognition.

— Karl Polanyi, 1947

I have no faith in 'curealls' but I believe that we can greatly influence economic forces. I have no sympathy with the professional economists who insist that things must run their course and that human agencies can have no influence on economic ills. One reason is that I happen to know that professional economists have changed their definition of economic laws every five or ten years for a very long time.

— Franklin Delano Roosevelt, 1933[1]

The allegory of "Amazing Grace" and the metaphors of blood and survival are linked together by a common strand of secular pessimism. While the Conventional Wisdom is more optimistic than its critics on some issues, it has an underlying pessimism. All of human history is seen as a continuing struggle against unyielding nature, and this struggle is bound to continue regardless of our rate of scientific and technological advance. This is the secular version of the belief that human life is a continuous struggle against temptation and sinfulness.

In the allegory of being lost and then found, it is possible through great effort to remain on the path of the straight and narrow, but the real reward that one receives will not be in this life. Earthly life remains — even for the righteous — a "vale of tears." By analogy, a society in which most individuals are hard working and frugal can expect to have a well-functioning economy, but the obligation to remain hard-working and frugal is permanent. There is not the slightest hint in this tradition of an earthly paradise of greater leisure and pleasure; such a vision remains a diabolical temptation.

The secular complement to this idea is an underlying "fear of affluence" that Barbara Ehrenreich has identified as an important theme in U.S. popular culture since the 1950s.[2] Despite deep aspirations for material prosperity, there is a strong fear that affluence will undermine the traditional values of hard work and self-discipline. Ehrenreich argues that when U.S. soldiers were unable to withstand North Korean brainwashing during the Korean War, it was immediately hypothesized that our improved standard of living had deprived our young people of the toughness needed to survive in a hostile world. The same theme persists to the present—our high standard of living has spoiled our children and left them more like the grasshopper than the ant. This popular ambivalence about affluence is one reason that the core economic allegory of the need for penitence and sacrifice resonates so strongly: While people want a higher standard of living, they are not so convinced that having it is really good for them or their children in the long term. Invoking the need for austerity allows people to have their cake and eat it, too; they can enjoy material goods while believing that there should not be so many. However, politicians who take the rhetoric too seriously and actually impose austerity on the broad middle classes usually find that people have a greater appetite for the rhetoric than for the reality.

THE QUESTION OF ALTERNATIVES

To say the least, this secular pessimism is not a helpful way to think about a conscious process of social adaptation to our expanding capacity to produce goods and services. On the contrary, it encourages sleepwalking—stumbling around in a dreamlike state in the vain hope that talking tough about austerity and repentance will solve our problems.

Yet, there are few obvious alternatives to this secular pessimism. There is, in fact, an important strand of contemporary thought—postmodernism—that is even more pessimistic about our prospects. Postmodern thinkers argue that the whole Enlightenment tradition that held that we could consciously create better societies has been severely mistaken. In this view, such visions of progress lead inevitably to abuses of political power and the victimization of one or another population. Some postmodern thinkers advise that all we can and should do is wage local struggles against oppression.[3]

This dour turn in Western thought seems to be a direct response to the collapse of Marxism as an alternative to the secular pessimism of the Conventional Wisdom. For close to a century and a half, Marxism reigned as *the* alternative way of thinking about human economy and human prospects. Marx's genius was to elaborate a critique of capitalism that stood the standard allegory on its head to construct a counter-allegory of secular salvation. As with Christian thought, Marx also began with the idea that humans had "fallen" from an initial state of grace—what he called "primitive communism"—but he argued that socialist revolution would begin a historical era in which the development of human productive powers could produce an earthly paradise. In place of the Christian eschatology in which "the last shall be first" only at Judgment Day, Marx insisted that the working class's day would come with the ending of class society.[4]

But the persuasiveness of Marx's formulations derived from combining this inversion of the Christian allegory with the Victorian era's belief in the tangible achievements of science and technology. If human ingenuity could revolutionize the means of production, then surely human intelligence could produce a society that eliminated poverty and exploitation. In a word, Marx's vision of an earthly paradise was rooted in the human acheivement of expanding production through scientific advance.

This belief in science and progress made "planning" one of the central metaphors of Marxism. Just as city planners could establish a design for the rebuilding and future growth of the great European cities, so could economic planners develop a design for the reconstruction and management of the economy. And during those fourteen decades in which Marxism was *the* alternative, the conscious "planning" of human society was the organizing vision of those who rejected the secular pessimism of the Conventional Wisdom. The appeal of this idea of "economic planning" extended beyond the working class and socialist political parties. From the 1920s through the 1940s, leading capitalists in a number of developed economies also embraced the idea of economic planning.

Today, however, the idea of economic planning sounds like an antique notion, and the secular optimism of Marxism appears to have lost its ability to mobilize intellectuals, workers, or peasants.[5] What happened? Everyone knows the obvious answers. The failure and ultimate collapse of Soviet-style Socialism discredited both Marxism and the belief that economies could be planned. More generally, the boundless faith in science and technology of the Victorian era has given way to profound skepticism. While Newt Gingrich and his futurist pals promise that we will all be liberated by the information superhighway, most people no longer believe that technology will save us.

But it is useful to probe a bit further. It was not only the experiences of the former Soviet Union that discredited the idea of central planning, but also the experiences in the developed economies which made it harder to believe that an economy could be planned like a nineteenth century city. The most obvious problem is that of innovation: how can one possibly plan for such an inherently chaotic and unpredictable process as that of technological change? As we have seen, individuals and firms are constantly faced with choices among a number of competing products with different technologies for performing a particular task. Should one switch one's music collection to compact disks or wait for the new generation of digital tape players? It is often extremely difficult to avoid the technology that will soon be orphaned and to choose the one that will provide maximum flexibility in the future. If such decisions are so difficult for the individual, how can they possibly be planned for the whole economy? The fatal weakness of that traditional concept of economic planning was its *hubris*—its exaggerated notion of the capacity of human rationality to comprehend and anticipate something as mercurial and dynamic as economic activity.

But disillusionment with central planning and the collapse of Marxism has left critics of market societies virtually disarmed; there is no longer an effective language to challenge the allegories and metaphors of the Conventional Wisdom. For this reason, the antistate crusade continues to triumph year after year even in the absence of any evidence that the wholesale dismantling of government programs makes the economy work better. But without an alternative narrative and a set of countermetaphors, it is very difficult to challenge the pessimism of the Conventional Wisdom.

CONSCIOUS SOCIAL ADAPTATION

But there is a third position or intellectual tradition. This third view, that has been largely forgotten or ignored in recent years, avoids the hubris of the Marxist faith in human reason and the earthly pessimism of the Christian allegory and embraces a cautiously optimistic belief in the possibilities of social evolution based on the conscious adaptation of societies to changing circumstances. This view rejects the inevitability of progress, while still imagining that advances in the human capacity to produce could lead to social innovations that would reduce poverty, inequality, and oppression. In this third view, however, the attitude toward social innovation is tentative, experimental, and democratic. A society needs to evaluate carefully its institutional changes and adaptations to make sure that the long-term consequences are benign and consistent with continued democracy. This kind of guarded evolutionary optimism has been an important current in twentieth century intellectual history; it is a recognizable element in the traditions of both New Deal liberalism in the U.S. and Social Democracy in Europe.[6]

At the level of rhetoric, this third position evokes the imagery of successful social evolution. Changing physical environments require that human societies adapt their institutions and cultural practices to meet these new challenges. But unlike the imagery of the "survival of the fittest," the evolutionary challenge is not mere survival, but the enhancement of human capacities. This imagery of social evolution was effectively captured in the psychologist Abraham Maslow's concept of the "hierarchy of needs." Maslow argued that while needs for food, water, and shelter were primary, the satisfaction of those needs made it possible for people to satisfy higher-level needs, such as those for social connection, meaning, and aesthetic experience. Social evolution means changing our institutions so that we can satisfy these higher-level needs for an ever larger portion of the population.[7]

But thinking about conscious social evolution also forces us to consider the problem of degeneration. When we think biologically of a favorable environmental shift for a species, the threat of degeneration looms large. For example, if a species that eats many different things suddenly faces a great increase in the supply of one type of food, it is easy to imagine that species adapting by concentrating on that one food source. The species might even give up an evolutionary advantage such as mobility because it can get enough of the new food supply by staying rooted in the same place. But the risk of such adaptations is that if the species were faced with a sudden shortage of one food, it might have lost characteristics such as mobility and the ability to digest a variety of foods that would allow it to adapt again. An environmental improvement can lead directly to a degenerative form of adaptation that diminishes the species' future adaptability.

The danger of degenerative adaptation is close to the fear of affluence discussed earlier. For at least the last 200 years, each successive generation fears that it has made life so easy for its children that they will be unable to flourish in a more challenging environment. But notions of conscious evolution recognize the danger of degenerative adaptations and seek to avoid them. For example, an increasingly productive agriculture frees more people from farming, but the danger of wide starvation is limited as long as knowledge about effective farming methods is retained and the cognitive skills of the population are improving. Movement up the hierarchy is consistent with society retaining the capabilities of dealing effectively with new kinds of environmental challenges.

The task is to avoid those forms of conscious social adaptation that would risk degeneration. For example, one society might handle a reduction in socially necessary work by creating a surplus population of the unemployed that has little incentive to develop its skills or capacities. But writing off this group would certainly diminish the society's ability to adapt in the future. It would be a far preferable strategy to organize work opportunities so that as many people as possible were developing their skills and capacities. But such strategies can only be pursued if we have a notion that we can and must effectively reshape our institutions to adjust to our advancing technological powers.

9 —— A Family of Countermetaphors

The metaphor is probably the most fertile power possessed by man [sic].
—Jose Ortega y Gasset, 1948[1]

This narrative of an ongoing and successful process of conscious social adaptation can be linked to its own family of metaphors to create a viable alternative to the pessimism of the Conventional Wisdom. To be sure, persuasive metaphors cannot simply be pulled out of a hat; they are persuasive only if they resonate with people's experiences. It was not a coincidence, for example, that the economy came to be thought of as a giant self-acting mechanism at the beginning of the Industrial Revolution: the experience of complex machinery gave people a tool that they could use for thinking about the economy. Hence, the countermetaphors proposed here are offered only provisionally, in the hope that others will suggest more persuasive imagery for communicating the underlying ideas.

TREASURE TROVES AND BARGAIN LUNCHES

For a generation, economists have proclaimed that there is no such thing as a free lunch. Everything has a price; it is just that sometimes the costs are not immediately apparent. For example, it is a mistake to think that raising the minimum wage is a costless means to combat poverty. Such a measure will inevitably diminish the number of jobs, so that some previously employed people will be pushed out of work. The lunch isn't free after all; those thrown out of work are the ones who have to pay for it. It hardly requires a stretch to get from the "no free lunch" slogan to the Christian allegory. Even if the lunch were free, the person would probably go off his or her diet, overeat, and end up with heart disease. Our pursuit of worldly pleasures can never lead to good results.

But despite the considerable influence of the "no free lunch" slogan, it contains a logical flaw. It is certainly true that most policy initiatives will have some unintended negative consequences, but there are no laws equivalent to the laws of thermodynamics that say that those costs will always equal the benefits. To be sure, many economic models incorporate the idea that every policy measure will produce an equal and opposite reaction, but such models rest on highly problematic assumptions. In the minimum wage case, for example, the number of people who benefit through higher wages vastly exceeds the number who are hurt by slower job creation.[2] And most reasonable metrics for comparing the costs and the benefits show that the former is substantially greater than the latter. If the result is not an entirely free lunch, it is certainly a bargain lunch; the new policy has produced a visible increase in welfare.

Actually, the rhetoric of "no free lunch" is simply a variant of the vampire state metaphor. Conservatives insist that even if there is a visible gain in welfare from raising the minimum wage, this is offset by expanding the power of the state to "intervene" in the economy. Sooner or later, this enhanced power will be used to suck the lifeblood out of the economy, and we will all be worse off. Hence, in order to move beyond the Conventional Wisdom, it is important to establish that in economic life, lunches might not be completely free, but there are some pretty good ones available at bargain prices.

Let us simply call these bargain lunches "treasure troves," because they are extremely valuable hordes of resources that are hidden from plain view. As long as we wear the blinders of the Conventional Wisdom, we cannot see them. But when we remove the blinders, we can find previously unknown treasures that can be used to finance our social adaptation.

The first treasure trove is that of unutilized output. If the economy is tooling along with 10% unemployment and lots of excess productive capacity, treasure can be created by putting many of these resources to work. This was the core Keynesian insight during the Great Depression: we would all be substantially better off if we could find some way to put more purchasing power into the hands of the unemployed. As Keynes said at the time, even if we employ people to dig ditches and then fill them up again, those so engaged will have money to purchase other goods and services, and that will lead firms to hire back workers and increase investment. As a consequence, total output will be substantially higher than it would be without the initial decision to put some of the unemployed to work.

The second treasure trove comes from increasing coordination efficiency in the economy. Simply bringing the worst managed firms up to 70% or 80% of the efficiency of the best managed firms would expand economic output dramatically. Or imagine, for example, a country that has a chronically high level of labor-management conflict. Not only is time lost in strikes, but the trade-offs between labor effort and compensation are generally poor because distrust is so high on both sides. If a series of government initiatives succeeded in creating a new labor-management framework that reduced conflict and increased cooperation, many firms would be able to develop more productive bargains with their employees. The resulting increase in coordination efficiency could be enormous, leading to significant growth in both labor income and profits. From any economic standpoint, those income gains are another bargain lunch.

There are also many other ways of increasing coordination efficiency in a contemporary economy. Improvements in the telecommunications infrastructure can make a big difference in improving coordination within and between firms. The result can be dramatic reductions in inventories as production is more closely linked to orders, so that labor and equipment are used much more effectively. Hence, countries that strengthen their telecommunications infrastructure through public spending might be able to reap economic benefits that far exceed the initial outlays.

There is still a third treasure trove that has not been mentioned. These are outlays for what can be called "productive consumption." In theory, all expenditures can be divided between consumption and investment, between immediate gratification and the expansion of productive capacity for the future. There is, however, a significant category of expenditures that are ambiguous; they provide both immediate satisfaction *and* they expand future productive capacity. For individuals, two obvious instances of these types of productive consumption are expenditures for education and for psychological counseling or therapy. In national income accounts, these are both counted as pure forms of consumption. But with any luck, these services will provide the consumer with some immediate satisfaction while also providing him or her with productive tools that can be used for many years. Similarly, a firm that offers its employees the benefit of extensive opportunities for training is simultaneously improving the employee's level of consumption and investing in its workforce. The result in both cases is the miracle that people have their cake and eat it, too — obviously the biggest lunch bargain of all.[3]

If a society can persuade people to place more emphasis on productive consumption, it has a powerful means to assure both short-term and long-term improvements in welfare. And, in fact, productive consumption represents the perfect form of social evolution in response to a richer environment. If, for example, a society provided its citizens with more leisure time *and* with more opportunities for productive consumption, it would be adapting itself to a decline in necessary labor time while strengthening the collective capacity to do productive work in the future.

STEERING THE ENTERPRISE

But if the treasure troves are in plain view, they are not right in front of our noses. To mine the treasures — to reap their advantages — means we have to be in the right places at the right times. This is where the second countermetaphor comes in; it is designed to replace the state-as-vampire image with a more realistic metaphor of government action. Our society is like the Starship Enterprise — of *Star Trek* fame — navigating its way through a dangerous universe on a mission of mining treasures and conscious adaptation. But the success of the mission depends on how well those on the flight deck perform the delicate task of steering. The flight crew of the Enterprise is analogous to the government, and steering the Starship is equivalent to what governments do.

The more familiar challenge of steering a car does not adequately convey the complexity of the task of steering a complex market society. While the driver of a car does have to adjust the steering wheel and the speed, it is usually not that hard to stay on the road. But with the Starship, there is no road. The flight crew has to chart a course through deep space that is filled with myriad unknown dangers. Effective steering requires constant and vigilant attention and the ability to make continuous adjustments in speed and direction. The famous diversity of the Starship's flightcrew suggests the range of different skills and types of intelligence that are required for this complex steering task.

The point of the metaphor is that the steering function is utterly indispensable; nobody in his or her right mind would think of relying on "the invisible hand" to steer a spaceship. But the vital role of the flight crew does not assure that it will perform its duties wisely or well. Steering can be haphazard or reckless with disastrous consequences. Moreover, the flight crew could easily abuse its power and take the craft in directions that are very different from where its passengers or headquarters wish it to go. Yet, these dangers cannot be averted by eliminating the job of steering; the only solutions are to choose the flight crew with great care and develop mechanisms for replacing crew members who fail to live up to their responsibilities.

An effective flight crew that steers wisely is able to improve the lives of those on the spacecraft and those dependent on it. For one thing, the flight crew plays a critical role in developing and enforcing the basic rules that allow the population on the spaceship to live and thrive. As was argued earlier, a well-functioning economy does not spring up naturally; it requires clear rules and understandings as to what constitutes property, valid contracts, and appropriate competitive behavior.

Second, the flight crew helps the spaceship community to locate and exploit the various treasure troves. A good crew can help the community take advantage of unutilized productive capacity. Government spending, and even government deficits, can strengthen total demand so that labor and capital that would not otherwise be used are put to productive use. The flight crew can also help realize the treasure trove of increased coordination efficiencies. Government regulations and policies, for example, can place strong pressure on firms to adopt labor policies that contribute to much higher levels of efficiency. Germany's manufacturing economy, for example, is well known for its highly efficient production based on high levels of skill and strong cooperation between workers and employers. But this productive German system was carefully nurtured and supported through governmental actions. Government policies can also contribute to coordination efficiencies by encouraging the development and effective use of new technologies. Free marketers do not like to admit it, but U.S. defense spending was the critical factor in launching the U.S. computer industry. Not only did the government underwrite the costs of the initial research, but it was government purchases that made it possible for the industry to lower prices gradually until private firms could afford the technology. More recently, government has helped to fund manufacturing outreach centers that are designed to teach small- and medium-size enterprises how to use cutting-edge technologies.[4]

The flight crew can also help exploit the treasure trove of productive consumption. Most obviously, effective public education produces high levels of skill and the ability of employees to learn how to learn. There is little debate that the Japanese, Taiwanese, and Korean successes in world markets have been linked to strong national commitments to upgrading education. But effective government policies can also encourage individuals and firms to invest more in the continuous learning of the adult population.

To be sure, not all government actions are productive in these ways. Program inefficiencies or bad decisions can squander resources and actually diminish the efficiency of private firms. If the vampire metaphor is wrong, so too is a view of government as a benevolent father who always knows best. But the steering metaphor captures the key idea that any particular set of government policies will not be effective for all times; there has to be a constant process of adjustment to make sure that the state's policies are strengthening the economy.[5]

STEERING AND UNCERTAINTY

This idea of steering is closely linked to uncertainty. When a business firm invests, there is always some uncertainty over whether or not the investment will pay off. There are multiple sources of this uncertainty: competitors might develop a better product, consumer tastes might shift, government regulators might block sales of the product, the new equipment that is being purchased might never work, and so forth. When levels of uncertainty are too high, firms are unlikely to make investments.

For example, when the political situation in a country is highly unstable, the level of uncertainty goes through the roof, and firms become extremely reluctant to take any risks because the chances of success are hazy. But it is also a serious problem if the level of uncertainty is too low. When a firm knows that demand for its products will continue no matter what it does, there is little incentive either to make new investments or to devote any effort to maintaining product quality. This is precisely why economists always preach against the dangers of monopoly. A firm in a monopoly situation faces very low levels of uncertainty, so there is no incentive to use resources efficiently.

The goal of governmental steering can be seen as an effort to achieve levels of uncertainty that are at the desirable intermediate level. In fact, most governmental economic policies can be reinterpreted as efforts to reduce the uncertainty that private investors face. Policies that shift resources to lower-income households have the effect of lowering uncertainty for firms that produce for the mass consumer market; they can be more confident that demand will be there for their products. Education and training programs reduce uncertainties surrounding the recruitment of an appropriate labor force. Environmental and other regulations reduce the danger that unscrupulous competitors will conquer market share by imposing pollution or other costs on third parties. And government spending on infrastructure, such as roads and bridges, simultaneously creates more certain demand for firms that win government contracts, and it creates more predictability for investors seeking to develop real estate projects.

The problem is that any particular policy runs the risk of reducing uncertainty too much. For example, U.S. defense procurement policies worked for many years to reduce uncertainties so that private firms would be more willing to invest in plant and equipment and help develop new military technologies. However, at a certain point, the levels of uncertainty for military contractors became too low. Defense firms became completely dependent on government contracts, and they lost the ability to compete in civilian markets where price competition is intense.

This is why the steering process is so complex and requires continuous adjustments. Maintaining the same course often risks either a fall in effective investment because uncertainty is too high or because it has become too low. Moreover, the standard political polarization between advocates of "activist" government and defenders of "laissez-faire" misses the real issue. The important question is not how much the government does to shape the economy because both "intervention" and "nonintervention" are policy choices that have real consequences for levels of uncertainty. Even the most extreme advocates of "deregulation" are arguing for a particular policy mix. The real questions are, what effect does any particular policy mix have on levels of uncertainty for firms making investments? And what changes in policy might return uncertainty to the optimal levels?

The need for continuous adjustment is also the reason that democracy is so critical for this process. Any political regime — whether it espouses free market rhetoric or believes in a command economy — is bound to develop substantial investments in the particular mechanisms that it develops for steering the economy. These mechanisms inevitably become part of the repertoire of devices through which this regime builds and holds on to its base of political support. The problem is that any particular regime will have a strong tendency to preserve its favored mechanisms even when they are obviously no longer effective. For example, an established regime that has a large and inefficient state-owned productive sector will be reluctant to make big changes because it relies on the plant managers and the employment they generate as a critical base of political support. But similarly, a free-market-oriented regime that has had some successes in selling off state-owned enterprises is unlikely to know when to stop because it has created powerful constituencies who benefit from the privatization process.

This is another reason that periodic competitive elections are so important. By allowing for periodic changes of regime, they assure that a government does not become permanently wed to one set of mechanisms or another. If, for example, a privatizing regime has gone "too far," a new election can produce a different government that pursues a more balanced policy. In this way, elections can force governments that have steered too far in one direction or the other to adjust their course and make changes in the mechanisms of economic adjustment.[6]

To be sure, recent history has been characterized by countries making very sharp swings in their economic policies from one political extreme to the other. Much of this has occurred in response to the hegemony of antistate ideology with its explicit references to the workings of the "invisible hand." When people come to understand that all complex economies require a great deal of steering by quite visible hands, we can get past the sterile debate between opponents and proponents of steering. But there will remain much room for intense and fruitful debate over the precise steering mechanisms to be used, since different political groups will correctly see their fortunes linked to the choice among these mechanisms.

10 —— The Logic and Illogic of Austerity

Mere parsimony is not economy....Expense, and great expense, may be an essential part of true economy.

—Edmund Burke, 1796 [1]

The difference in conceptualizing the economy between the Conventional Wisdom and the counter-metaphors suggested here is most obvious in the proposed remedies for economic weakness. The remedy that is favored by the Conventional Wisdom is generally a new round of austerity. Austerity is any systematic effort to depress average consumption levels either by reducing real wages, lowering government services, or increasing effective tax rates on most households. [2]

Austerity plays the same role as penitence in the Christian allegory. Just as the individual cannot return to righteousness without a period of more intense self-discipline, so a society cannot restore its economy to health without a period of austerity — belt-tightening and sacrifice is the sure path to prosperity. The mechanism is clear from the capital-as-blood metaphor. The weakness of the economy is understood as a consequence of too little blood; the life-giving supply of money capital is depleted. But if people can be persuaded to limit their consumption either directly or by curbing the appetite of the vampire state, there will be more blood/capital available to finance the life-giving investment that the economy needs. In short, austerity means more private saving and more restraint in government spending, and that will restore a healthy flow of blood capital through the economy's veins.

This is precisely the logic that underlies the current enthusiasm for balancing the federal budget. The deficit is seen as dangerous because it is drawing down the pool of capital that should be used for private investment purposes. If we can successfully drive a stake through the heart of the deficit monster, private investment can be expected to boom, providing more rapid growth and more vigorous job creation. But the effort to reduce the deficit is simultaneously a moral crusade. The deficit has become a glaring symptom of a society that has grown profligate; our inability to match government expenditures with revenues is proof that we are unable to control our appetites. Nobody

Chart 1: Total Government Spending as % of GDP

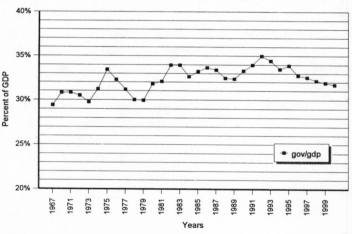

This chart shows state, local, and federal spending as a percentage of GDP for the period from 1967 to the year 2000. Data for the years from 1967 to 1994 are from Tables B-1 and B-83 in *Economic Report to the President 1995*. Estimates of GDP and Federal spending for the years from 1995 to 2000 are taken from the Clinton Administration's 1996 budget proposal, *Budget of the United States Government, Fiscal Year 1996, Historical Tables*, Table 1.2. The calculation assumes that state and local expeditures will remain constant at 11% of GDP. Since the Clinton Administration has given considerable ground in the budget battles since these estimates were released, the projected decline of government spending as a percentage of GDP is likely to be even steeper than this chart suggests.

imagines that it will be easy to balance the federal budget—even over seven years. But the claim is that the sacrifice that we will have to make—as we suffer from reduced government spending on health care, legal services, education, and dozens of other programs—will most certainly make us a better people. We will be forced to become more self-reliant, and the cold shower of austerity will do wonders for our collective moral character.

THE DEFICIT
AND FEDERAL SPENDING

Despite all of the huffing and puffing about the deficit, one simple fact is rarely mentioned. During the period of post World War II economic expansion, government expenditures rose rapidly as a share of GDP. In 1947, government expenditures had returned to their pre-WW II level of 18.5% of GDP (see Chart 1). Over the next twenty years, the ratio rose to 29.4% of GDP. But in the entire period from 1967 to 1994, the ratio has risen only 5% to 33.5% of GDP.[3] In other words, the ratio of government spending to total output grew three times faster per year during the prosperous years from 1947 to 1967 than during the troubled years between 1967 and 1994. And with current plans for budget cutting, this ratio is expected to decline by the end of the decade to 31% or 32%—just barely above the level of the early 1970s. This success—both already accomplished and projected—in slowing the growth of government spending is even more remarkable since government transfer programs, such as Social Security and Medicare, have grown substantially as a share of total government spending. In fact, the nontransfer part of government outlays—purchases of goods and services and government employment —has been declining as a percentage of GDP for more than twenty years and that decline will accelerate as current budget cuts take hold.

But what has been our reward for this remarkable success in restraining the growth of government spending? The obvious answer is a far weaker economy than we had during the period in which government outlays were rising more rapidly. By restraining the growth of government spending, we have successfully limited total demand, so that the economy's output is substantially below what it is capable of producing. Yet, we are continually told that the real problem is that the government continues to gobble up too large a share of GDP, and that we will never return to prosperity unless we make a serious effort to reduce spending on big transfer programs such as Medicare and Social Security. The basic claim is that if more than twenty-five years of budgetary restraint have not yet made the economy stronger, then the obvious solution is an even more drastic dose of the same medicine.

THE MISTAKEN LOGIC
OF AUSTERITY

The point is not that we would definitely be better off had these ratios grown more rapidly; much depends upon the wisdom with which the government steers the economy. But once we reject the vampire state view that government funds will always be used destructively, it is easier to see the central point. Government spending is one of the most important mechanisms through which our society adapts to a richer environment.

We do this primarily by using our resources to produce public goods that we think will improve our lives and make us more productive in the future. Among these public goods are national defense, education, scientific research, public safety, environmental improvements, and the protection of individuals and families from economic insecurity. The full value of many of these items is not included in our statistics on GDP because they are things that cannot easily be bought and sold on the market, but they are very significant determinants of our collective level of well-being. Moreover, the fact that these items are public goods means that private producers left to their own devices will be unable to suppy them at anywhere near optimal levels. When we decide to expand production of one or another of these public goods, we are finding ways to utilize productive capacities that might otherwise lie idle. In short, expanding the production of public goods puts resources to work without the risk of glutting the market with goods and services that nobody will buy.

In effect, the advocates of budgetary austerity are urging us to adapt to our expanded capacity to create goods and services by simply producing less and living less well. Imagine, for example, if a tribe had discovered an agricultural technique that allowed it to produce the same crop with half the labor. Assuming that the tribe simply redistributes output, the labor that was freed could then be used to produce works of art, public buildings, and other public goods. The tribe would be twice as rich as before. But what would happen if there were a religious taboo against nonagricultural labor? If we assume that there were no available trading partners, the community would either have to forget the new technology and forego the increased wealth or it would have to struggle with the problem of a shortage of productive work. The effect of the taboo is to turn something that was potentially positive into a disaster. But today's apostles of budgetary austerity are doing the same thing as the priests who enforce the religious taboo; they are imposing entirely unnecessary hardships on a community.

This issue should have been settled during the Great Depression. At that time, conservatives argued that a failure to keep the federal budget balanced would make recovery from the economic slowdown impossible. They reasoned that any lack of governmental budget discipline would postpone indefinitely the revival of private business investment that must be the key to recovery. But, of course, balancing the budget in a period of severe economic depression requires large cuts in spending levels since a government's revenues are much reduced. Balanced-budget policies only deepened the deflationary dynamic, and the promised spontaneous recovery never materialized.

Nations that pursued the alternative strategy of running government deficits to revive the economy correctly understood that all of the developed market economies were suffering from vast amounts of unused capacity. It obviously made no sense to tell people to tighten their belts and reduce their consumption at a moment when the economy's major problem was the weakness of consumer demand. The only thing that could possibly justify such a policy choice was the religious imagery that always defines penitence and self-sacrifice as desirable.

To be sure, today's economic conditions are nothing like those of the Great Depression either in the level of unemployment or general misery. But there is a basic similarity that makes austerity as irrational today as it was sixty years ago. As in the 1930s, the U.S. has vast amounts of productive capacity that are not being utilized effectively. Think, for example, of both the labor force and the plants and machinery in the defense industries that are now experiencing huge cutbacks with the end of the cold war. Just to keep these defense cutbacks from being even more devastating, the U.S. has significantly increased its sales of military equipment to other countries around the world. Everybody knows that arming other countries is a foolish short-term policy that will probably cost us dearly in the future, but the government keeps doing it because it needs to preserve jobs and defense firms.

Suppose that we were able to convert both the unused and the unwisely used defense capacity to produce civilian goods.[4] The immediate problem is who would buy the resulting flow of goods. If, for example, former defense plants started turning out attractive electric cars, they would inevitably cut into Detroit's sales and that would lead to new rounds of automotive job cuts. We could try to export a lot of the goods, but our major trading partners would not be very eager to absorb a huge new flow of imports.

The reality is that we leave these plants idle or use them to produce arms for export because we know that there would not be markets for the civilian goods that they could produce. We fail to pursue conversion because there is not enough consumer demand in the economy to make conversion viable. But then the leading advocates of the Conventional Wisdom insist that we must cut our levels of consumption in order to restore our economy to health. But will reducing what Social Security recipients receive by 10% create demand for the products of converted factories? Obviously not; it would instead dampen demand even further. Similarly, capping health care entitlements will also not add to demand; it will do the opposite since people will be forced to give up discretionary spending as they pay more out of their own pockets for health care. In a word, because austerity policies are designed to dampen consumption, they are inappropriate in an economy that has too much productive capacity relative to consumer purchasing power.

INCREASED UNCERTAINTY AND DIMINISHED PRIVATE INVESTMENT

Austerity policies also have other bad consequences. The efforts to restrain the growth of government spending over the past twenty-five years have produced a long-term decline in government spending on physical infrastructure. This includes outlays for airports, harbors, roads, as well as water and sewage treatment, and other kinds of physical facilities. During the 1992 presidential election, Bill Clinton made a big issue of this infrastructure spending gap, and he compared the U.S. unfavorably to other developed market economies whose governments spend a much larger share of GDP on these items.[5] Unfortunately, the pressure on Clinton after his election to reduce the federal budget deficit has meant that he has been unable to reverse the twenty-five-year decline in infrastructure spending.

Declining infrastructure spending raises the level of uncertainty for private firms and thus dampens the rate of private-business investment. In California, for example, during the boom years of growth in the 1950s and 1960s, local governments would provide most of the infrastructure needed for new housing developments. Builders only had to worry about putting up houses and selling them, and new units were added at a phenomenal pace. But after Proposition 13—the property tax cutting initiative that was passed in 1978—local governments could no longer afford to subsidize private construction and were forced to shift more and more of the infrastructure costs on to the developers. Developers now have to bear the costs of sewers, roads, and even the construction of new public schools. The result has been a significant increase in the risk facing developers who have to worry about whether or not they can recover these added costs when it comes time to sell the units. Predictably, the rate of new housing construction has fallen significantly.

Similar dynamics occur with industrial production as well. Purchases by government can be a key mechanism for protecting manufacturers from crippling levels of uncertainty in the development of new products. As noted earlier, government purchases of mainframe computers for military and space purposes played an absolutely critical role in the early days of the computer industry.[6] It was during the period of fulfilling the government contracts that the industry learned how to produce a cost-effective product that private firms would be willing to purchase. In the absence of that kind of certain demand, private firms are unlikely to risk the development funds needed to launch important new products.

In short, high levels of public infrastructure spending help to sustain private investment. Hence, austerity policies that are supposed to end up encouraging private investment often do the opposite. By cutting public infrastructure spending, uncertainty for private firms is increased and the overall level of investment falls.

AUSTERITY AND INVESTMENTS IN EDUCATION

Another area where austerity has particularly perverse consequences is in spending on education and training. Everyone knows that people in the bottom part of the income distribution are very limited in both their marketable skills and their discretionary income. Moreover, business firms are generally reluctant to invest in training such employees because there is no guarantee that the employer will reap the benefits; the newly trained employee might well take his or her skills elsewhere. But if lower-income people cannot finance their own or their children's education and training, and if they cannot rely on employers to provide either free, they have no choice but to depend on government programs such as public education, community colleges, loan guarantee programs, and so forth. Yet, it is precisely these types of programs that are most likely to be cut in times of budgetary austerity. For example, twenty years ago, many states and some big cities provided free access to public higher education. If students met the admissions requirements, they could sign up for classes even if their financial resources were extremely limited. But federal budget restraint over the past twenty years has led to significant reductions in subsidies to state and local governments, which has forced budgetary restraints at those levels as well. Today, virtually all of these institutions have been forced to establish significant financial barriers to entry in the form of tuition or fees. Often, the imposition of these fees has been accompanied by scholarship and loan programs that are designed to help lower income students overcome these financial barriers. But while some of the most talented and crafty students from lower-income backgrounds are still able to jump the barriers, many others are not. With higher tuition and fees coming on top of continuing deterioration in family income, many of these young people will end up abandoning the goal of higher education.[7]

These barriers will lock many low-income people into life-long poverty, but the impact on society as a whole is also destructive. Instead of having a larger pool of people with high skills, we will have an expanding low-skill population. This is a dysfunctional form of adaptation since it undermines our flexibility and ability to produce in the future. But this is precisely what austerity does; it adapts us downward.

This is the complete opposite of exploiting the treasure trove of productive consumption. Instead of encouraging people to consume increased education and training, austerity policies put these types of productive consumption out of reach for more and more citizens. The result is lowered standards of living in both the short term and the long term.

CONCLUSION

If we think in terms of conscious social adaptation, treasure troves, and steering the Enterprise, it becomes obvious that austerity policies are deeply misguided. The steering metaphor, in particular, highlights that the critical question is not the amount of government spending, but the nature of that spending. When the economy is not working well, the critical task is to redeploy government spending in more productive and effective ways to produce those optimal levels of uncertainty and to take advantage of all three treasure troves.

In the next four parts of this book, these opposing sets of rhetorical devices are used to unravel some of the main controversies over the U.S. economy. Part II focuses on the domestic economy, Parts III and IV look at the role of finance and the world economy, and Part V returns to the question of where conscious adaptation should take us.

Part Two

THROUGH A GLASS DARKLY: THE DOMESTIC ECONOMY

11 —— Selective Mismeasurement

It ain't so much the things we don't know that get us in trouble. It's the things we know that ain't so.

— Artemus Ward[1]

The Conventional Wisdom is biased toward bad news, since bad economic news reinforces the need for repentance and austerity. In fact, much of the persuasiveness of the Conventional Wisdom derives from a continuing flow of economic statistics confirming that something is very wrong. This peculiar bias creates a serious dilemma for critics of current economic arrangements. These critics are generally eager to point out the failures of the economy — that the average real wage of working people, for example, has not risen for close to twenty years — in the hope that this will lead citizens to favor significant economic reforms. But this kind of bad news is just grist for the mill; it is simply further confirmation that we are living in a state of economic sin and that only a return to the straight and narrow will suffice to bring us back to the bygone days of rising real wages. Instead of weakening it, bad news only confirms the Conventional Wisdom and its perpetual prescription for belt-tightening.

It would be better if these critics recognized that the economic statistics are themselves systematically biased in a way that usually reinforces the most pessimistic views of the economy. The bias is not intentional; it is an unintended by-product of attempting to capture a continuously changing reality with measurement tools that are often a half-century old. It is the "buggy whip problem" writ large. Before the advent of the horseless carriage, sales of buggy whips were a good leading economic indicator; their rise would tend to predict good times and their fall, bad times. But those who saw the precipitous decline of sales after 1900 as an indication of an economy that was about to go into the tank were seriously mistaken. It was simply that when you bought a car, you no longer had need of a buggy whip. The constant change in the mix of goods and services that the economy produces creates parallel dilemmas for economic statisticians, and the normal ways of handling these dilemmas contribute to a pessimistic bias in our economic data.

MEASUREMENT AND THE PROBLEM OF QUALITY CHANGE

Three of our most important economic statistics are the measures of GDP, the measures of productivity growth, and the measures of the inflation rate. The first tells us how much our economy is producing, the second shows changes in the efficiency of production, and the third indicates what is happening to the purchasing power of the dollar. All of these measures are distorted by changes in the quality of economic output.[2]

Quality changes in goods and services can occur in both directions; products can get either worse or better. Candy makers can surreptitiously shrink the size of chocolate bars and home builders can use thinner and cheaper wallboards in home construction. On the other hand, new products, such as "miracle drugs" and fax machines, can come to market that could not be purchased at any price in an earlier era and established products can get better—improved gas mileage for cars, increased reliability for appliances—without corresponding increases in prices. Since quality downgrading and quality upgrading are always going on simultaneously, it is possible that the processes will exactly offset each other, so that quality changes can be ignored without compromising the accuracy of economic data.

Over the past twenty years, however, quality upgrading has overwhelmed quality downgrading in the U.S. economy. Three different dynamics are involved here, but the computer revolution plays a role in each of them. First, producers of many consumer goods more than ever compete with each other by making claims about the improved quality of their products. In the automobile industry, Japanese producers made enormous inroads in the domestic U.S. market by making cars that simply worked better. U.S. auto firms were slow to rise to the challenge, but they were ultimately forced to worry about such dimensions of product quality as defects, repair records, gas mileage, and comfort. Now, the typical automobile ad on television brags about how much that firm's workers care about the cars they put together. But the pattern in cars now characterizes many other types of consumer goods, such as appliances, furniture, foods, and so forth. Increased concern with quality means both intensified efforts to catch defects before the products leave the factory and greater attention to previously neglected product characteristics. Appliances are now made to run more quietly, foods are being reprocessed to reduce fat calories, and so forth. In many of these cases, the availability of relatively cheap computer technology has made it easier for manufacturers both to improve their quality control efforts and to provide consumers with a greater choice of different product features.[3]

A second area of systematic upgrading has occurred in capital goods such as computers, communications equipment, medical instruments, and machine tools. This point hardly needs to be belabored. It is widely known that computer power has been falling in price at rates of 15% to 20% a year; each new generation of computers offers dramatic advances in computational power with prices constant or falling. But the important point is that these costless improvements trickle down into many types of equipment that use computing power, so that manufacturers can offer qualitative improvements without corresponding increases in cost.[4]

The final area of systematic upgrading has occurred in the service sector where computerization has often improved the quality of service. In banking, for example, consumers now have access to services that were previously unavailable, such as cash machines, and a much broader choice among different financial instruments than was possible in precomputer days. In telecommunications, the last twenty years have also seen such innovations as relatively cheap cellular phones, telephone answering machines, faxes, and the beginning of video phones. Even if one allows for such detested new technologies as electronic switchboards with their "press 1 now" messages, the qualitative improvements have been dramatic. Even in the troubled health care sector, there are numerous examples of procedures that used to require hospitalization that are now done on an outpatient basis with improved results.[5]

That the dominant trend has been toward quality improvements in the mix of goods and services that we consume would not be a problem if the methodologies of economic accounting were adequate to the task, but they are not. In theory, any change in product quality — either upwards or downwards — could be related to the past price of the product to figure out whether total quality per dollar has risen or fallen. For example, when the size of the candy bar is cut from 8 ounces to 6 ounces, while leaving the price at 48 cents, it is pretty clear that this is a disguised price increase of 33% per ounce of candy bar. But the measurement task is a lot more difficult when this year's model of automobile has 6% better fuel efficiency, 5% better reliability, a slight decline in its performance in crash tests, and a 2% increase in price. How does one take all of these factors into account?

The answer is that we do not because government statistical agencies have limited resources to monitor quality changes in goods and services. In the U.S., this task is assigned to the Bureau of Labor Statistics (BLS), which is in charge of constructing price indexes for both consumer goods and producer goods. BLS employees check the prices on a broad range of different products on a monthly basis in different parts of the country to see how price levels are changing. Even without probing for quality changes, simply checking the prices on thousands of different products is a huge undertaking. So it is hardly surprising that the BLS misses even some of the more obvious quality changes such as shifts in product size, and it totally ignores most of the more subtle quality changes including shifts in the fuel efficiency and reliability of cars.[6]

If government agencies had more resources, they could, in theory, collect information on many of the characteristics of products and develop what are called "hedonic price indexes" — this is an econometric technique designed to compare products with shifting characteristics over time to figure out exactly how the ratio of price to qualities is changing. Government statisticians have used this technique for computers because the failure to account for quality changes was creating major distortions in all of the basic economic data. But creating these hedonic indexes is extremely time consuming because it requires a great deal of specialized knowledge about the product that one is evaluating. The analyst is supposed to weigh all of the qualities that matter to the product's consumers, not only the qualities that might appeal to the statistician. Yet, some of the qualities that might be most important to the consumer — such as the product's reliability and durability — are impossible to evaluate at the moment of the initial purchase. In short, the use of hedonic indexes on a broader basis is impractical; it is simply too difficult to monitor all of these important price and quality changes on a monthly basis.

Moreover, there is still another large problem. How does one account for the introduction of new products that cannot be compared to an older product category? For example, when electronic calculators were first introduced their price and quality could be compared to electromechanical calculators, but even that kind of comparison is impossible in the case of the fax machine. One cannot reasonably compare the cost of sending a letter by messenger when a fax can arrive on the other side of the world in seconds. The available techniques simply do not help us to measure the increase in a society's welfare that can come from totally new products.

It is helpful to think about this in relation to the basket of goods and services that is typically covered by a price index, such as the food a family buys each week. For example, in June 1994, a typical family's bag of groceries cost $80 and in June 1995, the same bag of groceries cost $84. The news would report that food prices had risen 5% in that year. But imagine that in June 1995, these families were able for the first time to purchase a newly developed bar of chocolate that is delicious, gives one a jolt of energy, has no fat or cholesterol, and is priced at $3 a pound. Obviously, a comparable product was not available for any price in the previous year. For a family of chocolate lovers, the value to them of their $87 basket of groceries in June 1995 — the standard basket plus the new chocolate bar — was significantly higher than what they could have purchased for the same amount of money a year before. The infinite drop in price of their dream snack food easily offsets the 5% increase on other grocery items.

Of course, this measurement problem has existed for decades; the introduction of completely new products is old news. But the uniqueness of the current period is that for millions of consumers in the developed market economies, it has become expected and routine that a significant share of their budgets will be used to purchase gadgets, devices, and services that were completely unavailable as recently as a decade ago. To be sure, many of these new products are utter flops; twenty might fail for every one that successfully establishes a new market. Nevertheless, the vast consumer market for continuous innovation means that this longstanding measurement problem is much more important than in earlier decades.

For example, if a society devoted 10% of its capital stock and

10% of its labor force to the development and production of entirely new products, what would this do to the accuracy of its economic data? As long as some of those new products were eagerly consumed, that society's economic data would consistently overstate inflation and understate both the growth of real GDP and the growth of productivity unless that society developed a mechanism for estimating the addition to welfare from these innovations. Without doing that, it would appear that 10% of the society's resources were just being flushed down the toilet because the improvements in quality from new products were not being measured.

This is an exaggerated version of what goes on in our society. The failure to account for quality change — both with existing products and innovations — leads to systematic distortions in our data on economic output. Price indexes overstate the extent of price increases — as in the example of the basket with the magical chocolate. When these inaccurate price indexes are then used to compare the growth of output over time, current output appears smaller than it acutally is.[7] The results are lower rates of growth in GDP and lower rates of productivity growth. This provides further confirmation that we need to tighten our belts and go through a period of austerity.

12 —— Why Wellbeing Does Not Count

Not only is GNP a poor measure of welfare, it is also a poor measure of income.
— Herman E. Daly and John B. Cobb, Jr., 1989

From personal experience I know that the policymakers, to whom figures such as per capital Gross National Product (GNP) are fed, are not educated in the uses and abuses of these statistics. Most with whom I worked over the years would not have known that the accounts exclude the services of housewives or that conservation and environmental issues are quite beyond the sphere of any so-called balanced economic analysis.
— Marilyn Waring, 1988[1]

The huge problem of quality change in goods and services is only a part of the distortion in our economic indicators. Another major distortion comes from all of those things that are not included in our measures of GDP. Here, again, the basic consequence is a steady flow of bad-news reporting about the state of the economy. The irony is that this unreliable bad news diverts attention from what is really wrong with the economy.

THE LIMITS OF GDP

The people who originally designed our system for measuring economic output understood that their measures were not good indicators of how well or badly people in the society were living. On the contrary, their intention was simply to measure the changes over time in the value of goods and services that were produced for sale on the market. Because of this definition, our measures of national output exclude all of the services produced by unpaid family members working in the home. No matter what the quality of the relationship, all that cleaning, child care, and cooking done by wives, husbands, roommates, and live-in lovers are not services produced for sale on a market.

But even beyond services produced by family members in the home, there are other large chunks of economic activity that are left out of this definition of economic output. For example, the output of broadcast media such as television and radio does not appear in GDP as a consumer good because consumers do not buy these services on the market. Television and radio shows are treated as an intermediate good—something that is used up in the process of producing a consumer good. Hence, the total dollar value of detergents or automobiles that are included in GDP incorporates all of the advertising budgets that were used to produce television and radio shows.

National income accountants did make a big exception for government. Even though government services are usually not produced for sale on a market, governmental output was included as a component of total output. But when they made this compromise, national income accountants also chose to value this governmental output as equal to the wages and salaries paid to government employees. The result, in keeping with the vampire state metaphor, is that government can never demonstrate productivity gains. The value of government output is always equal to the labor inputs of government employees. Hence, it is statistically impossible for government to show improvements in productivity.

But the central problem with this measurement framework is that an economy produces all kinds of outputs that are not marketable commodities.[2] One obvious set of these noncommodity outputs are environmental "bads," such as air pollution, water pollution, and the destruction of natural ecosystems. This exclusion means that a country's economic output as measured by GDP might rise even though it is using up precious nonrenewable resources at breakneck speed and jeopardizing any future economic growth. By the same token, an economy can produce environmental "goods," such as cleaner air, cleaner water, and the protection of natural resources; but any funds used for these purposes will not produce any positive effect on the economic output numbers.

Environmental "bads" and "goods" are only the most obvious examples of many different economic outputs that are by-products of production. These include the various nonmonetary satisfactions that are provided by work such as opportunities for learning, the chance for movement into better jobs, and voluntary leisure time (as distinct from unwanted leisure that results from unemployment). Others include economic security, the ability to live in a desirable neighborhood without the threat of crime, the level of comfort experienced by those who are sick and injured, and the aesthetic satisfactions that people gain from working in, living in, or simply frequenting attractive surroundings. There is good reason to believe that people's feelings of well-being have much more to do with factors such as these than with small variations in their ability to buy marketable goods and services. For example, when people are asked how much of a pay reduction they would be willing to take in exchange for a job with significant opportunities for learning, their answers suggest that such opportunities are worth a great deal to them.[3]

The importance of these economic outputs that are not produced for sale on a market looms largest when we seek to evaluate how different economies are doing. If, for example, we compare the rates of economic growth in the U.S. and Sweden, we usually look only at how GDP—the production of marketable goods and services—has grown in the two societies. But the fact that Sweden has invested huge amounts of money to provide its population with protections from economic insecurity does not enter into the comparison. An output that is obviously extremely important for the average Swede does not get counted as a part of his or her nation's total output.

Yet different societies regularly make the decision to increase some of these noncommodity outputs even if it means reducing commodity outputs. Making those trade-offs does not mean that the society is actually producing less; it is just producing differently. But our overemphasis on GDP makes it impossible for us to understand these trade-offs. For example, politicians routinely warn that protecting the environment will mean slower economic growth. What they really mean is that protecting the environment will result in slower growth of marketable goods and services, since a larger share of production would be devoted to noncommodity outputs such as a cleaner environment.

In fact, the decision to increase these noncommodity outputs is one of the fundamental ways that developed market societies have successfully adapted to the growing productiveness of labor. Most of these societies have dramatically increased the role of leisure and nonworking time in the individual life course, and they have also made significant improvements in the population's level of economic security and in the provision of various public amenities. There is every reason to believe that these forms of adaptation will loom even larger in the future, so that the relative importance of the goods and services produced for sale on the market will continue to diminish.

NONCOMMODITY OUTPUTS AND MEASUREMENT BIAS

One more example should suffice to show how these vitally important noncommodity outputs throw off our economic measures. One goal that this society has had for some time is to increase the comfort level of people who are sick or incapacitated in one way or another. The Americans with Disabilities Act (ADA) is a recent expression of this goal; barriers to full social participation are to be reduced for millions of people with disabilities. But this is a continuation of a long-term trend that includes developing medical techniques that make life more comfortable for the afflicted, reducing pain levels for the sick and injured, and investing in technologies that expand functioning for the disabled. If one compares the current situation of the disabled or the chronically ill with their situation fifty or one hundred years ago, it is obvious that tremendous advances have been made in expanding this particular noncommodity output.

Clearly, the value of this noncommodity output vastly exceeds the expenses incurred in producing it. But how does one value millions of people not having to live with crippling levels of pain? How does one value the expanded opportunities and life chances for millions of people who in an earlier epoch would have been relegated to minimal existence in a custodial institution or in someone's attic? Whatever dollar value one might attempt to put on this noncommodity output is not included in our GDP figure. Therefore, our estimate of the economy's growth over the last twenty or fifty years dramatically understates the total growth of utility or sastisfaction.

Moreover, as the substantial costs of the ADA atttest, it seems clear that with each passing year, we devote ever more resources to the production of this and other noncommodity outputs. Hence, the distortion in measuring only the commodity outputs tends to increase with each passing year. Or, to put it in other terms, we should expect the growth rate of commodity outputs to decline over time since our advanced economies are devoting increasing efforts to producing a whole series of noncommodity outputs. But this apparent slowdown in growth is not bad news; it is simply a logical consequence of emphasizing the production of things that we have not tried very hard to include in our measures of output.

THE FINAL IRONY
OF MISMEASUREMENT

In identifying the distortion of economic data that results from quality change and noncommodity outputs, the idea is not to suggest an entirely rosy or upbeat scenario. Our economy's production of some of the most important of the noncommodity outputs — economic security, voluntary leisure, safety from crime — has been falling in recent years, contributing to pervasive anger and discontent. Equally important are the significant increases in inequality in the distribution of both money income and noncommodity outputs. Income inequality in the U.S. has been rising rapidly for several decades; for example, the after-tax income of the top 1% of households grew from 7.3% of total income in 1977 to 12.4% in 1989.[4] Moreover, widespread concern about the "secession" of the rich from the rest of the society suggests that high-income households have been able to insulate themselves from rising crime, decaying cities, and other shortfalls in the production of highly desired noncommodity outputs.[5] The combination of these two trends — insufficient production of certain key noncommodity outputs and growing inequality — has fostered rising political discontent.

Yet, when observers complain that average real wages of working people have not risen in the U.S. for twenty years, they divert attention from these real and pressing problems. The fact is that if quality changes are accurately reflected in the data, those real wages *would* show an increase for people in the middle of the income distribution. Chart 2 shows the changes in the average real income level of different income quintiles with the conventional consumer price index (CPI), while Chart 3 shows the same pattern with a CPI that has been adjusted to take account of quality changes. The adjustment that has been made is a minimal one — the estimate of annual inflation has been reduced by just half of 1% per year. Most estimates are that the overstatement of inflation is substantially higher than that. But even this minor adjustment makes a major difference in the relative success of different income groups.

With the uncorrected data in Chart 2, all three of the lowest quintiles — 60% of the population — show basically stagnant income levels. Only the richest quintile shows significant gains; the second richest quintile shows only a modest improvement. With the corrected data in Chart 3, the richest quintile still experiences the most dramatic income gains, but the three lowest quintiles also experience income growth between 10% and 20% over this twenty-two-year period. This is hardly a spectacular improvement, but if one made a larger adjustment to the CPI, their income gains would be more impressive. The point is simply that the story of stagnant real income levels for most of the population is not true if the CPI overstates inflation.

But the main problem with the story told by the uncorrected data is that emphasizing the slow growth of commodity outputs simply reinforces the Conventional Wisdom that output is not growing fast enough because we are not investing enough, and that only a scaled back public sector and increased household frugality will get us to the higher rates of growth that we all want. The issues of noncommodity outputs and inequities in distribution disappear from the society's radar screen.

Yet, these are the real issues. If people are worried about their growing economic insecurity, no amount of economic growth is going to solve that problem. On the contrary, as recent job layoffs by large corporations attest, even in periods of growth, there can be diminishing job security. Moreover, nobody has yet explained how a smaller and leaner government will be able to protect people from this kind of economic insecurity.

Similarly, the problem of growing income inequality is not a self-correcting one. Once the distribution of income begins to shift in favor of the rich, the process takes on a life of its own. When many working people find that their wages are stagnating or growing slowly, they find it harder and harder to live within their budget. The obvious recourse is to increase the amount of labor time that the family contributes to the economy. A primary earner might take a second job, a wife increases her hours, or teenagers are sent out to work longer hours. But as all of these people crowd the labor market looking for work, the bargaining position of employees deteriorates further. When employers see the long queues of potential employees, they are emboldened to resist demands for higher wages. As the bargaining position of employers improves, the stagnation of wage levels continues and the vicious cycle of overcrowding at the low end of the labor market and worsening income distribution continues.

Despite the misleading data, our economy's capacity to produce has been expanding substantially. The problem is that mistaken priorities have led us to underproduce some very important noncommodity outputs and to stand by passively in the face of a deterioration in the distributional position of all but the wealthiest households. The basic strength of our economy's capacity to produce goods, services, and noncommodity outputs should give us confidence that these pressing problems can be solved.

Chart 2: Income of Quintiles with CPI

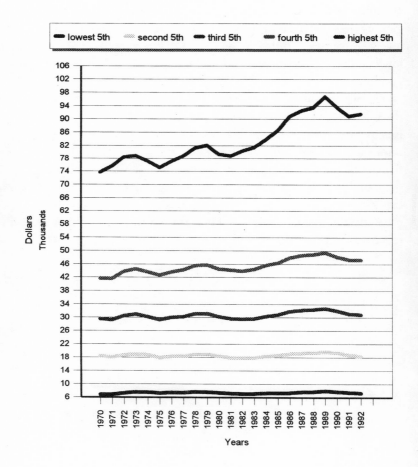

The data in Chart 2 are taken from the Department of Commerce, Bureau of the Census, *Money Income of Households, Families, and Persons in the United States: 1992.* Current Population Reports, Series P60-0184, Table B3.

Chart 3: Income of Quintiles with Adjusted CPI

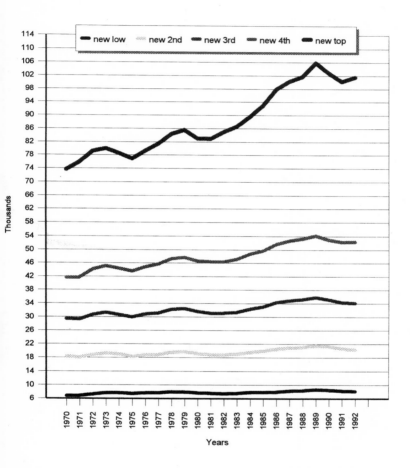

This chart uses the same data on income trends, but the annual increase in the Consumer Price Index as presented in Table B-1 of that report is adjusted downward by .5% each year.

13 —— What Will Getting Rid of the Deficit Do for Us?

A lot of us are worried that the government's appetite for credit tends to crowd out private borrowers—especially during periods when the private economy is expanding. America's industry must be able to secure credit on reasonable terms if it is to modernize and extend our productive facilities, regain international competitiveness, and create even more new jobs. Instead our recession-battered private sector—the real source of our nation's wealth and productivity—has shrunk even while the government has burgeoned. This is a disaster for any country predicated on free enterprise. And it of course helps to explain why so many American households must put in a total of well over 100 hours work per week—with two or more workers contributing—just to keep their heads above water financially. We must find a way to reduce the federal share of this country's economic pie because bureaucrats don't generate our nation's wealth. They just redistribute it and, in the process, they inevitably waste part of it.

— William Ford, President, Federal Reserve Bank of Atlanta, 1983

There is nothing as unsound as hoary doctrines that have acquired the support of authority simply because they are traditional and have stood for so long without genuinely critical examination. One of these mouldy fallacies is that regardless of the circumstances the government must balance its budget in each year. Why not in each month or week or hour?

— Jacob Viner, 1993[1]

M r. Ford's statement exemplifies the Conventional Wisdom's insistence that the federal budget deficit is the root of all evil; it is the explanation for slow economic growth and the deterioration of living conditions of many families. This is the reason that eliminating the deficit is now pursued with religious fervor; it seems that success in deficit reduction will restore both morality and economic prosperity.

The deficit is simply the difference between what the government takes in each year and what it spends. The gap is financed by borrowing, and the accumulated borrowings from past years constitute the national debt. But there is a big question as to what government is being discussed. Most of the discussion has been about the federal government's deficit. This is convenient for politicians because it helps them to play a shell game called "Who's got the blame?"

In our federal system, there is an extremely complex mixture of responsibilities and revenue flows among local governments, state governments, and the federal government. In education, for example, much of the financing of public schools is raised through local taxes, but state governments and the federal government make significant contributions as well. This complexity makes it possible for politicians at the federal or the state level to announce that they are going to cut spending and taxes with the consequence that if programs are to continue, taxes and spending will have to be raised at the local level. The idea is that the tax cutters take the credit for being kind to taxpayers while the state or local officials take the blame for either raising taxes or cutting back services. The game works particularly well if the participants are of different political parties. For example, if a Republican president makes big cuts in federal spending, he or she can create nightmares for Democratic governors who are suddenly made to look bad when they are forced to raise taxes.

The way to get beyond these games is to look at the whole picture — the total flow of revenues and expenditures of all levels of government taken together. It turns out that in most years, state and local governments taken as a whole run a surplus — their revenues exceed their expenses. In any given year, hundreds or thousands of government entities from local school districts to multistate agencies such as the Port Authority of New York will sell bonds to raise money for specific projects. However, other government entities will in any year have extra cash that they invest in bank accounts or bonds. When all of these are added together, it turns out that state and local governments end up with a surplus. Hence, when the balance sheet for all levels of government taken together is examined, the overall deficit is not as scary as the federal deficit by itself.

Chart 4: Combined Government Deficit as % of GDP

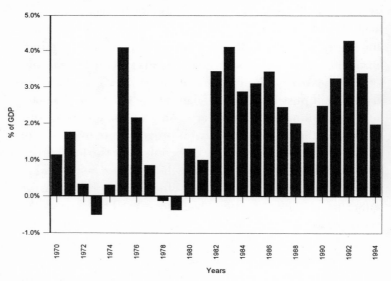

The chart shows the deficit of all levels of government combined as a percentage of GDP. The data for 1994 are based on the first three quarters of the year. Data are from Tables B-1 and B-83 in *Economic Report to the President 1995*.

WHAT IS THE DEFICIT
BEING USED FOR?

In thinking about this governmental deficit, it is useful to think in terms of the familiar analogy of a household trying to live within its budget. Imagine a family that earns $60,000 a year, but at the end of the year, it has spent $70,000, so that the family has been forced to increase its debt by $10,000. Before denouncing this family for its spendthrift ways, one would want to know how the family spent its money. One possibility is that it had $5,000 of gambling losses and spent another $5,000 on a cruise around the world. But it is also possible that the family bought a car that was indispensable for the wife's work and paid a large tuition bill for its oldest child's final year of college. In the latter case, the family's deficit financing would seem eminently sensible and rational.

Often, however, a close inspection of the family's finances would show a somewhat mixed picture. A financial consultant advising the family that had to finance both an automobile and a year in college might be able to identify $3,000 or $4,000 of discretionary expenditures that the family could have squeezed out of its budget. Therefore, its borrowing for the year should have been only $6,000 or $7,000. In short, one simply cannot tell from the family's overall budget situation whether it is spending money wisely or foolishly; one has to look at the actual expenditures.

The governmental situation is similar. While the overall government deficit has been averaging about $150 billion a year during the 1990s, there are a lot of quite sound expenditures being made by these different levels of government. State and local governments spend about $300 billion a year on public education and another $60 billion on maintaining the highway system. Somewhere between $70 and $130 billion of federal outlays are for nondefense infrastructure such as building dams, office buildings, and airports, and for financing education and research expenditures.[2] All of these are outlays that are comparable to the family buying a badly needed car or paying for college tuition; they are expenditures that will produce a stream of economic benefits in future years.[3] Think what our economic future would be like if we were suddenly to stop providing primary education to our children, or if we did absolutely nothing to slow the deterioration of our transportation infrastructure.

If we decided to eliminate the deficit from one day to the next by cutting $150 billion out of these types of expenditures, we would definitely be worse off in the future. As with the family, it is completely moral and rational for government to borrow to finance these kinds of worthy expenditures that will produce future benefits. But as with the family, one has to look closely at all of the other expenditures as well. In other words, whether or not the deficit is zero or $300 billion does not tell us if government is spending money wisely or foolishly.

When we start looking in detail at government outlays, it is obvious that there is significant waste and unnecessary extravagances. For one thing, nobody has provided a coherent explanation of why our defense budget has fallen only 10% below cold war levels even though our major military antagonist no longer exists. We could easily cut $100 billion a year from our defense outlays. Moreover, at both the state and the federal level, there are countless small agencies and offices that provide nothing but highly paid sinecures to political appointees. There has also been much recent attention given to various forms of "corporate welfare" that provide either direct subsidies or tax relief to various well-heeled corporations that could manage perfectly well without the assistance.

There is no dispute that some portion of government spending could be reduced or reallocated in more effective ways. But this is a different problem from the deficit question. In fact, the danger is quite real that we might eliminate the deficit without cutting out the most wasteful and unnecessary forms of government spending. In fact, all of the deficit-cutting plans that are under consideration leave military outlays at their current excessively high level while reducing expenditures for desperately needed infrastructure.

Here again the steering metaphor is extremely useful. We need the flight crew of the Starship Enterprise to recognize the need to use resources very carefully; we do not want them to waste tons of fuel flying to some distant corner of the galaxy without good reason. But it also does not make sense to give the flight crew a certain budget and say, do as good a job as you can with that amount of money regardless of the particular challenges and opportunities you face in a given year. Effective steering cannot be done within some rigid budgetary formula; it requires constant evaluation of the costs and benefits of each type of expenditure.

WHAT WOULD HAVE HAPPENED WITHOUT THE DEFICIT?

It is also important to explore the question of what would have happened to the economy had government not been running large deficits over the past fifteen years. There are two sharply contrasting answers to this question, both of which presume to know what would have been the consequences if the government had acted differently. While both of these standard views are flawed, it is possible to gain some useful leverage on this debate by looking more closely at the arguments on each side.

The first view—call it unreconstructed Keynesianism—is that the government deficits of the past ten years served to support aggregate demand in the economy.[4] The government's decision to sustain high levels of spending through deficit financing meant that the economy could acheive the strong rates of growth during the 1982 to 1987 period, and without the deficit spending, the slowdown from 1987 to 1992 would have been even more severe.

This argument is buttressed by the timing of the deficit. The deficit began to balloon in 1982 when the economy was in a severe recession. The government launched its program of vastly increased military procurement that year, thus contributing to the apparently strong recovery from the recession. ("Apparently strong" is a necessary qualification because the Reagan boom had weaknesses, such as the dramatic overbuilding of commercial real estate as well as other speculative excesses.)

But this unreconstructed Keynesian view needs some important qualifications. Government deficits can help sustain aggregate demand, but they cannot assure healthy economic growth, especially when the deficits are being used to finance massive increases in defense procurement. Moreover, deficits encounter the law of diminishing returns; the stimulus provided by $100 billion of deficit spending in Year 1 is much greater than the stimulus provided by the same amount of deficit spending in Year 4. As people come to expect that amount of deficit spending, they are less likely to keep expanding their investments. An economy might slip into recession even when the dose of deficit medication is being increased. In short, deficit spending cannot solve the problems of a weak economy where business is reluctant to invest. However, deficits can be useful in preventing a weak economy from sliding into a depression where 20% of the workforce is unemployed.

The contrary view embraced by deficit hawks is that government deficits actually serve to discourage private-sector investment, so that they actually weaken the economy.[5] The more sophisticated version of this argument acknowledges that a burst of deficit financing — as in the early Reagan military buildup — could boost the level of economic activity. However, such theorists tend to invoke a strong version of diminishing returns in which such an effect is likely to wear off very quickly. In just a few years, the deficits would make sustaining economic growth much harder.

Deficit hawks explain these negative economic consequences of government deficits with three arguments. The first is that deficit spending increases the risk of inflation, and that either the reality of inflation or the fear of future inflation will lead to increases in long-term interest rates that will discourage private investment. The second argument is that current deficits make future tax increases more likely, and the high probability of higher taxes in the future discourages private investment. The third argument is that government borrowing to finance the deficit directly drives up interest rates for private borrowers, and those higher interest rates discourage new investment. Different analysts emphasize one of these mechanisms more than another, but all three of these mechanisms could be working simultaneously.

Deficit hawks have their own account of the past ten years of economic history. They see the deficit as a ball and chain attached to the leg of the private economy. In the mid-1980s, the private economy was so strong that it could spurt ahead even with this handicap. By 1987, however, the inevitable began to happen: the private economy began to slow as a result of the government deficit draining resources. The next five years of recession and slow growth can be directly attributed to the private investment-reducing impact of the deficit. Deficit hawks insist that the only thing that is likely to restore a faster rate of growth is unambiguous evidence that the deficit will disappear soon. Projections that show a much smaller deficit by the end of the century are not sufficient, since everyone knows that politicians will have a million opportunities between now and then to launch irresponsible new spending programs.

MOVING BEYOND THE DEBATE

The contrast between these two positions could not be greater. On the one side, the unreconstructed Keynesians insist that if the government had suddenly eliminated the deficit in 1988 or

1990, the result would have been a disastrous economic downturn with rates of unemployment unheard of since the 1930s. On the other, the deficit hawks insist that the same choice would have led to a period of vigorous economic growth driven by a boom in private-sector investment spending.

This disagreement cannot be settled by an experiment. Even if one were set up, the losing side would have a thousand arguments about special circumstances that prejudiced the outcome. But there is a way to move beyond this stark disagreement. Both of these opposing predictions are built on assumptions about what determines the rate of investment by private firms. Unreconstructed Keynesians argue that business investment tends to follow demand, and that when demand is weak, investment will fall. Deficit hawks, in contrast, see that private investment is primarily shaped by current and future levels of interest rates and taxes. Of course, the actual economists who embrace one or the other of these positions acknowledge that factors emphasized by their opponent's theories have some relevance. But there is still a fundamental disagreement over the determinants of private-sector investment.

Moreover, it is a disagreement where actual evidence can be brought forth. One does not have to argue about counterfactuals — what would have happened had the government done something radically different? One can look instead at actual rates of business investment in different times and in different countries and analyze how those rates appear to respond to changes in different variables — demand, interest rates, tax policies, and so on. To be sure, the results one gets will be influenced by the precise ways that one sets up the study — what kinds of assumptions are used, which historical eras and countries one includes in the study, and what is the expected time lag between changes in the variables and changes in investment levels. Nevertheless, a number of technically competent studies point to the same conclusion — that rates of business investment are far less responsive to tax and interest rate variables than the arguments of the Deficit hawks would suggest.[6] But these studies also suggest that demand is also not as important as the unreconstructed Keynesians would have it.

A glance at trends in the U.S. economy since 1980 can help us make sense of this puzzle. Since 1980, nonresidential fixed investment—purchases of plants and equipment by business firms—in the U.S. has fallen sharply as a percentage of GDP (see Chart 5). From 1980 to 1992, the rate dropped from 13.1% to 9.4% of GDP. Two other important indicators have fallen almost exactly parallel to the decline in business investment. The effective rate of corporate income taxation dropped very sharply during this period as a series of "tax reforms" lowered the tax burden on corporations. Moreover, long-term interest rates also fell sharply during this period, from 11.5% to 7.0%. (These are the rates on ten-year government bonds.[7]) The key variables emphasized by deficit hawks—tax rates and real interest rates—have moved in the opposite direction than their accounts of the determinants of investment would suggest. Across this same period, demand in the economy was uneven, but it was hardly weak enough to account for such a sharp fall in business investment in a period when interest rates and corporate taxes were falling. It is significant, however, that something else was falling during this period—public sector tangible investment. The amount that governments at the state, local, and federal levels were spending on roads, buildings, and other civilian investment was falling as a percentage of GDP.[8]

The key change in the 1980s was a dramatic decline in government's ability to maintain the intermediate levels of uncertainty that encourage strong business investment. The level of uncertainty for U.S. corporations went through the roof in this period. For one thing, there was a substantial intensification of international competitive pressures, so that more and more industries were under direct pressure from foreign competitors.

For another, even though the business community had lobbied fiercely for the kinds of "free market" and deregulatory policies that the Reagan administration embraced, the actual implementation of those policies placed many firms in new circumstances where they faced either new competitors or a new and less predictable regulatory environment. The obvious instance is the commercial airline industry that has had enormous difficulties in finding a profitable path through a deregulated terrain. The result of uncertainty and declining profits were significant reductions in investments in new equipment. Finally, the ideological commitments of the Reagan administration led it to pursue a hands-off policy toward the great wave of corporate mergers and buyouts in the 1980s. While these transactions were fantastically lucrative for some, they created

Chart 5: Nonresidential Fixed Investment

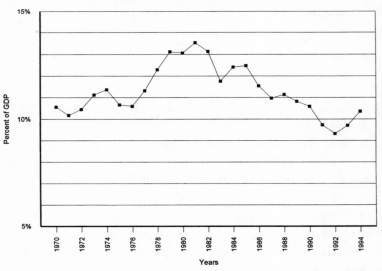

This chart shows nonresidential fixed investment as a percentage of GDP. Data are from Table B-1 in *Economic Report to the President 1995*.

another quantum leap in uncertainty in many corporate board-rooms where managers suddenly found it very difficult to plan for the next week, much less for the next year. Firms that faced an uncertain market situation and a threat of takeover by another firm or corporate raiders would inevitably be extremely reluctant to embark on any new investment initiatives.

The link between the turbulence on Wall Street and the declining levels of business investment in plants and equipment is now well established. For one thing, firms sought to avoid becoming takeover targets by keeping their stock prices high, which required strong quarterly profits. In order to assure these strong quarterly profits, firms developed strategies that placed short-term results over long-term results. It became common in many firms to demand that any new piece of capital equipment be required to pay for itself within two years if its purchase was to be justified. Firms also used techniques for evaluating new investments that established extremely high hurdle rates; the widespread capital asset pricing model (CAPM) technique often led firms to reject any investment that could not promise a 16%-a-year rate of return.[9]

At the same time, firms that were targets of successful takeovers were usually burdened with substantial amounts of new debt, since these takeovers were almost universally financed by bonds and bank lending. In order to service this debt, firms were under intense pressure to cut costs, including expenditures for capital equipment and research and development. This further discouraged all but the most obvious and risk-free investment initiatives.

But the impact of these financial mechanisms on investment were reinforced by the broader uncertainties that firms outside of the defense sector faced. Many industrial sectors were facing pressures to restructure as a result of intensified international competition and dramatic technological changes. But these industries could not turn to the federal government to help them reduce the uncertainties they faced. The Reagan administration was ideologically opposed to anything that smelled like industrial policy, such as support for an industry's research and development efforts or new regulatory policies. The only real help that these industries could expect from the Reagan administration was its support of antiunion policies designed to weaken the bargaining power of employees. Those efforts had the questionable effect of reinforcing a firm's orientation to gain greater productivity through "sweating" employees — simply intensifying the pace of work, rather than through investing in new technologies.

CONCLUSION

When one looks at the federal budget deficit without the scary imagery of vampire states, it is difficult to see what all the fuss is about. For one thing, it is easy to imagine circumstances under which a substantial continual government deficit could be economically justified. But even more importantly, the arguments that deficit hawks have made that federal deficits will depress private investment levels are decidedly unpersuasive. Even with large deficits, both the effective rate of corporate taxation and real interest rates declined sharply during the 1980s, and yet business investment fell anyway. The main cause of those declining investment levels was a significant increase in the uncertainty that business firms faced. This suggests an answer to the counterfactual. Had the federal government slashed the budget deficit by massive spending cuts in the mid-1980s, it would only have further depressed the economy because the levels of uncertainty faced by business would have been driven even higher.[10]

All of this brings back the centrality of the steering metaphor. Neither the exact level of government spending nor the amount of that spending that is financed by borrowing is really that important. What is really important is the quality of the spending. Does it help to produce those intermediate levels of uncertainty that business needs for high rates of investment? Does it help the society to use the treasure troves of unused capacity, increased coordination efficiency, and greater productive consumption? Does it help us to adapt effectively to our expanding capacity to produce? On all of these questions, the deficit hawks are dead wrong.

14 — The Alleged Savings Decline

Because of a secular downward trend in private saving rates, national saving will be inadequate to finance even the levels of investment that have been observed historically.

— Lawrence Summers and Chris Carroll, 1987

We are last in savings among our industrial competitors. Japan, Germany, Canada — they're all ahead of us, with our dangerously low personal saving rate of about 4 percent.

— Senator William Roth, 1991

Thus our argument leads towards the conclusion that in contemporary conditions the growth of wealth so far from being dependent on the abstinence of the rich, as is commonly supposed, is more likely to be impeded by it.

— John Maynard Keynes, 1936 [1]

The last critical piece of the Conventional Wisdom is the claim that a decline in saving by households in the U.S. has dramatically intensified the seriousness of government budget deficits. Because of insufficient rates of saving by households, our total pool of private savings is smaller than it should be. This means that there is even less left over for private business after government deficits draw down much of the pool. This argument gives added urgency to the task of reducing the federal deficit. The crisis could just as well be eased by persuading American households to increase their savings, but nobody is certain how this can be done. Hence, the preferable policy approach has been just to solve the problem by cutting the federal deficit.

The declining household savings argument gained wide credibility in the 1980s because the government's main statistic on household savings registered a dramatic decline — a decline that has not yet been reversed. Declining household savings fits perfectly with the core allegory of being lost and then found; the old virtues of frugality have been forgotten by many of us with dire economic consequences. Moreover, low rates of saving in the U.S. are often compared unfavorably to high rates in Japan and the rapidly industrializing countries of East Asia that have not suffered from moral decline.[2] And, of course, it does not make things better that the vampire state continues to suck the lifeblood from the economy. Since households are no longer doing their part to increase the blood supply, the government's thirst appears to be all the more illegitimate and threatening.

But when one looks closely at the data, the decline of household savings in the U.S. is a nonevent; it simply did not happen. That the data were so widely misinterpreted is a textbook case of how misleading metaphors and allegories can create misperceptions about the economy. For most observers, the story of the declining frugality of U.S. households made so much sense that it simply had to be true even if there was massive evidence to the contrary.[3]

THE MYTHOLOGY OF HOUSEHOLD SAVING

From reading the popular press, it is easy to imagine that Toyota has done better than GM because the average Japanese autoworker saves a good share of his or her income, while the U.S. autoworker spends everything that he or she earns. Because of its workers' thrift, Toyota can borrow the money it needs at relatively low interest rates, while GM is forced to borrow at substantially higher rates because its employees and other Americans are spendthrifts.

This comparative fairy tale is misleading in a whole series of ways. First, in Japan and the U.S., the stream of household savings is small compared to the stream of savings within the corporate sector itself. Most corporate investment in both countries is financed by corporate profits and by depreciation funds—revenues set aside to cover the wear and tear on capital goods. Household savings play a relatively minor role in both countries in financing corporate investments.[4]

Second, it has long been the case that most families in the U.S. never acquire any significant ownership of financial assets, other than what they get through pensions. Surveys done in the 1950s, '70s, and '80s all show that 70% or more of stocks, bonds, and bank account assets were owned by the top 19% of households. This does not mean that the bottom 81% of households do not save, but the direct acquisition of financial assets by this group has never been significant.[5] Aside from pensions and life insurance, the major form of savings by households in the U.S. occurs through home ownership. By paying off mortgage debts, households acquire equity in their houses, and this constitutes the bulk of household savings for most families.

Third, this story neglects the role of pension funds in the U.S. economy. While pension funds play a minor role in the Japanese economy, they are extremely important in the U.S. Over the past fifty years, there has been an extraordinary expansion in pension fund assets. Pension fund reserves went from $12.3 billion in 1945 to $5.0 trillion in 1994.[6] That amount is larger than the total net worth of all nonfarm, nonfinancial corporations in the U.S. Pension fund assets have reached this astronomical level because close to $200 billion flows into these funds *every year*. Since pension funds acquire stocks and bonds and lend money directly to corporations, one would think that the big story of U.S. savings would be the great expansion of household savings that has resulted from the growth of the pension system. Because of this growth, the role in the economy of savings originating in the household is several orders of magnitude greater in the 1980s than it was in the 1950s and 1960s.[7]

How then can we explain why the big story has been exactly the opposite—the declining frugality of the U.S. population?

Much of the credit or blame goes to a single statistic — the rate of personal saving that the Commerce Department reports as part of the national income and product accounts. During the 1980s, this measure showed a sharp drop in household savings from a high of 8.8% in 1981 to a low of 4.3% in 1987. What the measure purports to show is what percentage of disposable personal income was saved by U.S. households. (See Chart 6.)

UNTANGLING THE DATA

What most observers, including many economists, have failed to realize is that the Commerce Department's savings figure is generated without any direct information on household savings. The analysts do not consider how much people have salted away in bank accounts or pension funds. In constructing their estimates of GDP and national income, the government's statisticians generate an estimate of disposable personal income DPI — the amount that households have available to spend after taxes. They also estimate total consumer purchases — personal consumption expenditures (PCE). The savings figure is produced by subtracting PCE from DPI. This is logical; everything that is not spent on consumer purchases must be going somewhere, so it makes sense to assume that it represents savings.

At best, this kind of indirect residual measure of estimating household savings would be extremely sensitive to small measurement errors. Since both DPI and PCE are very large numbers, small differences in either of them would make a huge difference for the amount of the residual. But the difficulties are even more serious. The ways in which the Commerce Department analysts define both DPI and PCE are not the definitions that we would use if we were trying to estimate the amount of money households have left over to put into stocks, bonds, or savings accounts.

For example, the Commerce Department analysts treat home owners as though they are renting their houses from themselves. There are sound reasons for this technique, but it produces results that make no sense when one is trying to estimate household savings. This technique means that one important component of PCE — about 15% of the total — is an estimate of the rental cost of owner-occupied housing. It is very difficult to know how that estimate compares to the actual costs that home owners pay to maintain their homes and cover their mortgage payments. This technique also includes an estimate of the rental income that owner-occupiers pay themselves. The problem is that in calculating this rental income, the analysts subtract the cost of depreciation — the wear and tear on the house. The result is that in all recent years, the rental income that owner occupiers receive has been negative because the depreciation is greater than the revenue received. Again, this procedure is perfectly logical; owners of apartment buildings often report negative income from their properties because depreciation and other costs exceed revenues. However, if one is trying to estimate household savings, this procedure makes no sense at all. Most home owners tend to assume that if they keep their house in reasonable shape, the houses will appreciate in value. Most home owners do not worry about putting aside funds to rebuild the house in twenty or thirty years. It therefore makes no sense to subtract depreciation from rental income of households when one is attempting to estimate household saving.[8] Since the costs associated with home ownership are a very significant part of the economy, these Commerce Department techniques significantly distort reported levels of household savings.

A comparable distortion helps to explain why the Commerce Department savings figure hit bottom in 1987. In 1986, Congress passed a piece of tax reform legislation that increased the rate of taxation on capital gains starting in January 1987. Capital gains are the profits that one earns when an asset, such

Chart 6

Years	NIPA Personal Saving (Billions of current dollars)	% of Disposable Personal Income
1975	100.3	8.7%
1976	93.0	7.4%
1977	87.9	6.3%
1978	107.8	6.9%
1979	123.3	7.0%
1980	153.8	7.9%
1981	191.8	8.8%
1982	199.5	8.6%
1983	168.7	6.8%
1984	222.0	8.0%
1985	189.3	6.4%
1986	187.5	6.0%
1987	142.0	4.3%
1988	155.7	4.4%
1989	152.1	4.0%
1990	170.0	4.2%
1991	211.6	5.0%
1992	247.9	5.5%
1993	192.6	4.1%
1994	204.2	4.1%

The chart shows Personal Saving as measured in the National Income and Product Accounts as a percentage of Disposable Personal Income. Data are from Table B-27, *Economic Report to the President, 1995.*

as 100 shares of stock, increases in value. As expected, many investors "cashed out" in the final months of 1986 in order to take advantage of the lower tax rates that were to end with that tax year. Capital gains reported on personal income tax returns rose to a spectacular level of $295.8 billion in 1986, as compared to an annual average of about $150 billion in previous years. But in national income accounting, capital gains are not counted as part of DPI. Hence, the $300 billion bonus earned mostly by upper-income households does not appear in the Commerce Department figures. But it is only reasonable to assume that some of the $300 billion windfall was used to finance increased consumption by upper income households during 1987. Sure enough, DPI rose by 5% from 1986 to 1987, but PCE rose by 7.1% in the same period. With expenditures rising faster than income, the result was a very big drop in the Commerce Department savings rate. But what really happened was that about $50 billion of consumption was financed by capital gains income, while another $250 billion of capital gains income was put back into other financial instruments.[9]

Fortunately, the Federal Reserve Board provides more direct estimates of the accumulation of financial assets by households. For example, for 1988, the Commerce Department reports that the total of all personal savings in the economy was $156.2 billion, but the Federal Reserve reports that in the same year only pension funds and life insurance reserves increased their assets by $157.5 billion.[10] Briefly, the institutionalized savings of households reported directly to the Federal Reserve are greater than the sum of all household savings reported by the Commerce Department. In a word, the Commerce Department figure is not a good measure of anything.

UNTANGLING THE MYSTERY

Fortunately, there is also another source of data on this issue. The Federal Reserve Board organized surveys in 1983 and 1989 to ask a representative sample of people to report on their savings and their acquisition of various assets. The Survey of Consumer Finance (SCF) gives us a much better handle than the Commerce Department data on actual savings behavior, and it can also help us to understand why so many people believed that Americans had ceased to save in the 1980s.

The SCF provides the most solid data on the assets that are directly in the control of the household, while the Federal Reserve already has excellent data on the institutionalized savings controlled by pension funds and insurance companies. Between 1983 and 1989, the SCF shows that even after one controls for price changes, holdings of financial assets by all households increased by $890 billion. To be sure, household debt also increased during this period by $1.3 trillion, but most of that was offset by a $1.1 trillion increase in the value of owner-occupied housing. When one nets out the increase in borrowing that was not going to finance residential purchases, one is still left with a net increase of financial holdings of $690 billion. This translates into about $100 billion a year of household financial savings. To this must be added the annual increases in resources placed in pension and insurance reserves—another $260 billion per year in 1989 dollars. The result is an annual household savings figure that is more than twice the Commerce Department estimate.[11]

The value of these surveys is that they allow us to see how these flows were distributed across households. It turns out that the poorest 90% of households did experience an actual decline in the value of their financial holdings. The great bulk of the population added debt more quickly than financial assets; these households were "dissaving," but on a relatively small scale.

The next group—the households between 90% and 99% of the wealth distribution—was surprising in its behavior. These upper-middle-class households dramatically increased their borrowing; the value of their financial holdings dropped significantly. One can surmise that these households reduced their financial holdings in order to finance more expensive housing so that they could keep up with the Joneses in these high-spending years of the Reagan boom.

It is only in the top 1% of households, and primarily in the upper half of the top 1% — the very rich — that one sees a significant shift in the pattern. These most affluent households experienced a dramatic increase in their holdings of financial assets that far outweighed any increase in debt. In other words, the bottom 99% of households reduced their savings, but the top 1% saved more than enough to give the whole society a quite positive saving rate.

The richest half of 1% of households took in something like $1.9 trillion in income between 1983 and 1989 — an average of $372,400 per household in 1989. Further, these households managed to put 44% of this amount into the acquisition of additional financial assets. Of course, it is not that hard to save a lot when you are taking in that kind of money. Rather than being grateful to the very rich for their high propensity to save, it is more appropriate to speculate about what would have happened to overall savings rates if the distribution of income and wealth had been more equal in this period. It seems likely that in that case, savings by the bottom 99% of households would have been much stronger.

The point is that there was a sharp redistribution of income in favor of the richest households during the Reagan years. As a consequence, the bottom 99% of households had to struggle to make ends meet, leading to an increase in indebtedness. But this makes it far easier to understand why the Commerce Department data on household savings were so widely believed. It corresponded with the experience of much of the population, especially the professional middle class of journalists, academics, and politicians who knew that they themselves were borrowing instead of saving. But these people failed to understand two important things. First, their borrowing was being offset by the increased saving of the overpaid rich. Second, institutionalized savings through pension funds was extremely strong in this period.

15 —·— Alternatives to Austerity

Not one person in a thousand can tell you why either the debt or the deficit is a threat to the country, but four hundred and forty out of a thousand will tell you that both are America's most immmediate danger.
— Robert Heilbroner and Peter Bernstein, 1989[1]

The Conventional Wisdom sees slow economic growth, an increasing federal deficit, and low rates of household saving as the main pathological symptoms that justify policies of austerity. In arguing that each of these so-called dangerous symptoms has been profoundly misunderstood, the idea is not to suggest that the U.S. economy is problem free. The U.S. economy is broken and desperately needs major repairs. But we have to move beyond thinking that balancing the budget and belt-tightening will solve all of our problems.

IDENTIFYING THE PROBLEMS

The U.S. has done a terrible job in adapting our economic institutions to fit our expanding productive capabilities. On the one hand, the technological progress of recent years has been spectacular. Science fiction fantasies of robotic factories assembling products are now a reality. Computerized systems can instantly route billions of phone calls and messages across the global telecommunications web. And the capabilities of the computers that now sit on millions of desks are truly staggering. But, on the other hand, millions of our citizens live in terrible poverty and millions more have been facing mounting economic insecurity as stable jobs disappear and wages and working conditions deteriorate. There is no need for this misery in the midst of historically unimaginable plenty.

The inequalities in our society present us with a profound moral and spiritual challenge. But it is also a profound economic challenge because the problems generated by deepening inequality threaten to undermine the future vitality of our economy. If things continue to move in the current direction, the poverty in the midst of plenty could well obliterate the plenty.

There are two dynamics of decay that threaten to undermine our future collective well-being. The first comes from the interaction of growing inequality with increased international competition in the production of both goods and services. This increased competition means that our labor force must be able to "work smarter" — achieve higher levels of productivity — or production will simply shift to low wage areas of the world economy. If, for example, garment production is going to be organized with the same technologies as in early twentieth century sweatshops, production in the U.S. will disappear because labor will be cheaper in poorer parts of the world. It is only if those domestic garment workers are able to "work smarter" with more advanced technologies that garment jobs in the U.S. will survive. The same is true for machine tool production, automobile production, movie production, and software production.[2]

But in technologically advanced production where employees "work smarter," labor costs can represent as little as 5% or 10% of total production costs. If, for example, it costs $8,000 to produce an automobile, the cost of the production labor might be only $400 per car.[3] At that point, it is much more critical for profitability to economize on other costs — transportation, inventories, managerial costs — than on direct labor costs. In short, when employees "work smarter," there is much less incentive to shift production to low-cost areas.

But the big question is how can American workers "work smarter" if they have not learned to *be* smarter? The 30% of the students in each high school class who drop out before graduating are not good candidates for working smarter, but neither are the substantial numbers who graduate with skills in math and science that lag far below the standards achieved in much of Europe and Asia.

The school achievement of children, however, is linked directly to the economic security or insecurity of their parents. It would be nice if every child who saw his or her parents struggling with layoffs and unemployment resolved to get such a good education that he or she would never have to worry about these things. But that is not the way the world works; it is far more likely that those children will, in fact, respond to their parents' economic distress with behaviors that make them underachievers at school.

The mechanisms are not just psychological. Those more economically insecure families are not going to have resources to spend on their children's education, and they are more likely to have to move frequently, creating breaks in their children's schooling. They are also likely to need the children to make a greater contribution to the household income. And as young people work more, they are likely to devote even less energy to their studies.[4]

In a word, growing economic inequality threatens to make us less educated as a society at just the point where it is more urgent than ever that we "work smarter" if we are to keep significant amounts of high value-added productive activity within our borders. This dynamic is not the great "sucking sound" that Ross Perot evoked in the battle over the North American Free Trade Agreement (NAFTA). It is a far slower and more subtle process than the sudden movement of factories across the border. And, most importantly, it is a dynamic that can be reversed.

The second decay dynamic comes from our collective loss of faith in the possibilities of steering our economy. Over the past two decades, citizens of the U.S. have repeatedly expressed their frustration with the status quo by embracing the view that less government is the solution to our problems. Proposition 13 in 1978 in California, Reagan's landslides in 1980 and 1984, and the Republican sweep in 1994 all rested on the idea that everything would be fine if we could only drive a stake through the heart of the vampire state.

This is one of the cases where metaphors make all of the difference. If people understood that the state was the steering mechanism for a complex starship making its way through a dangerous and threatening universe, it would be obvious that leaving the steering to an "invisible hand" is utter folly. But the ongoing argument about whether it is necessary or desirable to steer the starship makes it impossible for the society to agree on the direction in which we want to head or the missions we want to accomplish. As a result, government policies become more short term, more uncertain, and devoid of any consistent guiding ideas.

The whole problem is intensified by the expanding influence of business lobbyists who further distort public policy toward a quick fix. A corporation that might need to spend $10 million to develop a long-term solution to a problem of environmental pollution now prefers to spend a tenth of that amount on campaign contributions to gain a loophole in congressional legislation that would allow it to continue polluting. As a consequence, both our environment and our politics are debased.

But the growing incoherence of government policies simply raises the level of uncertainty for economic actors, and the result is that levels of new investment in plant and equipment remain low. Moreover, under these circumstances, the government is also incapable of making many of the investments in infrastructure and "human capital" that the economy needs, further limiting our ability to take advantage of the treasure trove of improved coordination efficiency.

Finally, of course, disappointing economic results — exaggerated by the Conventional Wisdom — serve only to undercut further public confidence that the government can act effectively. The results are intensified efforts to shrink state spending so that a weakened government—constrained by insufficient revenues and a legitimacy deficit—becomes even less effective. And the whole downward spiral continues to accelerate.

THE POSSIBILITIES AND THE OBSTACLES

Neither of these downward cycles is necessary or inevitable. Neither represents the ineluctable working out of some powerful economic or social logic. If we can find better ways to adapt to our economy's productiveness, we can reverse these cycles and create an economy that increases well-being for almost all of the population.

The key is to steer the starship economy so that we can take maximal advantage of the three treasure troves—unused capacity, increased coordination efficiency, and more productive consumption. If we do that, we can produce an expanding supply of both goods and services and noncommodity outputs that are distributed more equitably. With more equal distribution of this expanding output, it should be possible to reduce the level of economic insecurity of the bottom half of the population, and that, in turn, should make it easier for both current and future generations to learn how to "work smarter."

But why are we not pursuing these possibilities? The first and most obvious answer is, because our vision has been clouded by the Conventional Wisdom; its logic and its metaphors prevent us from seeing our situation clearly and it constantly pushes us toward the false remedy of austerity. But the hold of the Conventional Wisdom is directly linked to powerful institutional forces that limit our political choices. While these institutional forces are powerful, they are not insurmountable. Once we understand their nature, it is possible to develop effective strategies to overcome these forces.

These powerful institutional forces result primarily from the organization of the financial system—both domestically and internationally. The domestic financial constraints were evident in the period immediately after Bill Clinton's election in 1992. The financial markets experienced a period of uncertainty when faced with the first Democratic president elected in twelve years. Similar periods of uncertainty had occurred after the election of John Kennedy in 1960 and after the election of Jimmy Carter in 1976. The uncertainty is felt by the participants in the financial markets—the people who trade large quantities of stocks, bonds, and related instruments on a daily basis. These people worry that a Democratic president might be tempted to make changes in government policy that are perceived as bad for the markets.

The key word here is "perceived." The participants in the financial markets are—with relatively minor exceptions—slaves to the Conventional Wisdom. They believe that expansion of the state's role in the economy—through higher taxes or greater regulation—will suck the lifeblood from the economy. They also believe that any swing toward a more "activist" government policy—one that tries to put more people to work or that redistributes income towards the poor—will increase the risk of inflation.

When these partipants are uncertain about the direction that a new president will take, they are likely to become cautious in their investment strategies. They will not buy stocks or bonds agressively, and they are likely to buy gold and foreign currencies to protect themselves from a possible fall in the value of the dollar. Generally, newly elected presidents respond to this uncertainty by signalling the markets that they need not worry—that the new administration will cautiously adhere to the Conventional Wisdom. The time-honored way that this signal is usually sent is by nominating a respected man with conservative credentials as secretary of the treasury, such as the venerable Lloyd Bentsen who was Bill Clinton's initial appointee to that office.

It is useful, however, to think about what would happen if a newly elected president refused to send that signal. What if he or she said, "I completely reject the Conventional Wisdom, and I believe that unless we take bold new initiatives in redirecting our economy, we will face a dismal downward economic spiral. I know that in the short term these steps might scare the financial markets, but over the long term, they will give us a healthier economy that will benefit us all." The financial markets would most likely respond to such a speech with a major decline in prices for both stocks and bonds. Uncertainty would be transformed into fear and many market participants would start selling dollar assets. As we know from the crash in 1987, the huge scale on which large institutions trade can lead to extraordinary volatility. Such a wave of selling could easily produce a free fall in stock prices.

The newly elected president would then have a second chance to clarify his or her earlier remarks in order to reverse the market's decline. If he or she held fast to the previously stated position, the market's decline could be expected to continue. Further, there is a high likelihood that such a sharp decline would pull the economy into recession, since both consumers and many large firms would suddenly find themselves much less wealthy than they were before the crash began. Their decisions to limit spending would guarantee an economic slowdown.

This is a serious structural constraint. No president wants to begin a term with a serious recession, so the incentive to send the financial markets the message they want to hear is very strong. But sending the message they want to hear means that even before the new administration begins, it has to abandon certain goals and certain means to those goals.

In Bill Clinton's case, there was a further twist to this story. He was told that the participants in the financial markets wanted more than a simple signal that he would adhere to the Conventional Wisdom. He was told that if he failed to place a major emphasis on reducing the federal budget deficit, long-term interest rates would continue at historically high levels and that would probably discourage any significant recovery from the Bush recession.[5] President Clinton agreed to abandon his campaign promises of a middle-class tax cut and significant increases in government infrastructure spending and to concentrate instead on deficit reduction. The result was that long-term interest rates declined through 1993, allowing a vigorous economic recovery. But then at the beginning of 1994, the Federal Reserve Bank started pushing interest rates back up. So that despite his successes in reducing the federal budget deficit, the president still ended up with the kind of high long term interest rates that he had sought to avoid.

The international financial constraints operate in a parallel fashion. When participants in the global financial markets perceive that a particular country is pursuing policies that go against the Conventional Wisdom, they insist that those policies are likely to produce a surge of inflation. But when inflation accelerates in one country, it produces a relative decline in the international value of that nation's currency. Hence, just the prediction of more inflation makes it logical for traders to transfer assets out of that currency before the inevitable decline in its value occurs. This is the classic instance of a self-fulfilling prophecy. The action by traders in anticipation of higher rates of inflation produces a decline in the relative value of a currency — whether or not the predicted inflation ever materializes. And since a declining currency reduces consumer purchasing power, this often sets off an inflationary dynamic as different groups attempt to recoup their lost purchasing power. The traders pat each other on the back for being so prescient and go on to make sage evaluations of other country's policies.

In short, the international financial markets require constant signals that each country's leaders are pursuing policies that fit within the Conventional Wisdom. And in an era where there are few obstacles to the movement of capital across national lines, currency traders can instantly punish a government that fails to send the right signals. It is not surprising then that very few major political leaders have shown any interest in recent years in defying the Conventional Wisdom.

UNDERSTANDING THESE OBSTACLES

How did these participants in the financial markets accumulate this extraordinary power? They now have an effective veto over governmental decisions that they are not shy about using. It is almost as if these financial market participants have two-thirds of the seats in the legislature, and they can effectively force the chief executive to do their bidding. But, at least in my recollection, these people never actually won an election. It is worth some exploration to see how financial mechanisms — which emerged historically simply as a means to provide funds to businesses and governments — have become so politically powerful. This is the topic of Parts III and IV.

Part Three

DOMESTIC FINANCIAL STRUCTURES

16 —·— Finance: Growing Like a Weed

What are the distinctive aspects of capital markets that result in government regulation in almost all countries? Capital markets are different from ordinary markets, which involve the contemporaneous trade of commodities. As I have noted, what is exchanged is money today for a (often vague) promise of money in the future.
— Joseph Stiglitz, 1994

Finance has not simply been spreading into every nook and cranny of economic life: a sizeable portion of the financial sector, electronically liberated from past constraints, has put aside old concerns with funding the nation's long-range industrial future, has divorced itself from the precarious prospects of Americans who toil in factories, fields, or even suburban shopping malls, and is simply feeding wherever it can.
— Kevin Phillips, 1994[1]

I n early modern Europe, it was common for financiers to lend money to kings or queens, usually to help them finance military expenditures. Monarchs could raise more money by increasing taxes, but that was an inherently slow process and there was always the risk that sharply increased taxes could incur resistance. So it was often easier to borrow from a banker on the assumption that the debt would be repaid with future tax revenues.

Such royal bankers became important personages who could rely on a grateful crown to grant them various privileges. Yet, these bankers also knew that there was considerable risk in their position. The monarch had an option that other borrowers lacked: the sovereign could always repudiate the loan. Even worse, the crown could strip the banker of his wealth, throw him in jail, or even have him executed. Even some relatively benevolent rulers resorted to this strategy from time to time because victimizing the banker might be the simplest way out of a budgetary crisis.

But this kind of brutal use of royal prerogatives did serve a broader social need: it helped to contain the role of finance in society. Financial institutions are similar to a fast-growing plant in a garden. If carefully tended and contained, the financial plant makes a very significant contribution to the beauty of the garden. But if the garden is neglected, the financial plant will grow like a weed and begin to choke the other plants. In recent years, the quality of our collective gardening has diminished and our economy is seriously threatened by powerful and fast-growing financial weeds. Elaborating this metaphor requires a close look at the productive roles that financial institutions can play in the economy.

PURPOSES OF FINANCIAL SYSTEMS

The functions of a financial system fall into two categories — facilitating flows of money and creating flows of information in the economy. This chapter addresses the first, and the informational role is taken up in the next chapter. Facilitating flows of money means transferring funds from savers to those who need help financing a project — whether it be a home owner wanting to add a new room, a business adding a new factory or office, or a government needing to build a school or a highway. A distinction is usually made between raising money by borrowing and raising money through the sale of equity or shares. Since an enterprise that fails has no obligation to pay back its shareholders, this type of financing is usually not considered borrowing. The discussion that follows, however, encompasses both types of financing.

In order to get the funds to the right places, the financial system has to resemble the body's circulatory system — as the otherwise problematic capital-as-blood metaphor suggests. But the metaphor actually leads in a quite different direction than the Conventional Wisdom implies. Just as the circulatory system has to be able to deliver blood to both the largest organs and the most distant extremities, the financial system needs both large arteries as well as tiny little capillaries to bring small amounts of credit to households and small enterprises. Moreover, the financial system should be able to balance the demands of different parts of the society. In the body, it simply will not do to stop flows to the brain just because the leg muscles are demanding unusually large amounts of blood. Hence, even if the rates of return on certain instruments are very high, finance should still be flowing to other vital activities. As we shall see, financial economists often forget about this level of complexity; they seem to imagine that one large financial artery is sufficient to serve all of the society's different needs.

As an intermediary that shapes the flow of finance from savers to users, the financial system does not create any new resources. Financial institutions do not produce savings, they simply channel it from one place to another. Even when banks and other financial institutions create credit, this works because there are already existing resources that might not otherwise be used. And when banks create credit too rapidly, so that demand exceeds the economy's productive capacity, there is likely to be inflation. When financial institutions are not available, individual economic actors can sometimes find ways to provide finance on their own. For example, it was mentioned earlier that the small firms in Taiwan often make use of postdated checks as a means to create the financing that they need.

OTHER PEOPLE'S MONEY

It is inherent in this capital allocation function that financial institutions make substantial use of Other People's Money. For example, the bank takes depositors' funds and lends them to various borrowers. The insurance company collects people's insurance premiums, and then invests them in various assets. Whenever substantial use is made of Other People's Money, there is what economists term an agency problem. Why should the agent to whom I entrust the money act in my interest? In fact, the agent who gets the money has the opportunity to walk away with it. This is what happens in many cases of financial fraud; investors entrust millions to a financial adviser who suddenly disappears with all of the cash.

But even if the agent does not want to engage in outright theft, there is still a question of how careful he or she will be with someone else's funds. After all, the agent's goal is to make a profit with the money above and beyond the returns that are paid to the owner, and he or she knows that profits might be greater by pursuing a riskier strategy for investing the funds. And, of course, if the agent bets wrong—if the assets fall in value rather than rise—the agent can give the owner back a smaller amount of money with sincere apologies. "Despite the best of intentions, the investment strategy did not pay off and there is now less money than before." This is what the treasurer of Orange County said after his risky investment strategy led to several billion dollars of losses for public agencies in that county.[2]

This agency problem, which is built into the very nature of financial institutions, can only be managed through a legal and regulatory framework. One part of this framework are those legal rules that make it very risky for financial agents to walk off with Other People's Money. This includes the enforcement of legal contracts and various statutes that define and outlaw financial fraud. The recent experience in the former Soviet Union of an entrepreneur who promised huge returns to people who bought his worthless shares is a vivid reminder that all developed market societies have laws that make it possible to throw such people in jail.

The regulatory framework also includes rules that define the kinds of risks that various agents are allowed to take with Other People's Money. In general, banks, insurance companies, pension funds, and other financial intermediaries are required to exercise "prudence" in their use of Other People's Money, and regulatory agencies devise specific rules to give concrete meaning to the idea of prudence. This need for regulation exists whether or not government authorities decide to provide insurance for certain kinds of accounts. And since new types of financial instruments are constantly being created, there is a continuous regulatory task of deciding whether it would be prudent or imprudent for various intermediaries to hold this kind of asset.[3]

The problem is that competition among financial institutions creates ongoing pressures to reduce the prudence with which Other People's Money is used. When financial institutions compete with each other to offer the highest return on the funds of savers, they have a powerful and ongoing incentive to increase risk and reduce prudence as a way to assure that they will command a larger share of the total pool of savings. Hence, financial markets cannot be self-regulating because the rewards to prudence come only over the long term, while many savers are attempting to increase their returns over the shorter term. The old-fashioned prudent banker who keeps risk to a minimum might very well be able to offer customers a 3% annual rate of return year after year, but his or her bank is likely to find its depositors shifting to the bank across the street that offers a 7% return this year. If this market continues without regulation, both banks are likely to be out of business by the end of the year—the first because it took on too little risk and the second because it took on too much.

The recent vogue for "financial deregulation" was based on a profound misunderstanding about the nature of financial activity. Financial intermediaries can only be kept on the path of prudence through some kind of external pressure from regulators.

To be sure, there is some place for collective self-regulation, since external regulation will be more effective when colleagues are willing to turn each other in for violating the rules. But ultimately, there has to be the threat of serious regulatory and criminal sanctions or financial institutions will not treat Other People's Money with the appropriate respect and caution.

This is the first meaning of the gardening metaphor. The ongoing activity of prosecutors and regulators in limiting financial fraud and imprudence is necessary to keep the financial plant from turning into a noxious and destructive weed. The belief that financial markets will regulate themselves is a lot like imagining that a formal garden can be effectively maintained with an invisible hand.

WHERE THE MONEY IS

Willie Sutton's reply to the question of why he robbed banks was simple: "Because that is where the money is." Financial activity deals with money on a wholesale scale as contrasted to the retail nature of most production or trade activity. The consequence is that profit opportunities are almost always quicker and more dramatic in financial activity. Imagine, for example, that you are in business and you get to keep a tenth of a penny of every dollar that flows through your hands. So, for every billion dollars you see, you get to keep a million. With such an incentive, you would definitely choose to engage in financial activity since there are literally thousands of financial institutions that rack up billions worth of transactions in a given year, but only the very largest nonfinancial corporations operate on that scale. This is the reason why even the most brilliant manufacturing or retailing entrepreneur takes at least five to ten years to transform his or her initial investment into personal wealth of a milion dollars or more.[4] But it is not uncommon for an individual who plays the financial markets correctly to generate a million dollars in trading profits within a year or two. And, of course, if you are persuasive and criminally inclined, you might be able to bilk people out of that amount of money in a few weeks with a clever scam.

The fact that finance is where the money is creates an incentive problem for market societies. Why should anybody who wants to make money take the slow route of producing or selling goods or services when finance is obviously the fast track to earning big money? But if most of the talented people take the fast track, the productive economy will suffer. It is ultimately the talents and energies of the people who actually produce goods and services that make us all better off. The most vibrant and energetic financial economy cannot forever make up the difference for a real economy that has become stagnant and unproductive. To be sure, the history of the world economy records instances of powerful nations whose financial expertise allowed them to extract wealth from other countries even after their own economy's productive strength was gone.[5] But that game cannot go on for very long. Sooner or later, a new global power with a more productive real economy emerges and the citizens of the declining financial power face a significant fall in their living standards.

The U.S. appears headed for this kind of fate. In the period from 1950 to 1970, when the U.S. was the dominant economy in the world, total employment in the financial sector of the economy grew from 4.2% of nonagriculture payrolls to 5.2%. From 1970 to 1990, when the U.S. was subject to increasing economic competition, financial employment accelerated to 7% of total nonfarm payrolls.[6] And even these figures might understate the magnitude of the shift since one of the great changes in the economy has been the spectacular growth of "nonbank banks."[7] These are divisions of major corporations that derive their income from traditional banking activities such as lending money to consumers and to other businesses. Employment in the financial sectors of these nonfinancial corporations has grown rapidly, but the official statistics often code these employees by the main line of business of the firm.

To avoid the unhappy fate of societies that allow their financial sector to grow too large, any well-ordered society takes steps to keep financial employment from growing too quickly. One common strategy is for the government simply to limit the number of banks and other financial institutions that are given permission to operate. Another strategy is to rely on some form of class selection, so that only "gentlemen" with a certain kind of social pedigree are allowed to staff the responsible positions within financial institutions. Neither of these strategies makes sense in the contemporary world for obvious reasons, but there are other means to acheive the same end of keeping the financial vegetation under control.

But without an active program of financial gardening, financial activity will ultimately displace all other kinds of economic activity. In his chronicle of life on Wall Street, *Liar's Poker,* Michael Lewis claims that 40% of the Yale class of 1986 applied for jobs at one particular investment bank.[8] Even if one discounts this figure by half, the image of large numbers of the best and the brightest heading toward foreign exchange trading desks and mergers and acquisitions groups is not a good indicator of the future economic vitality of the U.S. economy.

17 —— Bad Information Drives Out Good

The social object of skilled investment should be to defeat the dark forces of time and ignorance which envelop our future. The actual private object of the most skilled investment to-day is 'to beat the gun,' as the Americans so well express it, to outwit the crowd, and to pass the bad, or depreciating, half-crown to the other fellow.

—John Maynard Keynes, 1936[1]

Another dimension of the horticultural metaphor becomes apparent when one examines the other major function of the financial system—the production of high-quality information. Much economic analysis assumes that the financial system *only* channels funds from one part of the economy to another. But such a view is based on utterly unrealistic assumptions. In the real world, one of the central tasks of financial institutions is to generate information about the individuals and firms that want to borrow funds. But the quality of the information that financial institutions generate varies substantially. The difference between a financial sector that produces high-quality information and one that produces low-quality information can make a major difference for a national economy.

The complexity is that when financial institutions are under competitive pressure, market participants have strong incentives to economize on the production of high-quality information. Instead of spending the considerable time and energy required to produce such information, participants decide instead to rely on rules of thumb, signals, abstract formulae, or the performance of impersonal markets. The consequence is a degradation in the quality of financial information that can weaken the performance of the entire economy.

THE PRODUCTION OF INFORMATION

Economic models often assume that economic actors have perfect information.[2] This means that if somebody comes to my bank to borrow a million dollars to start a business, I will know by looking at that individual the precise probability that his or her new business will be successful. With the assumption of perfect information, all bankers are geniuses who can instantly tell a charlatan from an eccentric but brilliant entrepreneur. Having staffed financial institutions with genius bankers, these analysts then assert that the only role of financial institutions is to channel funds to the people who will make the best use of them.

But in reality, it is extraordinarily difficult to figure out who is deserving of credit and who is not. Even bracketing outright fraud, some who are attempting to raise finance are doing so on the basis of hare-brained schemes that could never work. Others might have great ideas but lack the temperament or expertise to realize them. Financial institutions need to compare the relative riskiness of the different projects asking for finance so that they can direct their funds to those with the best prospects for success.

It used to be thought that this task of allocating capital among those competing for credit could be handled by the price mechanism.[3] If the demand for loans at a bank exceeded the available supply of credit, the bank would simply raise its interest rate until enough prospective borrowers would be discouraged and the supply and demand would then be in balance again. But the problem is that when the interest rate goes from 8% to 12%, the bank might very well discourage a sober businessperson with a realistic sense of the immediate market prospects. But the daring entreprenuer with a scheme for commercial applications of low-temperature fusion will be completely undaunted by a higher interest rate. In a word, allowing the interest rate to balance the supply and demand of credit increases the likelihood that banks will finance only the least creditworthy projects. While interest rates can be expected to vary with the riskiness of loans, the interest rate cannot be expected to balance the supply of borrowers and the supply of lenders. Banks have no choice but to balance supply and demand by rationing—by denying access to credit to certain borrowers.

But in order to make sound rationing decisions, bankers should know a lot about the specific activity in which the potential borrowers are engaged. If ten borrowers come through the door all wanting financing to start a new business on the World Wide Web, the banker making the decision has to know how the Web works and how it is likely to evolve. This kind of concrete and specific knowledge of the business situation is indispensable and far more valuable than the mechanical exercise of running the borrower's numbers through a set of formulae designed to predict the likelihood of business success.

Being able to make these rationing decisions effectively is only the first part of the informational role of financial institutions. After the credit is provided, these institutions need to continue to monitor the borrower to make sure that he or she is making good use of the funds. Producing a steady flow of information about how the borrower is doing is doubly important. For one thing, it informs the institution's lending decisions in the next round; borrowers frequently have an ongoing need for credit. Equally important, monitoring the borrower can work to avert bad economic outcomes. If a bank sees, for example, that a business has grown beyond the entrepreneur's managerial skill, it can exert strong influence for the hiring of professional managers. If the bank recognizes that changes in the broader environment make the original business plan obsolete, the bank can exert pressures on the borrower for revisions of the firm's strategy.[4]

When financial institutions play these two informational roles well, they can actually increase economic output. They do this by avoiding the wasteful allocation of credit to units that will squander it and by assuring that more promising borrowers receive the funding they need. When they play the monitoring role well, financial institutions contribute to coordination efficiencies in the economy; they exert pressure on firms to make the best possible use of their resources. Once it is recognized that competition does not automatically force producers to adopt the best available business practices, it becomes obvious that financial institutions can make a major contribution to coordination efficiency by coaxing firms into adopting more effective business practices.

But the Conventional Wisdom generally ignores these critical informational tasks; it simply assumes that these tasks are handled perfectly in the process of allocating capital. Instead of worrying about how to design financial institutions to maximize the production of high-quality information, conventional analysts imagine that the only issue is how to assure that finance will get to the activities with the highest rate of return. This mistaken perspective leads to a variant of Gresham's Law — bad information drives out good. Gresham was a sixteenth century businessman who recognized the principle that "bad money drives out good." When a government deliberately debases the currency, people will hoard the older, undebased coins and circulate the coins of dubious quality. But as we shall see, a similar process occurs with information.

THE POWER OF BAD INFORMATION

While the informational roles of financial institutions are extremely important, they are also expensive. Both of the core activities — rationing credit and monitoring the performance of creditors — are labor-intensive. Even more important, they are activities where experience really counts. Whether or not the job is to approve loan applications or to monitor lenders, it usually takes years of experience before an individual becomes a real expert. One can give these employees intensive training or require advanced degrees, but it is the experience of actually doing the job that is most important in learning skills such as how to read other people, how to assess the prospects to make money from an innovation, and how the business cycle influences the prospects of different types of economic activity. Developing, retaining, and compensating this kind of expertise becomes a major managerial challenge for financial institutions.

When financial institutions operate in a competitive environment, they are usually under pressure to economize on this costly process of producing good information. One common way to economize is to rely on some kind of simple device to screen potential creditors. For example, if a bank decides that it will only lend to people who wear three-piece suits, fewer loan applications will have to be processed and one can manage with fewer experienced loan officers.[5] But these screening rules can seriously distort the flows of capital in an economy by arbitrarily cutting off certain categories of borrowers.

Another popular way to economize on this costly production of information is for market participants to rely to a greater degree on impersonal markets for credit rationing and monitoring. The stock market and the bond markets are the obvious instance of such impersonal markets. Instead of going to a bank to borrow, a firm goes to an investment banker to sell securities. To be sure, a reputable investment banking firm will not issue shares or bonds for any firm that comes along; it will try to screen out those firms that are unlikely to use the funds productively. But since the investment bank is usually not risking large amounts of its own funds for any extended period, it generally has less incentive to produce high-quality information than a banker making a direct loan.

According to theory, these impersonal markets generate high-quality information that is produced collectively by the investing community. For example, the price of a firm's shares is supposed to reflect the investment community's collective wisdom about how well that firm is run and how well it is likely to do in the future. If a firm is poorly managed, investors will find this out, and the firm's stock will fall in value. This price decline will send a signal that there are problems with the firm, and that will make it more likely that either the current management will change directions or that the firm's board of directors will choose a new management team.

But once one gets away from models that assume perfect information, there is a question of how the investment community is supposed to find out that the firm is being poorly managed. Here again, the dominant perspective in financial economics is not helpful; it simply assumes that impersonal markets will establish prices that fluctuate around the firm's real value. One possible explanation is that brokerage houses and large institutional investors hire analysts who follow the prospects of different firms in different industries, and the analysts will figure out which firms are poorly managed.

But these analysts are at a distinct disadvantage when compared to bank monitors. First, the banker has more of a direct claim on management for information; he or she can get a more "inside" view by threatening to deny or cancel the loan if certain information is not forthcoming. The analyst has only the much weaker threat that he or she will say something bad about the firm unless certain information is provided. Second, the analysts are generally responsible for keeping up on a lot of different firms; they have limited time to delve deeply into any particular firm. In practice, they often do little more than monitor the business press, so that if a magazine or newspaper does not call attention to problems with a firm, the analysts are unlikely to find out about them.

The choice between knowledgeable bankers and impersonal markets as ways of generating information about firms really comes down to the old aphorism—when everybody is responsible, nobody is responsible. It is expensive for banks to monitor firms, but in that system, it is clear where the responsibility lies. When a shift is made to impersonal markets, the responsibility is diffused and everybody can take a free ride by relying on other market participants. Nobody has a very strong incentive to spend time and energy generating detailed information on the skill and effectiveness of a particular management team.

But that is only part of the problem of relying on impersonal markets. The other problem is that because market participants tend to economize on information gathering, they often rely on very specific signals as a means to select among different stocks. One signal that has become overwhelmingly important in the U.S. market are quarterly earnings reports. If a firm reports strong quarterly earnings, a very strong buy signal is sent through the market and vice versa. Analysts who work in the markets attempt to predict quarterly earnings figures for firms since that is the best way to predict the performance of the stock. So, if a firm's results are better than what analysts expected, the price will shoot upwards; if results are below what analysts anticipated, the shares will likely drop sharply. The latter danger is so great that many firms will make analysts aware —in advance—of bad news so that they have a chance to adjust their predictions downwards.[6]

All of this substantial investment in predicting quarterly results would be fine if quarterly results were a good indicator of how well a firm is being managed. However, they are not. Badly run firms are sometimes able to use a wide variety of tricks to make their quarterly results look good for several years while the firm is heading downhill fast. And firms whose future prospects are excellent can have bad quarterly results either intermittently or for several years. There are so many different variables—including arcane accounting decisions—that can shape quarterly results that they become an unreliable indicator.

Nevertheless, once managers understand the importance of this particular signal, they have very strong incentives to concentrate their energies on improving quarterly results. Good quarterly results mean a higher stock price and that means both greater job security for managers and probably higher compensation. But focussing a firm's strategy on improving quarterly results leads to an emphasis on the short term over the long term, which has weakened U.S. firms in international competition.

The most dramatic example of this weakening is in new-product development. Introducing an entirely new product usually takes many years. During that long start-up period, the new product is generating lots of costs and very little revenue. Firms that are too strongly oriented to short-term results will sacrifice the potential gains from new-product development in favor of the immediate gains from cutting expenditures that have no likelihood of producing returns this year or next. Japanese firms, in contrast, have been far more willing to nurture new-product research, and in some cases, they have been able to take commercial advantage of products that were originally invented in the U.S. or Europe.[7]

SUMMARY

Instead of producing the kind of high-quality information that can make an economy work better, the present financial system in the U.S., with its heavy reliance on impersonal markets, produces information of a much poorer quality, such as elaborate predictions about quarterly profit figures. This poor-quality information feeds back into the real economy and distorts managerial incentives toward short-term time horizons.

Here, as well, the idea that the financial system must be kept carefully pruned and tended is useful. When financial institutions are free to respond to market pressures, they will have strong incentives to economize on the production of high-quality information. But with an effective regulatory system, financial institutions can be persuaded to invest resources in improving the quality of financial information. As these institutions develop considerable expertise in evaluating and monitoring different categories of borrowers, there can be a marked improvement in the economy's ability to take advantage of coordination efficiencies.

18 —— The Problem of Financial Dictatorship

At the president-elect's end of the table, Clinton's face turned red with anger and disbelief. "You mean to tell me that the success of the program and my reelection hinges on the Federal Reserve and a bunch of fucking bond traders?" he responded in a half-whisper.

Nods from his end of the table. Not a dissent.

Clinton, it seemed to Blinder, perceived at this moment how much of his fate was passing into the hands of the unelected Alan Greenspan and the bond market.

— Bob Woodward, 1994[1]

The quality of the information generated in the financial sector is an enormous problem precisely because control over capital allocation places so much power in the hands of financial institutions. When the financial sector has been allowed to grow out of control, bad information drives out good. And when powerful overgrown financial institutions are distributing resources on the basis of bad information, the society suffers under a kind of financial dictatorship.

THE TYRANNY OF THE CONVENTIONAL WISDOM

One of the most important informational problems in financial markets was identified by Keynes in the 1930s. He showed that in the short term, investors make money not by accurately predicting economic fundamentals, but by accurately predicting how the mass of other investors will behave.[2] Imagine, for example, that Controversial Technologies, Inc. (CTI) announces its plan to introduce a new product that will revolutionize the telecommunications industry. A particular investor might know with a fairly high degree of certainty that this new technology is actually a dead end that will not generate any profits. That person might be tempted to bet that this stock will fall in value as other investors come to recognize the folly of CTI's technological choices. But the bulk of the investor community might well be bamboozled by CTI's smooth-talking chief executive officer (CEO), so that purchases of the stock will drive its price up. In that case, the knowledgeable investor might lose a lot of money betting against the stock, and by the time the stock price actually nose-dives several years hence, he or she will have already left the market in disgust. In a word, the markets reward not whose judgment is correct over the long term, but who makes the best guess about what other investors will do in the next few weeks.

This is the source of the herdlike behavior in the financial markets that is captured in the familiar imagery of large beasts — bulls and bears — stampeding in one direction or the other. Market participants have to keep their antennae alert to every latest shift in collective sentiment because it is costly to sit on the sidelines when a wave of optimism passes over the market. Even if one knows full well that there is no sound basis for this optimism, when prices are moving sharply higher, there are significant profits to be made, and the same thing is true when the markets are engulfed in pessimism. To be sure, the trick is to catch the shift in mood before others do, but the premium is always on figuring out the direction in which the crowd is going.[3]

But crowds — whether animal or human — are notoriously bad at serious thinking; they tend to rely on emotions and some relatively simple ideas. In the financial markets, these simple ideas are the Conventional Wisdom of the day. It hardly matters whether the ideas of the Conventional Wisdom are true; what is important is that when these ideas are shared among the bulk of market participants, they represent a good basis for making money.

For example, in recent years the Conventional Wisdom has held that many U.S. corporations hired too many employees and that excess staff both at the production level and in middle management was eroding corporate profitability. It followed from this piece of wisdom that if a firm announces a significant program of staff reductions and layoffs, its future profitability will improve. Hence, as firm after firm announced these staff reductions, the market has responded enthusiastically, thus driving the firm's share prices higher.

But why would anyone believe that firing a group of long-term employees would automatically make a firm more profitable? It is just as easy to imagine that the loss of valuable human capital and the demoralization and speedup among the surviving employees would set the firm on a downward spiral. Therefore, it is hardly surprising that research on the economic effects of downsizing shows quite divergent consequences. In some cases, firms become stronger, but in others, downsizing has had disastrous impacts.

The point is not simply that downsizing became a managerial fad that often did not produce the promised effects. More important, the fad was literally imposed on the managerial class by a stock market that pushed down the share values of firms that were slow to jump on this particular bandwagon. In such a climate, the quality of the arguments for current staffing levels do not matter. The market simply "knows" that it is better to downsize. This is the sense in which the Conventional Wisdom can exercise dictatorial power over the whole society.

THE POWER TO RATION IS THE POWER TO DESTROY

These dictatorial powers are even more evident when financial institutions are unwilling to provide credit to certain categories of borrowers.[4] The classic instance is the process of redlining — marking a section of the city where banks are unwilling to risk lending funds for home mortgages or small business development. (While redlining is now prohibited by law, more subtle forms of credit denial to poorer communities continue.) As with other instances of financial dictatorship, redlining and similar practices create a self-fulfilling prophecy. The banker argues that it is too risky to lend in that part of the city because it is going downhill rapidly and property values are likely to deteriorate. While the prophecy by itself might or might not prove accurate, the decision to redline the neighborhood assures that the anticipated decay will occur because the neighbors are now unable to borrow.

In theory, if one or two banks were to engage in redlining a neighborhood, then other banks believing in the prospects of that neighborhood could take advantage of the opportunities and grab all of the available business. Competition among financial institutions is supposed to prevent any kind of arbitrary or irrational withholding of credit. But here again, the theory diverges from the reality. The first difficulty is the problem of collective sentiment. If Bank A and Bank B have redlined a neighborhood because they think that property values are going to decline, then employees at Bank C have to take very seriously the likelihood that prices will decline. As in the stock market, going against the prevailing sentiment can be a costly proposition. The second difficulty is that all of the banks share the common problem of wanting to economize on the costs of gathering information, and so often adopt the same time-saving conventions, such as automatically saying no to applications from neighborhoods where the median income falls below a certain level. If all the banks in an area adopt the same conventions, then no amount of competition will make funds available to neglected areas.

Another glaring instance of this kind of systematic denial of credit has been the historic reluctance of banks to lend money to employee cooperatives. Even when such cooperatives have been able to provide collateral for loans, banks have generally refused to lend them money. Most bankers share the conventional view that only standard privately owned firms will be economically viable, so there is still another self-fulfilling prophecy. Without any access to credit, employee cooperatives will certainly not be viable. So as bankers see cooperatives fail, they feel completely justified in their prejudices.

But it is not only nonconventional firms that find it difficult to raise capital. Many small businesses have been poorly treated by existing financial institutions. The creation of the Small Business Administration in the U.S. was a direct response to the reluctance of banks to provide loans for smaller firms. If anything, this problem appears to be worsening because of the economics of the banking industry.

Making small-business loans is a labor-intensive retail business. One loan officer making loans of between $20,000 and $100,000 to small businesses will probably have difficulty handling a portfolio of more than $5 or $10 million worth of loans in any given year. But if the bank were to concentrate on real estate development loans or the purchase of securities, one individual could easily handle a portfolio that is ten or one hundred times that size. Since loan officer salaries constitute a significant share of bank costs, the advantages of going with larger portfolios are pretty overwhelming. This means that the bank economizes on the essential role of producing high-quality information, and that many deserving small businesses find it impossible to raise the finance they need.[5]

The damage that results from the reduced access to credit for small businesses is considerable. Beyond the obvious lost opportunities, there is also a systematic diversion of entrepreneurial energy away from the actual production of goods and services. Banks are generally much happier financing the acquisition of rental properties because the properties are a safer form of collateral that reduces banks' risks. Hence, many an aspiring entrepreneur will choose real estate acquisition over other possible businesses simply because of the greater availability of credit.

POWER OVER THE PUBLIC SECTOR

But the most dramatic examples of financial dictatorship are the limits imposed on governments. For state and local governments, and even some national governments, these limits are embedded in the rating system for establishing the riskiness of bonds. Two major rating agencies issue periodic reports on the creditworthiness of both public and private issuers of bonds. A reduction in the rating generally means that the borrower will have to pay a higher rate of interest when issuing new bonds in order to compensate the bondholders for the higher level of risk. The rating process is supposed to be a purely technical exercise based on such variables as total accumulated debt and expected cash flow. But inevitably, the rating process is deeply influenced by the Conventional Wisdom about the proper responsibilities of government.[6]

If, for example, a local government decides to become very involved in the provision of low-income housing, and it becomes clear that some of the proceeds of a bond offering are to be used to help finance actual construction, there is a good chance that the rating agencies will respond negatively. They will argue that such initiatives should remain in the private sector and that housing finance is beyond the capacity of local governments. This is supposed to be a completely nonpolitical argument for downgrading that community's bond rating. But once the word gets out that the community will have to pay more interest on all of its borrowing because of its commitment to the affordable housing project, it is likely that political support for the low-income housing project will evaporate. In short, the power to rate is often the power to veto.

The irony of this is obvious in the aftermath of the Orange County fiasco. In that case, the county treasurer had borrowed close to $10 billion from Wall Street firms to hold a portfolio of financial instruments that included some extremely exotic securities that were highly sensitive to changes in interest rates. When interest rates rose, the value of the portfolio dropped sharply, and the county had to declare bankruptcy. But the rating agencies had taken all of this borrowing for speculative purposes in stride; they did absolutely nothing to warn that the county's creditworthiness might be slipping. The priorities are obvious; if the county had been trying to build low income housing, its credit rating would be jeopardized. But as long as the county was just gambling with taxpayers' money, there was no problem at all.

For the federal government, the dynamics of financial dictatorship are somewhat different. When the financial markets do not like the direction of policy in Washington, traders become reluctant to buy the government's bonds. The government has to issue these bonds both to cover current deficits and to refinance past deficits. (Even if the federal budget were miraculously balanced tomorrow, the government would still have to go to the capital markets to refinance the accumulated national debt.) When the markets are reluctant to purchase the government bonds, the interest rate that the government has to pay rises. If this rise is steep enough, it can force the government to change course to regain the confidence of the bond market.

Here again, the herdlike quality of the financial markets explains this dynamic. When key players in the markets express a lack of confidence in the direction of government policy, this translates into the idea that government bonds will fall in value. The Conventional Wisdom usually assumes that bad government policies will lead to higher rates of inflation. Higher future inflation makes the yields on already issued government bonds look unattractive. As the price of those bonds falls, the yield will improve. As soon as traders begin acting on this view, bond prices will fall. Even if a minority in the trading community thinks that the government's policies are sound and that bonds are a good buy at the current price, the minority is likely to be trampled in the rush to bid bond prices down.

It was precisely this dynamic that Bill Clinton was warned about after his election. If the bond markets did not like the president's policies, then long-term interest rates were likely to move sharply higher. But higher rates on government debt also meant higher rates for all private borrowing as well. And the danger was acute that those higher interest rates would block any significant recovery. Clinton was also warned that even traditional efforts to stimulate the economy with fiscal policies would probably prove unsuccessful in the face of higher interest rates. Some of these warnings were certainly exaggerated; there is evidence that high interest rates are not sufficient in themselves to keep the rate of economic activity low.[7] But the risk was great enough that the president quickly abandoned his campaign promises.

Clinton heeded these warnings by making deficit reduction a priority in his first year in order to gain the confidence of the bond market. The policy "worked" in the short term; the bond market was reassured, interest rates came down, and the economy recovered. But the issue here is not whether it was politically or economically smart for Clinton to listen to the bond market in his first year in office. Rather, the question is how can one justify placing that kind of power in the hands of bond traders. By what theory should the preferences of a handful of bond traders operating within a flawed Conventional Wisdom have a veto over a president's campaign promises?

In metaphoric terms, the financial weeds are threatening to strangle democracy itself. If local and national governments have to worry more about the financial markets than the desires of their constituents, then the principles of self-government are endangered. The choices are stark. Either we try to restore democratic self-government by restraining the ability of finance to exercise this kind of political power, or we might just as well establish the bond traders as a third and dominant house of the Congress with a complete veto over all government decisions.

19 —— Weeds Running Wild: Speculative Frenzies

Most important is the distinctive nature of the financial mind; this rather remarkable manifestation of human intelligence is characterized by a very short memory span. In consequence, the recollection of the economic effects of past disaster that has occurred because of past errors of optimism eventually dissolves. In its place comes a new confidence in the unique and extraordinary genius of a new generation; the impression of such genius is always held most strongly by the favored individuals of themselves. Usually, there will be some variant in the speculative object or emphasis — as in the past, enthusiasm moving from program trading in securities to commodity futures, to stock options, to junk bonds, to urban real estate, to art.

—John Kenneth Galbraith, 1992[1]

In economic terms, the periodic shocks brought about by speculative excesses are the largest cost from the failure to contain the financial sector. In 1995, for example, the Japanese economy was still struggling to recover from a severe economic slowdown. The slowdown was a direct result of government efforts in 1989 and 1990 to halt a fantastic boom in real estate and stock prices. The boom drove both land prices and stock prices to levels that were ridiculously high. After waiting too long to intervene, the government finally opted for a strategy of letting the air out of the bubble slowly instead of waiting for a potentially disastrous explosion. The price that Japan has paid for the runaway boom has been enormous. Its economy has been in the doldrums for five years, resulting in hundreds of billions of dollars of foregone economic output.[2]

Closer to home, the costs of the speculative excesses that caused the Savings & Loan (S&L) disaster were huge. U.S. taxpayers had to spend more than $150 billion to insure the deposits at failed S&Ls. For other episodes of speculative excess, it is more difficult to develop specific cost figures. We know, however, that U.S. commercial banks had to write off $100 billion in bad loans between 1987 and 1991.[3] Most of these bad debts were linked either to failed real estate transactions or the boom in leveraged buyout deals that were fueled by junk bonds. Imagine, for example, had that $100 billion been used instead to finance real investments that actually strengthened the economy's ability to produce. (Net nonresidential fixed investment averaged between $100 and $120 billion per year in this period, so an increment of $20 billion per year would have been dramatic.)

Episodes of financial excess are inevitable when financial markets are left to their own devices. It is only when those markets are carefully regulated and contained that these destabilizing economic booms and their costly aftermaths can be avoided. A closer examination of the dynamics behind these booms will make clear the necessity of regulation.

ASSET PRICE BOOMS

Herdlike behavior in financial markets is a significant part of the explanation for speculative booms. The fact that making money requires bracketing one's judgment and concentrating instead on the likely behavior of others creates an environment in which prices can become unreasonable. An investor might know that United Magic's shares are wildly overpriced at $100 a share, but since others are still buying at that price, the temptation is strong to hold on to the shares and see how high they will go. Moreover, traders gamble in such situations by promising themselves that as soon as they see signs that the market has arrived at a more realistic evaluation of United Magic, they will move quickly to sell their shares before a big decline sets in.

But herdlike behavior is not sufficient in itself to create an asset price boom. Under normal circumstances, United Magic might go to $110, but at that point, the dominant view is likely to be that it is overpriced. It is quite unlikely that the shares would keep going up until they reach $200 unless the company had announced a major breakthrough. Herdlike behavior is similar to stretching a rubber band—when prices go too far in one direction, the elastic begins to pull them back in the other direction.

The additional element that is needed to set off an asset price boom is a large inflow of new money into the market. A useful example is a group of collectors who have been trading baseball cards for some time. The price of a particularly desirable card might have been rising rapidly, but the rubber band principle places a limit on how high it will go. But if a new group of wealthy collectors suddenly becomes interested in baseball cards, all of the old bets will be off. Prices that had been rising at 10% a year could suddenly start rising at 20% or 30% a year.

At this point, the capital gains dynamic begins. If established collectors start selling at the higher prices and reinvesting their profits in more cards, the price rise can be even more dramatic. As individuals see the value of their holdings rising spectacularly, they are likely both to pour more of their own money in and to tell their friends to do the same. A card that last year was priced at only $10 could now trade at $200, *and* it is completely reasonable to imagine that it might go to $400 before the year is out. A full-scale speculative bubble is now in progress, and it can continue for quite some time. Ultimately, however, the inflows of new money will slow and some market participants will try to sell their holdings at the peak prices. This selling pressure can then trigger a panic and price levels will start to fall precipitously as the herdlike mentality shifts from blind optimism to extreme pessimism.

When the influx of new money into the market begins, it forces established market participants to reevaluate their assumptions about proper valuations. Their old rules of thumb about reasonable prices no longer make sense. As they see prices rise, they are likely to embrace one or another explanation for why the new price levels are justified and make economic sense. For example, a study might show that the price of baseball cards lagged behind the prices of other collectibles over the past ten years, leading to the argument that the market was now simply catching up to the higher prices of more traditional collectibles. The combination of the new theories and the money they are making from the price rises is likely to give market participants a false sense of security about how long the prices can continue to rise. This helps explain how otherwise rational economic actors can come to believe that the much higher price levels are sustainable.

NEW BORROWER ENTHUSIASMS

A second type of speculative boom can occur when financial institutions suddenly discover a new category of borrowers. The precipitating circumstance is that lending institutions have money available to lend, but the competition for existing categories of borrowers has kept profit margins down. Somebody gets the bright idea that the financial institution could make money by lending to a category of borrowers who had not previously been seen as creditworthy. And since this is an unfamiliar and somewhat more risky type of lending, the financial institution can charge higher rates of interest.

The institutions who are first to innovate in this way are likely to be somewhat cautious in lending to this new category of borrowers and they are often rewarded with improved profits. But when other financial institutions become aware of this success, some of them will decide to imitate the front-runners. The result is a race among multiple financial institutions to get in on the action. The latecomers have less high-quality information than the institutions that pioneered the market, and they tend to be less cautious because they are determined to grab a share of this newly found market.

The entrance of this new group of players changes the calculus for the borrowers. They suddenly see institutions competing to offer them deals, and their mind-set shifts from "How can I convince a banker to make me a loan?" to "How quickly can I put together a proposal to take advantage of this extraordinary situation?" Moreover, with much easier access to credit, it becomes relatively easy for borrowers to handle problems by borrowing even more. When a borrower finds it hard to meet the interest payments on loans that are currently due, there might be an opportunity to borrow even more and use some of the proceeds to cover those interest charges.

This kind of lender enthusiasm characterized the explosion of bank lending to developing countries and Eastern Europe in the 1970s. The result was the debt crisis of the 1980s when loans had to be renegotiated and country after country suffered a crippling period of austerity to atone for the earlier borrowing sprees.[4] But the same dynamic also occurred with lending for management organized leveraged buyouts in the 1980s. Some combination of bank lending and "junk bonds" provided the management of firms with enough capital to buy all of the existing shares of stock. These new owner-managers were then supposed to run the firm far more efficiently and use the higher profits to pay down their accumulated debt. Many of the deals of this nature that were put together in the early 1980s were relatively successful. But from 1985 on, as institutions competed with each other for this business, the quality of the deals deteriorated sharply.[5] Many of these firms went bankrupt, and banks were left holding large quantities of uncollectable loans.

Here, also, it is relatively easy to understand the mental processes that underlie these enthusiasms. When a few institutions suddenly make profits even though they are violating old industry understandings about who is a worthy borrower, it forces others in the industry to reevaluate their previous assumptions. As they reevaluate, they are likely to embrace one or another theory that purports to explain why this previously overlooked category of borrowers is really quite creditworthy. And once they are swept up in the business of making these deals, then there is no time even to question whether the new theory makes sense. The rude awakening only comes when the flow of loans slows and the new borrowers are suddenly revealed to be insolvent.

FROM REALITY TO THEORY

That these speculative episodes have occurred repeatedly over the last twenty years is undeniable, but the Conventional Wisdom treats each episode as a special case with its own unique causes. The Third World debt crisis, the S&L debacle, the overbuilding of commerical office buildings in the 1980s, the leveraged buyout mania, and the Japanese land and stock price bubbles are treated as entirely independent events with no common causes.

There is an obvious reason for this analytic myopia. The Conventional Wisdom cannot make sense of speculative episodes because they contradict three of its most treasured premises. The first of these premises is that financial markets generally do a very good job in pricing assets and managing risk. The second is a belief in the desirability of tightly linking financial markets within countries and across countries. Such financial integration is attractive because it increases the likelihood that funds will be able to flow to the activities with the highest rate of return. The third premise is that the regulation of financial markets should be kept to a minimum because regulation tends to interfere with the integration of markets.

Each of these premises is dangerously wrong. The frequent

occurrence of speculative bubbles indicates that there are very significant occasions when financial markets establish utterly unrealistic prices. And if it is relatively easy for financial markets to get prices wrong, then it also follows that the integration of financial markets is not an unequivocal good. Financial market integration actually increases the likelihood of speculative bubbles. The baseball card example shows the important role in a bubble of new money coming into an asset market and shaking up both the prices and the traders' perceptions. But financial integration means that funds that had previously been dedicated to another purpose will be available for new purposes. In the S&L scandal, it was the "deregulation" of the industry that suddenly gave S&Ls the opportunity to diversify their portfolios beyond residential mortgage lending. The result was that S&L funds flowed in large quantities into real estate deals and into junk bonds. In both cases, the newly available funds fueled speculative excesses. Similarly, one of the dynamics behind the overbuilding of commercial office space in the 1980s was that banks suddenly found themselves competing to finance these deals not only with other banks but also with insurance companies and pension funds that had not previously been involved in real estate development.

Metaphorically, financial market integration is similar to the idea that the circulatory system does not have to be a complex array of blood vessels of different sizes with different purposes. One size fits all, and money should be able to just slosh around to where it has the highest rate of return. Arguments for financial integration are utterly insensitive to the information-producing function of financial institutions. If a particular financial institution is dedicated to a particular task such as providing small business loans or funding municipal infrastructure projects, it is likely to develop considerable expertise in that area. But if the same institution is suddenly told that it can invest wherever it wants, the incentive to economize on information production will likely be overwhelming, and impersonal markets with their lower-quality information will replace higher-quality information.

But if financial integration makes the economy more vulnerable to speculative excesses, then the argument that financial regulation should be kept to a minimum is also wrong. A developed system of regulation is necessary both to keep financial institutions from becoming carried away with new enthusiasms and to assure that financial institutions have strong incentives to develop high-quality information about specific markets. Instead of creating one huge integrated financial market, regulators must strive to segment financial markets so that different participants develop different kinds of expertise.

The tasks that financial regulators face are daunting. Not all forms of financial market segmentation are productive, and a financial system has to evolve as the economy changes. It is inevitable that even if a structure of rules functions well for some time, it will eventually become inefficent and counterproductive and will need to be revised. Moreover, overly rigid regulations can kill financial institutions; the goal rather is to keep them pruned and in their proper place. As with the most demanding types of gardening, regulating the financial sector is a complex mix of art and science.

But financial regulators cannot hope to be effective if the whole society is operating on a series of fundamental misconceptions about the proper role of finance in the economy. And the potential economic and political costs of these misconceptions can be staggering. The recent experience of Orange County exemplifies the general problem. One man, the county treasurer, bet wrong in the way that he handled his investment portfolio and the entire county will have to pay the costs. Hundreds of public-sector workers have been laid off, and the quality of services that millions of others receive is deteriorating. The same fate awaits the rest of us if we fail to tend the financial plants in our national garden.

A few years ago, a well-known advertising campaign bragged that a particular brokerage firm made money the old-fashioned way, through hard work. This is the way that the financial sector is supposed to work; employees of financial intermediaries diligently acquire concrete information about particular markets and firms and improve their evaluative skills so they can identify and monitor productive users of funds. But in recent years, the financial sector has become preoccupied with a search for the Holy Grail — mathematical formulae and techniques that will allow participants to make money consistently in these markets. The result has been an intensification of the substitution of bad information for good. Absract formulae and complicated trading strategies now substitute for concrete knowledge of what goes on in specific markets. Knowledge of the dynamics of global markets increasingly displaces understandings of what is going on in specific regional markets. To be sure, the quantity of financial information is growing apace. Newspapers' financial sections grow progressively larger so they can provide reports on dozens of new financial instruments. But the quality of that information, and its usefulness for productive economic activity, continues to deteriorate.

Hence, there is no good reason why we should accept the constraints this system places on our domestic politics. Those constraints are not indispensable for economic prosperity. In reality, the current financial system distorts our politics and fails at its central economic tasks. Strategic reforms could simultaneously make our political system more democratic and make the financial system work more effectively. But before discussing those reforms, it is also important to analyze the international constraints on our domestic political choices.

Part Four

THE GLOBAL ECONOMY: COSTS EXCEEDING BENEFITS

20 —— Global Overdosing

There is no such thing as free trade... You have to have rules of the road.
— Mickey Kantor, U.S. Trade Representative, 1993[1]

The Conventional Wisdom makes the same logical error with the global economy that it makes with finance — it assumes that something that is good in small quantities will be even better in large quantities. This is the dosage fallacy; if a teaspoon of medicine makes you better, then why not drink the whole bottle. There are indisputable advantages to making national economies responsive to international markets, but it does not follow that those same economies will benefit from being totally integrated into one global market. The Conventional Wisdom rests on mistaken views about the nature of international trade and finance.

THE BENEFITS OF OPENNESS

The "openness" of an economy to international trade can be thought of in terms of a continuum. North Korea or Albania — before the collapse of Eastern Bloc Communism — represent one extreme: economies that are basically closed to market-driven transactions. Consumers in these countries are simply not allowed to buy Western consumer products. And when those countries do engage in foreign trade, goods and services move across their borders through intergovernmental arrangements. Prices in such deals are generally set through official negotiations rather than being determined by markets.

At the other end of the continuum are countries that allow both their own and foreign citizens broad freedom to move goods and services across their borders in order to make a profit. But there are no examples of "real" nations in recent memory that have been as close to the absolutely open end of the continuum as Korea and Albania were to the absolutely closed end.[2] Even the most open nations still maintain many restrictions on trade, such as prohibitions on the export of national treasures, bans on the import of certain drugs and weapons, and rules against trading in human beings. And the major developed market societies such as the U.S., Japan, and most European countries are farther from the open end of the continuum because of consumer safety, environmental, public health, and other regulations that prohibit various transactions.

Since the fall of Soviet-style Communism, it is often assumed that the failure of Soviet Socialism proves that the closer a society is to the open end of the continuum, the better its economic performance. But there is no real support for this assumption. All that one can learn from the failure of economies that were on the closed end of the continuum is that they would be better off being somewhat closer to the open end. To date, there has been no convincing empirical work to show that economic performance improves as nations move closer to the completely open end of the continuum.[3]

The obvious disadvantage of being near the closed end of the continuum is that a nation's producers have no need to worry about foreign competition. Hence, domestic producers can remain terribly inefficient by international standards and yet consumers will have no recourse because they are not allowed to purchase goods from abroad. East German state industry, for example, could continue to sell 1950s style automobiles in the late 1980s; but when the Berlin Wall collapsed, so also did the market for Stalin-era vehicles.

A society does not have to adopt state socialism to suffer from this problem. A combination of high tariffs and collusion among domestic producers can create the same situation. Many developing countries have seen a handful of domestic producers take advantage of a shared monopoly in a certain product line to force consumers to accept poor-quality goods at internationally uncompetitive prices.

The benefit of being more open is that domestic producers face foreign competition. Without such competition, the pressures on domestic producers to seek out more efficient practices will depend entirely on the existence and energy of domestic competitors. And we have already seen that markets within countries often do not work in such a way that only the fittest firms survive. This is the powerful argument for some kind of system of international free trade in goods and services. It provides a simple mechanism to force producers in all parts of the world to move toward the most efficient possible production techniques. But while the arguments for a moderate dose of free trade or international openness are very strong, arguments for a large dose of free trade are quite problematic.

LARGE DOSE ARGUMENTS

Large-dose advocates generally argue that the only desirable system of free trade is one that keeps government regulation of the economy to an absolute minimum.[4] In their view, real free trade requires that economic transactions be determined only by relative prices. If, for example, I want to buy a container of fruit juice, the only thing that should matter to me is the quality of the juice and its cost. Whether or not the juice was bottled in Mexico, the U.S., or Italy should be utterly irrelevant, and anything that draws attention to the product's place of origin represents a distortion of the way economic transactions are supposed to work.

However, governments in developed market economies long ago realized that they had to take steps to protect the quality of the food supply because consumers inevitably lack important information about a product's contents. To this day, there are reports of unscrupulous businesspeople who dilute fruit juices with various chemicals and then attempt to sell them as pure and natural. As long as such tampering is difficult to detect by the individual, market competition by itself cannot eliminate the problem. On the contrary, the profitability of tampering puts pressure on other producers to tamper as well. The only effective way to eliminate such practices is through a system of legal enforcement. Even though a firm with an established brand name might think twice before damaging its reputation through tampering, ownership of the brand name could easily fall into the hands of a new management that was interested only in quick profits.

The complexity comes if particular nations are known to have laxer procedures for inspecting juices. Consumers in a nation with stricter regulations might then have a strong preference for juices that are packaged domestically. Large-dose advocates would see this result as a distortion of free trade. Their worry is that governments can engage in disguised forms of protectionism by issuing complicated sets of regulations that are unreasonably biased against foreign providers. They go on to argue that the only way to avoid these types of interferences with the principle of free trade is to reduce government regulation to an absolute minimum. With far fewer regulations, governments will be less tempted to bend the rules in a protectionist direction. And usually at this point, large-dose advocates invoke the imagery of vampire states with overblown and wasteful regulatory bureaucracies.

But large-dose proponents completely ignore the fact that without regulations and enforcement, someone is likely to adulterate the fruit juices and pass them off as pure. Their preference for less regulation is rooted in an irrational distrust of the state rather than in any realistic sense of how markets actually work. Government regulations are not an interference in markets, but rather they are essential for making markets work.[5]

One additional example should suffice to make this point.

There is a long-standing debate over labor standards in international trade, and the same arguments are also relevant to international environmental standards. Labor advocates have argued that a free-trade regime should include certain basic labor standards such as prohibitions against child labor, guarantees of trade-union rights, and certain health and safety standards for workers. Nations that failed to meet these standards would face higher barriers to the international sale of their goods, while nations that met the standards would enjoy all of the benefits of free trade. They go on to argue that without such labor standards, there will be an international "race to the bottom," since countries that exploit child labor or tolerate unhealthful workplaces will have lower costs than their competitors and will have an unfair advantage over their more decent rivals. Soon, the pressure of this competiton will force other nations to roll back previously instituted protections.

Large-dose free-traders tend to dismiss these arguments for global labor standards as self-serving efforts by workers in richer countries to protect their positions of relative privilege. The expressed concern for employees in poorer countries is seen simply as a pretext to keep lower-cost producers out of the global marketplace. For large-dose advocates, a regime in which there are elaborate labor standards is not a system of free trade but some kind of managed global competition.

Here, however, the large-dose arguments miss the point that any trading system has a set of ground rules, for example, that parties will pay their bills and that intellectual property rights such as patents and copyrights will be respected. There is no logical reason why those ground rules should not include certain basic rights for working people. In fact, the expectation that nations will not permit chattel slavery is already a ground rule of the existing trading system. To further specify the rules governing the employment relation or environmental policies is completely consistent with the idea of ground rules.

In fact, it is possible to have a free-trade regime with no labor standards and a free-trade regime with quite stringent labor standards. The preference of large-dose advocates for the former is simply a reflection of their value system in which protecting workers has a very low priority. But the basic advantage of a free-trade regime—that participating nations will be under continuous pressure to upgrade their techniques of production —will be available under both types of free trade regime. But the one with labor standards has the obvious advantage that employers will not be tempted to compete by degrading working conditions and wages. Competition will focus instead on capital investments that improve labor productivity.

CLOSING THE INFANT INDUSTRY LOOPHOLE

A second line of argument by large-dose advocates is that protection for "infant industries" is a violation of the concept of free trade. The protection of infant industries is often used to get a new industry started. For example, without tariff protections, no entrepreneur would bother to start a steel firm in a nation that lacks even a rudimentary steel industry because of the certainty that foreign steel firms would market their steel so aggressively that the new firm would be unprofitable for years and years. However, an entrepreneur might be willing to make the investment in exchange for tariff protections that will disappear after five years. The hope is that after a protected infancy, the firm should be strong enough as an adolescent to face foreign competition.

Large-dose advocates argue that countries will generally find excuses to extend infant protection into adolescence and adulthood. The political clout of the industrialist and the desire to protect jobs will assure continued protection and the principles of free trade will be subverted. Hence, the world will be better off by not allowing these exceptions in the first place.

Yet, the argument that infant industry protections will be extended indefinitely is an empirical claim that is not strongly supported by evidence. What large-dose advocates forget is that there are other parties to trade policies within countries. The firms that purchase steel, for example, are unlikely to support continued protection for the local steel industry if it interferes with their ability to get their materials at the best price. Also, international organizations that oversee the ground rules can also help to assure that the temporary exception is truly time limited.

Moreover, there are other circumstances in which these types of temporary protection might be appropriate. An established industry in one country might suddenly face devastating competition from foreign producers who have developed a dramatically new production technology. In such a case, there could be considerable benefits in giving the domestic industry several years of partial protection so that it would gain some time to meet the challenge. The alternative of immediate unemployment for the industry's labor force might be too high a price to pay.

MORE IS NOT BETTER

In each of these cases, large-dose advocates assume that if some free trade is good, then a system of free trade that reduces government activity to a minumum will be even better. But that does not follow at all. Once one recognizes that international trade requires ground rules, then it is logical to include in those rules labor standards, environmental standards, and provisions for temporary protection of industries. In a word, it is possible to have all of the benefits of free trade without some of the more noxious side effects.

21 —·— Overselling the Cure

It is crucial to keep in mind the new reality of world trade: mass-pro-duction technologies have grown so productive and so portable that one of the world's major trade areas all by itself could easily meet major consumption demands of the entire world, given the present distribu-tion of purchasing power. If the United States permitted totally free entree to all goods, the Far East could easily supply all our textiles and apparel, all our cars and trucks, and all but the most sophisticated con-sumer electronic products. Or the United States could happily supply most of the world's cars, televisions, and consumer appliances, as we did in the short happy decade after World War II.

—Robert Kuttner, 1984[1]

Those who advocate a large dose of global free trade are also guilty of making exaggerated claims for their med-icine. They resemble snake oil salesmen who claim that their medicine will cure everything that ails you. Large-dose advocates of international free trade have repeatedly insisted that free trade is the best way to assure global job growth. Both George Bush and Bill Clinton have repeatedly insisted that dis-mantling trade barriers through agreements such as NAFTA and the General Agreement on Tariffs and Trade (GATT) is the best way to expand domestic employment. But while a small dose of free trade can help expand employment, free trade can ulti-mately play only a minor role in helping societies to solve their major employment problems. The problem of conscious social adaptation to rising productivity cannot be solved by free trade.

FREE TRADE AND
EMPLOYMENT GROWTH

In a society that closes itself off to international trade, firms will generally have little incentive to innovate. The productivity of labor in steel mills or auto plants will likely remain about the same year after year, and so workers' wage levels can also be expected to remain stable. Since workers' income levels are stagnant, there is not much incentive to try to produce new consumer goods since nobody will be able to buy them. Hence, there is little chance of expanding employment in new industries.

If, in contrast, firms are under competitive pressure to innovate, then productivity will rise and wage levels can also be expected to improve. With rising income, consumer demand will also be increasing. Entrepreneurs who provide consumers with goods and services that were previously unavailable are likely to expand their operations and create new jobs. It is in this sense that free trade creates jobs through increasing average incomes.

But it has to be remembered that this rising productivity is also a double-edged sword. If, for example, productivity in the steel mills is rising at 4% per year but demand for steel is rising at only 2%, then it is to be expected that steel mills will reduce their total employment. Whether the reduction in steel employment is greater or less than the growth of employment in bowling alleys, movie theaters, and other expanding industries depends on the relative labor intensity of these different activities. In fact, it is entirely possible that an economy with rising productivity and rising income will also experience a decline in the total hours worked by the labor force. In recent years, for example, the economy of the former West Germany has had growing output and declining employment.[2]

The paradox is that productivity growth is indispensable for increasing consumer incomes and the growth of new branches of employment, but productivity growth can simultaneously shrink employment in established industries. As was argued earlier, developed market economies have worked out a number of techniques to cope with this paradox. First, there has been a dramatic reduction in the total amount of paid work performed over a lifetime by the average person in the labor force.

This has been accomplished both through shorter workdays and work years and through the combination of earlier retirement and later entrance into the labor force. The second mechanism has been the growth of many types of employment that are not really necessary for human survival but that mobilize labor to improve the quality of life.

But free-trade advocates argue that if we had a lot more free trade — NAFTA, GATT, and so forth — we would not have to worry about these kinds of adaptations or coping mechanisms. They insist that the vigorous growth of international trade will create a rising tide of employment everywhere in the free-trading world. Their logic is based on the idea that vigorous trade will contribute to rapid growth in productivity and income and that will assure the creation of new jobs. The problem, however, is that free-trade advocates utterly ignore the other side of productivity advance — its role in diminishing employment.

The case of agriculture is one example in which advances in productivity can lead to declining employment. The U.S. has been extremely effective in expanding international markets for its agricultural products, and the result has been long-term growth in agricultural exports. But agricultural employment has continued its long-term decline precisely because of steady productivity advances in farming. The same pattern can be expected for manufacturing industries such as automobiles, aircraft, and machine tools. Even if international trade allowed us to increase production in these industries by as much as 3% or 4% a year, it is still likely that total employment in these industries will shrink.

THE ZERO-SUM PROBLEM OF GLOBAL TRADE

When politicians such as George Bush or Bill Clinton insist that growing international trade will expand domestic employment, they invoke a vision of the U.S. as the workshop of the world producing computers and other high-tech gadgets for all of the world's citizens. But such imagery leaves out the basic reality of international trade — that trade is and has to be reciprocal. (While our trade with Country A does not have to be balanced, our total exports and imports must come close to balance.) For example, if we export vast quantities of computers to Mexico and the rest of Latin America, we would have to buy goods or services from these countries so that they can earn the dollars with which to purchase our computers. And if we buy large quantities of clothing and packaged foods from these countries, then we have to expect that our domestic employment in those industries will contract.

In fact, there is a good chance that expanding reciprocal trade might actually reduce domestic employment. The industries in which our exports are most likely to rise tend to be capital-intensive — employing relatively few workers. And the industries where our imports are likely to rise — resulting in a contraction of our domestic production — are likely to be far more labor-intensive. Hence, the growth of jobs in the expanding industries is unlikely to offset the loss of jobs in the declining industries.[3]

Even so, this growth of high-tech exports in exchange for an increase of low-tech imports is still a desirable deal. Our collective wealth as a society will be greater when we expand production in capital-intensive industries and contract it in labor-intensive industries. This is what people, such as Secretary of Labor Robert Reich, mean when they emphasize the importance of expanding our high value-added industries. But it is also important that we shed the illusion that some automatic market forces will take care of those people who have lost their jobs in labor-intensive industries. Their chances of being reemployed in one of the expanding export industries are very small. And because trade has to be reciprocal, the sacrifice of low value-added employment is actually necessary to expand high value-added employment. For this reason, the society has a moral obligation to find ways to shift some of its wealth to those who have been forced to sacrifice their livelihoods to facilitate greater import flows.

THE GREAT JAPANESE EXCEPTION

The argument is a little more complicated because Japan and some of the other Far Eastern economies have—for a sustained period of time—violated the principle that international trade must be reciprocal. Japan has run huge trade surpluses year after year. This means, in essence, that when Japan increases its exports of automobiles to the U.S. and other nations, it has not opened its markets to comparable flows of imports. Instead, Japan has chosen to export capital to finance its trade surplus. Instead of buying an equal dollar amount of goods from the U.S., Japan instead invests billions of dollars each year in U.S. treasury notes, real estate, and other assets.

What Japan has done is optimal for its own domestic employment. Many thousands of new jobs have been created in Japanese export industries, but Japan has been slow to contract employment in older industries such as agriculture and apparel where more imports would destroy jobs. This helps to explain why Japan has consistently had one of the lowest levels of reported unemployment in all of the developed market economies. Still, even with its success in running these large trade surpluses, Japan's total employment has grown slowly over the past ten years. In short, trade surpluses are still not sufficient to overcome the employment-reducing impact of high rates of productivity advance in the more developed sectors of the economy.

So, if Japan can consistently run this kind of trade surplus that protects its economy from some of the negative consequences of expanding trade, why cannot the U.S. do the same? The answer is that for every dollar that Japan's trade is in surplus, there must be other countries who are in an equal trade deficit position. This is the meaning of the idea that trade has to be reciprocal across all trading nations. Japan has been able to run its consistently large surplus only because the U.S. has been willing to run a consistently large trade deficit. If both Japan and the U.S. sought to run trade surpluses of a $100 billion a year at the same time, they would have to find a group of other nations willing to import more than they export to the tune of $200 billion a year. But there are no nations that want to have that kind of an import surplus. The reason is obvious: If you import much more than you export, the domestic employment effects will be terrible. The nation will lose jobs in industries where import competition is strong without gaining jobs in export industries.

In a word, it is utterly impractical for the U.S. to have an export surplus like the Japanese. The only realistic goal for the U.S. is to try to eliminate its import surplus and return to a rough balance between imports and exports. This means, as well, persuading Japan and some of the other East Asian countries to give up their export surpluses. Progress in this direction would improve our domestic employment situation because we would be using our own workers to produce the $150 billion of goods and services by which imports currently exceed exports. This is worth doing, but again, it is important to be realistic about the size of the expected employment effects. They are likely to be small—after all, $150 billion is only 2.5% of a $6 trillion economy. And even the expected 2.5% growth in jobs would be reduced by continuing productivity gains.

But it is not that easy to eliminate our trade deficit and Japan's trade surplus. The U.S. has spent years applying pressure on Japan to expand its imports of U.S. goods, and while there have been gains, the Japanese trade surplus persists. For Japan to live by the rule of reciprocal trade would require some fundamental changes in Japanese society, and there has been no political will in Japan to carry out those changes. Moreover, the

U.S. government has been consistently reluctant to push the Japanese very hard.

In the absence of Japanese agreement to balance its trade, U.S. options are extremely limited. If the U.S. were willing to violate existing trade agreements, it could slap high tariffs on imported goods, but that would only lead to retaliation by other nations against our exports. Within the rules of free trade, the only alternative is to reduce our imports by slowing our entire economy. It is possible, for example, that if domestic unemployment were pushed up to 15% or 20%, then the U.S. could achieve balance in its trade account, but that is a price that nobody wants to pay.

But whatever happens on the trade front, it is only modestly relevant to our problems of domestic employment. Whether or not the U.S. overcomes its trade imbalance with the Japanese, the U.S. will still have difficulty finding jobs for everybody who wants to work. Whether or not U.S. trade with the rest of the world expands at 1%, 2%, 3%, or 4% a year, the U.S. economy still has to find ways to adapt to the unrelenting advances of productivity that shrink employment in established industries.

CONCLUSION

The damage done by the snake oil salesmen of free trade is of two kinds. The first is that they have persuaded people of the legitimacy of large doses of free trade—a cure that can have disastrous consequences for the world economy. The resulting arbitrary rejection of international labor and environmental standards and the opposition to temporary relief for infant industries reduce living standards globally. The second type of damage is the diversion of our attention away from the real problems of conscious adaptation. It is pure fantasy to believe that trade will solve employment problems, but the popularity of this fantasy makes it harder to mobilize the political will needed to devise creative responses to our expanding productivity.

22 —— Upping the Dosage: Free Trade in Finance

Because services have become so vital a part of the domestic and international economy, the United States has insisted on including the liberalization of trade in services in the Uruguay Round [of international trade negotiations]. It took a strong position that commitments would be necessary not only with respect to the usual border restrictions on trade but also with respect to rights of establishment for U.S. service enterprises abroad and their treatment once established. Without such assurances (including national and non-discriminatory treatment), trade liberalization for service industries, such as banking and insurance, would be meaningless, since the bulk of foreign sales of such services can, as a practical matter, be accomplished only through an established presence in a foreign country.

—Research and Policy Committee of the
Committee for Economic Development, 1991

There's a growing worry among the Clinton Administration, Federal Reserve officials and top Wall Street financiers that the international money markets could trigger a major financial crisis they might not be able to control.

The problem, as they see it, is the rise of what is called 'hot money,' a multi-trillion dollar pool of capital that races around the world's stock, bond, and security markets in search of the highest returns each day.

—John M. Berry and Clay Chandler, 1995[1]

The most important move by large-dose advocates has been to argue that a system of global free trade also requires maximum freedom for capital to move across national boundaries in response to market signals. Sometimes this argument is actually made in trade terms by arguing that banking services, brokerage services, and insurance services are no different from the steel or apparel industry. A regime of international free trade requires that countries dismantle barriers that prevent foreign banks, brokerage firms, or insurance firms from doing business in other countries. But if such financial intermediaries are going to be able to do business in other countries, it is only logical that they have maximal freedom to move their raw material—money—back and forth as freely as possible.

Over the last twenty years, these large-dose arguments have carried the day. Many countries have moved to dismantle systems of capital controls that had previously limited or restricted capital movements. The consequence is that the world economy has acheived a level of global financial integration that has not been seen since before World War I.[2] In addition, U.S. trade negotiators continue to be active in deepening financial integration by pushing other nations to grant greater freedom for foreign financial institutions within their domestic economies. In late 1994, for example, when the U.S. was contemplating a major effort to support the Mexican economy after a dramatic fall in the value of the peso, one quid pro quo that the U.S. considered was an accelerated timetable for permitting U.S. banks to expand their role in Mexico.[3]

Despite the political triumphs of this large-dose argument for free capital movement, its intellectual foundations are quite flimsy. In fact, in this case, too much of the free-trade medicine might end up killing the patient. The dangers of the present level of global financial integration are enormous, and the arguments for moving back to a regime of capital controls are extremely compelling.

THE POLITICAL CONSEQUENCES OF GLOBAL FINANCIAL INTEGRATION

The extension of the free-trade argument to cover capital movement rests on the same logic that is used to justify the integration of financial markets domestically. Eliminating barriers at national boundaries is supposed to allow capital to move to wherever returns are highest, and this is supposed to assure the most efficient use of global resources. As we will see, these arguments are no more persuasive at the global level than they are domestically. But advocates of free capital movement also invoke a political argument in which freedom to move capital across national boundaries is seen as a basic human right.

Free international mobility of capital has been defined as an essential component of human liberty. If governments have the power to impose capital controls that keep a citizen from moving his or her wealth abroad, they are radically limiting that citizen's property rights. This is seen as a critical step down the slippery "road to serfdom" since property rights are one of the main bulwarks that protect people from an intrusive state. The claim is that once property rights are compromised, it becomes much more difficult to limit the state's power over the individual.[4]

One problem with this slippery-slope argument is that it lacks any real historical support. Most of the democracies of Western Europe maintained extensive systems of capital controls in the period from the end of World War II to the mid-1970s. And all but the most conservative of thinkers would be hard pressed to argue that those societies moved irrevocably during that period to stamp out individual liberty. On the contrary, most observers would agree that there were significant extensions of personal liberty in most of these countries during that period.

But an even deeper problem with this line of argument is its elevation of the liberty of the few over the rights of the many. It is, after all, only a small percentage of the population that has enough wealth in liquid form to be personally affected by capital controls. However, when the rich decide to shift capital abroad, the consequences are felt by every citizen. Large outflows of capital lead inevitably to a devaluation of the national currency that translates into a reduction of the standard of living. Moreover, when capital controls cannot be used as a means to stem the outflow, governments have to respond to these outflows by raising domestic interest rates. Such interest rate increases usually mean an economic slowdown and a big increase in unemployment. By what calculus is this a reasonable trade-off—that the rich have liberty to do whatever they want with their wealth, but as a consequence, the rest of the population can suffer significant economic hardships?

The political consequence is that the liberty of the few gives them inordinate power over the many. Overwhelming majorities of the electorate might vote in favor of parties advocating certain policies such as an economic stimulus package and increases in taxation on the wealthy. However, it is probable that if the government attempts to carry out that policy, holders of liquid wealth will insist that the new policies will have inflationary consequences that will lead to a devaluation of the currency. The result will be a massive outflow of capital that will force the predicted devaluation—whether or not there are any signs of the predicted inflation. And almost every time that this has happened, the government has been forced to retreat from its initial economic program.

The only way that proponents of the liberty argument can defend this obvious violation of democratic principles is by insisting that the market evaluations are always correct. If vast amounts of capital suddenly flee a particular country, it is an indication that the country's government is pursuing wildly impractical policies that will end up hurting the citizenry. In this view, the capital flight is an effective early warning system that prevents significant policy mistakes.

Yet, this position is also indefensible. Precisely because impersonal markets are prone to herdlike behavior, it is easy to imagine circumstances under which asset-holders are stampeded irrationally into capital flight. After all, if the preponderance of opinion in the marketplace is that a currency will fall in value, then it will fall in value. That means that market participants will be watching for any loss of confidence in a currency, and they will be quick to move when they suspect that others are moving.

In this jittery situation, market participants are not going to be able to make subtle evaluations of the long-term soundness of government policies. One has to remember the example of Franklin Delano Roosevelt who repeatedly insisted that the purpose of the New Deal was to stabilize capitalism. The conventional view in the business community, however, held that FDR was a dangerous radical and that his reforms were likely to wreak economic havoc. Fortunately, capital flight from the U.S. was not a realistic option during the 1930s because of the lack of safe havens; but if it had been, it would have hampered FDR's ability to win reforms that did strengthen the economy.

This is precisely the problem. The liberty argument gives an effective veto over government policy to a group of people who are very likely to be consistently wrong in their views about what is really good for the economy. These are people who have persuaded themselves that impersonal markets can be relied on to get prices right and that unregulated markets will produce good outcomes for everybody. In short, the opportunity for capital flight gives the Conventional Wisdom dictatorial power over the whole society.

PUTTING THE NATION UP
FOR AUCTION

The global financial integration that large-dose advocates have favored means that nations are continually up for auction in the foreign exchange markets. Transactions in these markets have now reached $1.2 trillion a day, and 90% or more of these transactions are for speculative purposes.[5] Large banks and other financial institutions both in the U.S. and abroad have dedicated billions of dollars for taking positions in these markets. Some foreign-exchange traders will buy or sell $1 billion at a time in dollars or marks, so that if they guess right on a movement of only 1 cent in the price of the dollar, they stand to make $10 million on the deal.

Moreover, there are other investors with vast resources at their disposal who are ready to jump into these markets with huge amounts of money. In 1992, George Soros, an important financier, was able to borrow $10 billion to bet that the British pound would have to be devalued. Since other speculators with even more billions of dollars were willing to follow his lead and also bet against the pound, the British government capitulated and devalued. Soros had the double triumph of forcing a government to its knees and walking away with a profit of more than $1 billion.[6]

The resources that Soros and others have at their disposal vastly outstrip the foreign-exchange reserves that governments hold for emergencies. In earlier days, these reserves could sometimes be used to prop up a currency that was falling in value, but now the resources in the markets are simply too great. In the peso crisis in early 1995, the Mexican government could easily have exhausted its total reserves of $12 billion without making any impact on the market.[7] But the same impotence exists for the developed market economies as well; it is easy to imagine circumstances in which the British or French government could spend $50 billion in reserves without effectively reversing the slide in its currency's value.

But a country's exchange rate is a major determinant of its standard of living. If imports represent 50% of what Mexicans consume, then the 40% devaluation of the peso that occurred in January 1995 represented a 20% across-the-board reduction in the standard of living of Mexico's people. This is an enormous shift to occur in a matter of days, but it is an obvious and logical result of a system in which the price of currencies is determined on an impersonal market. The country's standard of living will rise and fall with shifts in the confidence of the international investor community.

The irrationality of this arrangement is obvious in the case of natural disasters. If a country suffers from earthquakes or floods in its central regions, international investors could easily decide that they had overestimated the country's economic prospects since rebuilding would take away energy and resources from other economic activities. In fact, the Kobe earthquake in Japan in 1995 led to a temporary decline in the value of the yen.[8] If such a decline were more substantial, the country's standard of living would fall, adding a second human disaster to the natural one.

THE WEAKENING OF GOVERNMENTS

As a consequence of this ongoing currency auction, governments have been forced to recognize that they have no choice but to accept the foreign-exchange market's valuation of their currency. They have to avoid any policies that the foreign-exchange markets might consider unconventional or radical. Governments also have far less room to maneuver in stimulating a weak economy with high unemployment. If the government tries to lower domestic interest rates to encourage borrowing for new investment, the probable result will simply be increased capital outflows in search of higher interest rates in other countries. If the government tries instead to cut taxes or increase government spending, the larger budget deficit will lead to fears of inflation and capital will flow out in anticipation of a decline in the currency. In both cases, the resulting capital outflows will probably produce a decline in the value of the currency.[9]

A government that is trying to stimulate its economy might actually welcome a small decline in the value of its currency. After all, a cheaper currency will make its country's exports more competitive abroad, and an export boom could also help to jumpstart the domestic economy. The difficulty is that once the markets start to lower the value of a currency, it is never obvious where the stampede will end. A 2% decline in the currency's value can lead other investors to panic that it is not safe to leave assets in that currency. By the time the investors have liquidated their positions, the decline is 8%, and then still other investors panic. A government that might have initially welcomed a 5% devaluation can easily find that its currency has dropped 20% with quite drastic domestic consequences.

Since government authorities know this scenario very well, they understand the importance of avoiding any action that might lead market participants to reassess the value of their currency. The safest strategy is to avoid any fiscal or monetary stimulus that might create doubts in the foreign exchange markets. This situation is radically different from the period from World War II to the late 1970s when governments had far more ability to steer their economies. It is hardly surprising, therefore, that average unemployment levels have been consistently higher in the developed market economies from 1980 to the present than they were in the three decades before global financial integration.

This decline of activist government intervention is extremely important. During the Great Depression, the Conventional Wisdom was that governments should try to balance their budgets despite the dramatic fall in revenues, and that sooner or later the spontaneous forces of the business cycle would bring about an economic recovery. As long as this advice was heeded, nations suffered huge and unnecessary declines in their levels of economic output. Once FDR's administration disregarded the Conventional Wisdom, it was able to use government spending to stimulate the economy and take advantage of the great treasure trove of unutilized resources.

But now, the nations of the world have been forced by global financial integration back to where they were before the Keynesian Revolution. If the business cycle turns down, nations have to try to limit budget deficits and hope that the spontaneous forces of recovery will assert themselves again. But those spontaneous forces could take ten, twenty, or even forever to produce a return to full employment. In the meantime, in the developed market economies alone, twenty-five million people were unemployed in the middle of the business cycle.

The simple reality is that global financial integration does not work. The pressures of the financial markets operate to keep nations from moving close to full use of their supplies of capital equipment and labor, and there is absolutely no countervailing mechanism that pushes toward full employment because governments have lost most of their ability to pursue fiscal and monetary policies. The dictatorship of international financial markets has become a powerful obstacle to conscious adaptation and effective steering.

23 —— Weakening Local Economies

A flood of foreign capital can destroy a developing economy by creating a crippling current-account deficit — the difference between what is taken in from exports and what is paid for imports and interests on foreign debts. Foreign investors are also likely to pull their money out in a crisis, further destabilizing the economy.

—Ronald I. McKinnon, 1995[1]

T he large-dose arguments also have the ironic consequence of lowering the quality of financial information that is being produced within nations. Global financial integration accelerates the already-noted tendency for bad information to substitute for good information in financial markets, and it can even diminish the supplies of capital available for local purposes.

GLOBAL BANKS REPLACING LOCAL ONES

Most nations have gotten along quite well with rules that restrict most types of financial activity to domestic firms. But the push toward free trade in financial services requires that those restrictions be eliminated so that foreign financial firms will be able to compete on a level playing field. But when this happens, it creates a situation analogous to the arrival of the large national pizza chain in a small town that has its own family-owned pizzeria.

No matter how well the family-owned pizzeria has been serving its customers, the national chain, Deep Pockets Pizza, has a number of critical advantages in the competition. The local Deep Pockets Pizza store can capitalize on national advertising campaigns that have made everybody familiar with its product. Moreover, the national firm is willing to sustain some months of unprofitable operation in this new store in order to establish itself in a new market. This makes it possible to undercut the competitors' prices for a good period of time through wide use of coupons that offer two pizzas for the price of one. Often the family-owned pizzeria will not be able to survive months of that kind of competition. If it does not cut its prices, the family-owned pizzeria loses business, but if it does, it loses profits. Its only chance of survival is if the pizzeria has very loyal customers, or a very lean operation that is capable of surviving through a prolonged period of low or zero profits, or quite substantial financial reserves.

When the same scenario plays out in the competition between a local bank and a new branch of Global Financial, the established local firm has even less of a chance. Global Financial has all of the advantages that come with a state-of-the-art global communications and computer system while the local bank is lucky if it has any computer system at all. But the difference between banking and pizza is in what the community loses. When the pizzeria shuts down, the community loses a familiar and comfortable place to eat; but when the local bank shuts down, the community is likely to lose the high-quality information about the local economy that the bank had built up over the years.

The loss of that high-quality information about the local economy will reduce coordination efficiencies and deprive some local firms of effective monitoring. Moreover, there is a good chance that Global Financial will be far more reluctant to make loans to local businesses than the bank it replaces. For one thing, its branches are likely to apply formulae that were developed at its international headquarters that could well be insensitive to local conditions. For another, Global Financial is going to compare the returns and risk on those loans with the returns and risk of investments that it could make anywhere else in the world.

In addition, Global Financial will also make it easy for its new depositors to acquire assets abroad. Since Global Financial's strength is its link to the global financial markets, it will offer its clients the opportunity to diversify their portfolios internationally, which has the obvious advantage of protecting them against a devaluation of their own currency. In short, Global Financial's presence in the local market is likely to accelerate outflows of capital from that particular economy. The result is that the availability of capital for local investment could drop sharply.

THE DOWNSIDE OF INTERNATIONAL EQUITY INVESTMENT

For advocates of global financial integration, one of their success stories has been the explosive growth of stock markets in emerging economies. These stock markets have allowed businesses in developing economies to attract tens of billions of dollars from investors in the developed economies. Since banks —whether foreign or domestic—have had an uneven record in providing finance to businesses in these economies, the expanded availability of equity financing seems to be an ideal way to spur economic growth in developing countries.

Advocates of these emerging stock markets go on to argue that it is far more appropriate to finance firms through equity investments than through bank loans. After all, banks insist on repayment, but equity investors know that the value of their share holdings can fall to zero if the firm fails. Given the risks of doing business in emergent economies, it makes sense for the firms to raise capital in a form that does not have to be repaid if the firm falls on hard times.[2]

But who is left to do the monitoring of firms that sell shares on these new impersonal markets? Investors in the developed economies lack specific information on firms that are listed on these emerging market exchanges. They tend to rely on mutual funds that acquire portfolios of stocks in various countries. These mutual funds hire analysts whose job it is to gather information about the merits of different firms, but these analysts are unlikely to have the time or energy to probe very deeply. It is more likely that they will rely heavily on the local business press and on a few obvious signals such as the periodic earnings reports that companies issue.

The weakness of monitoring combined with the very large sums of money controlled by these global mutual funds create additional problems. When global money managers are eager to invest in a particular emerging economy, the best new stock issues are likely to be grabbed up quickly. Dishonest operators can be expected to take advantage of the seller's market by offering shares of marginal firms with no real prospects. With weak or little enforcement of security laws, and the possibility that accountants, journalists, and regulators might be effectively bribed, such frauds can be relatively easy to perpetrate.

Yet, even reputable and successful entrepreneurs will be sorely tempted to sell their stakes in a firm when international investor enthusiasm pushes prices far above what the firm might otherwise command. In some cases, the entrepreneur might literally walk away, leaving the firm in far less competent hands. In others, the entrepreneur might stay on in a managerial position, but having "cashed out," he or she might lose interest in aggressively building the firm. Either way, the global mutual funds who own a large share of the firm's stock are not likely to be terribly effective in getting the firm's managers to serve the interests of the owners.

A similar problem exists with the enthusiasm for privatizing state-owned firms. In those cases, where share ownership is widely dispersed around the globe, the new managers of these firms are likely to face little active monitoring by the owners. This creates the distinct danger that those new managers will simply loot the firm for a couple of years, and then quit before the stock value drops precipitously.

A second problem is the distortion of incentives in the

countries that receive these equity inflows. Building an effective firm in manufacturing or retailing in emerging countries is a difficult entrepreneurial challenge, especially when free trade requires direct competition against established firms from abroad. In contrast, it is relatively easy to make a lot of money by buying and selling assets when global money managers have become enthusiastic about your economy. Even if such periods of enthusiasm were to come as rarely as once every ten years, a rational individual interested in maximizing his or her wealth would have a better chance of success preparing for the next period of enthusiasm instead of pursuing the very risky path of attempting to build a productive firm.

A third problem comes from the volatility of these international capital flows to purchase equities in emerging markets. The tendency of impersonal markets to produce herdlike behavior by investors is intensified when those investors have to worry about both the foreign exchange market for that emerging nation's currency and the equity market. Drops in either one can diminish the value of holdings, so that some important fraction of global investors will be ready to reduce their position in that stock market if either of these markets shows signs of weakening. And once such a period of selling begins, there is a good chance that it will bring a sharp decline in equity prices in that market.

How might that certainty of volatility in the stock market influence well-managed firms that have raised money through stock offerings? Imagine, for example, a firm whose owner-entrepreneur has resisted the temptation to "cash out" and has held on to a significant share of the equity in the firm, for example, 25% of the shares. Even if this entrepreneur took the long view and was not distracted by big swings in his or her net worth as the stock markets went from highs to lows, he or she would have to worry about losing control of the firm during the lows. A rival entrepreneur would be able to buy a controlling quantity of shares at the artificially low stock price established during periods of international disfavor, and our forward-looking entrepreneur would be out of luck.

In short, this kind of forward-looking entrepreneur who actually cared about building up a business over the long term would tend to be quite cautious about going to these new equity markets. Those markets can provide vast amounts of cash, but they also involve a very significant risk. These new stock markets can suddenly lower the value of a company's shares for reasons that have nothing to do with the entrepreneur's own effectiveness. As a result, the entrepreneur could lose control of his or her firm.

The irony of these emerging equity markets is that they will be very effective in channeling funds to entrepreneurs who want to disengage from a firm, but they will not solve the financing needs of entrepreneurs who are still strongly committed to a firm. This hardly seems like a good financing mechanism to encourage real economic growth.

THE ABSENCE OF A LENDER OF LAST RESORT

Despite all of the metaphors about vampire states that suck the lifeblood out of the economy, all participants in financial markets understand that these markets require a lender of last resort. This indispensable role can only be played by some kind of governmental agency. Hence, the normal antistate rhetoric has to be suspended long enough to assure that government plays this essential role.

The lender of last resort is necessary to deal with the extreme of herdlike behavior — financial panics.[3] Panics occur when investors are so eager to get out of one or another type of financial instrument that they begin to trample each other as they rush to the exits. Panics will move from one asset to another like falling dominoes unless somebody steps in and starts lending large amounts of money.

A run on a bank is one type of financial panic. Depositors hear that their local bank is in trouble and they rush to withdraw their funds. But banks hold cash representing only a fraction of their depositors' funds; the rest is held in assets that cannot immediately be transformed into cash. So, the only way that the bank can meet depositors demands for cash is by borrowing from somewhere else. If a small local bank borrows from a bank in a large city, the run might spread to that bank's depositors. In the absence of a lender of last resort, these panics can lead to a collapse of much of the banking system—something that happened routinely in the U.S. in the nineteenth century. When a lender of last resort exists, the panic can be stopped. If, for example, the second bank in the chain were to be provided an open line of credit by the Federal Reserve bank, then it would be able to hand out cash to its depositors until they are reassured that the funds are there. Once the panic stops, depositors return, and the bank can repay the funds that were used to help it through the crisis.

The dynamics of a stock market panic are similar. As prices fall, more and more investors decide that it is time to sell their holdings. The rush to sell is intensified by margin calls— those who have borrowed to purchase stocks are asked to put up more money since the value of their collateral has fallen. This intensifies selling pressures. On some stock exchanges, specialist firms are supposed to be buyers of last resort whose purchases will help stop the fall. But specialist firms will need some kind of open credit line to finance these purchases.

The dilemma of the specialist firms points to the danger that the stock market panic will spill over into a bank crisis. If banks have leant heavily to finance stock purchases by individuals or institutions, then a market crash makes it likely that many of those loans will not be repaid. The resulting fears of bank insolvency can lead to a run by depositors. Here, as well, the role of the lender of last resort is critical. If the central bank makes it clear to the large banks that they will have an open credit line, they do not have to fear a run and they can afford to make loans to specialist firms and others who might be willing to go back into the stock market and buy shares. With any luck, a sudden drop in share prices can be largely reversed as the herd suddenly becomes persuaded that stocks at this low level are now a bargain.

Within nations, this lender of last resort role has been played by central banks, and they have become increasingly expert in responding quickly to financial crises. But with global financial integration, it is not clear who will play this vital role when a panic involves an entire national economy. When the Mexican peso and stock markets went into freefall in early 1995, the Mexican Central Bank could do little to stem the crisis. Since both foreign and Mexican investors were rushing to get their assets out of Mexico and into harder currencies, a peso credit line was of no use. The lender of last resort had to be willing to make dollars available in vast numbers to persuade investors that the panic was unnecessary. Just as in the bank panic, when investors are reassured that they can get their funds, they have less reason to withdraw them. Hence, when investors realize that they can cash in their Mexican assets for dollars at a reasonable exchange rate, the panic should stop.

Despite extensive moves toward global financial integration, such a global lender of last resort does not exist. The International Monetary Fund does not have the resources or the authority to provide that kind of open credit line. The central banks in the major economies cooperate extensively and are prepared to lend each other money, but they are also ill-equipped to serve as global lender of last resort. Not surprisingly, then, the role has fallen onto the U.S. Treasury. Both in the Third World debt crisis in the early 1980s and again in the Mexican crisis of 1995, the pressure has been on the U.S. to provide a line of credit large enough to restore confidence in the large international banks and in the Mexican economy.[4]

This is, however, a fragile and unsatisfactory solution to the problem. For one thing, as Congressional opposition to the Mexican bailout in early 1995 indicated, it is too risky for this indispensable international role to depend upon the vagaries of domestic politics in a particular country. For another, a true lender of last resort has to play an ongoing regulatory role to make certain that the use of its services will not be abused. For example, the central banks that operate as lenders of last resort within nations monitor the credit markets to prevent the kind of excessive credit creation that will make a panic more likely. But nobody is suggesting that the U.S. government should be given that kind of regulatory authority over global finance.

The fact that the role of international lender of last resort has to be combined with some kind of global regulatory authority explains why it is politically difficult to fill this global need. Not only do nations have to be willing to give up sovereignty to a global agency, but global financial institutions also have to be willing to accept another layer of regulation.

But moving toward global financial integration without first solving the problem of creating a global lender of last resort is a little bit like trying to cross the Atlantic Ocean repeatedly in a small boat without any emergency equipment. Even if one completes one or even two trips without incident, it is a virtual certainty that one will soon be in desperate need of the emergency life raft, the radio, and the flares. The argument for turning back to shore and cancelling the trip is extremely strong. But why not choose another destination and another mode of travel with better long-term prospects of success?

THE NEW REGIME VS. THE OLD REGIME

Fortunately, it is possible to have a vigorous world economy with high levels of trade without the tight integration of financial markets. This was the situation in the 1950s and 1960s; international trade grew very rapidly, but the impersonal financial markets had a more restricted role and limited political power. What made this possible were two measures that were eliminated in the 1970s — fixed exchange rates and widespread restrictions on the international mobility of capital. The need is urgent to restore these two measures.

Under a fixed exchange rate system, governments keep their currency in some stable relationship to a baseline. For example, today a number of European countries keep their currency within 2% or 3% of a fixed number of German marks (DM). The government constantly intervenes in the foreign exchange market to keep the currency within that target range. In this system, it is legitimate for governments to change the value of their currencies. A currency that previously was equal to 5 DM might be reduced to 4 DM, but such shifts are supposed to occur infrequently and only with solid justification. In such a system, exchange rates are fairly predictable; one knows with a reasonable level of reliability that a few years from now the Dutch guilder will continue to buy the same number of German marks.

During the 1950s and 1960s, a number of "free market" economists railed against this system of fixed exchange rates because they perceived it as giving governments a central role in shaping the economy. They insisted that it would be much better to leave the determination of exchange rates to impersonal markets without government interference. Each day, the foreign-exchange markets would determine exactly how many DM each Dutch guilder should be worth. They went on to claim that such a system would be much smoother because it would eliminate the infrequent but large exchange rate adjustments that occur within a fixed exchange rate system. The claim was that if, for example, a particular currency were overvalued, the market would gradually bring it down to its proper value rather than having a one-time sharp adjustment.

In 1973, the U.S. and its major allies agreed to abandon fixed rates and to try a system where exchange rates were determined solely by the foreign-exchange markets. The result has been something like a laboratory test of the claims by the "free market" economists that such a system would be far more stable. The results are in, and a floating exchange rate system has proven to be far more unstable than a fixed-rate system. Over the past twenty years, exchange rates have become highly volatile with very large shifts occurring in relatively short periods of time.[5]

This volatility is a nightmare for firms that are engaged in international trade. With floating rates, there can easily be shifts of 8% to 10% in the relative value of two currencies within a given year, which makes planning very difficult. A German firm, for example, might sign a deal to sell products in the U.S. at a certain dollar price. This might look like a profitable deal when the contract is initially signed, but changes in the exchange rate could turn it into a money-losing deal. There are, of course, strategies that firms can pursue to protect themselves against such exchange rate shifts. They can buy insurance against the risk of an adverse shift in exchange rates. But while insurance against natural disasters has no effect on the probability of such disasters, increased purchases of foreign exchange futures—the mechanism by which firms insure themselves against this risk—end up increasing exchange rate volatility. So, trading firms are caught in a vicious cycle where foreign-exchange markets are volatile and they bear heavy costs to protect themselves from that volatility.

The other vicious part of this cycle is that the shift to floating exchange rates vastly accelerated the growth of international capital movements, and this acceleration, in turn, further increases the volatility in these markets. One can see this dynamic by thinking of the concrete example of U.S. investors and the German market. When the exchange rate between the dollar and the DM was stable, investors in the U.S. were likely to invest money in German assets only when they saw a particularly attractive opportunity. But with floating rates, the calculus of U.S. investors changes dramatically.

If the DM starts to increase in value relative to the dollar, then the change in value can easily reach the magnitude of 10% in a given year. Investors who stay entirely in dollars could end up 10% poorer at the end of the year than investors who shifted all of their assets into DM. In short, investors who want to maximize returns have to think seriously about acquiring some DM assets even if those assets promise no higher rate of return than dollar assets. DM become more attractive not because of their intrinsic merits, but because they are denominated in a currency that is likely to appreciate in value.

When exchange rates were fixed, most countries placed substantial restrictions on the ability of firms or individuals to send large quantities of capital abroad. And when these capital controls were in place, they worked quite well to reduce capital outflows. But with the arrival of floating rates and the increased exchange rate volatility, investors in countries with capital controls were suddenly placed at a disadvantage relative to investors who could send their capital wherever they wanted. Not surprisingly, investors who were subject to capital control began pressuring governments to dismantle the controls. From 1975 to 1990, most European countries dismantled all of their remaining controls over capital exports. Hence, many more investors were able to send capital abroad to protect themselves from exchange rate changes.

But the combination of increased freedom to invest abroad and increased incentives to protect oneself from exchange rate changes has created a huge increase in international capital movements. Ironically, the growth of these capital movements makes exchange rates even more volatile, and so even more investors start to establish internationally diversified portfolios to protect themselves from exchange rate changes. In a word, the shift to floating exchange rates has dramatically increased international capital mobility and that makes exchange rates even more volatile.

CONCLUSION

Those who have made large-dose arguments for free trade, including advocacy of global financial integration, have repeatedly claimed that a lot of free trade is the only reliable route to an expanding economy — both globally and domestically. But this argument is simply not true. We can have all of the benefits of free trade with a small dose, and that way we could avoid the horrible side effects of financial dictatorship and periodic financial meltdowns.

An international economy built on a small dose of free trade would have the following elements. First, the efforts of the past fifty years to establish an international free-trade regime would continue; nations would be encouraged through reciprocal trade agreements to reduce tariff and nontariff barriers to trade in most goods and many services. However, these international trade agreements would include a systematic effort to establish global labor and environmental standards with some real enforcement mechanisms. For example, nations that routinely exploited child labor or allowed plants to pollute freely would find their access to foreign markets restricted. Obviously, poor countries would not be expected immediately to provide the same protections that are available in richer countries, but the standards would require a gradual process of upgrading.

Second, this new trade order would also recognize the legitimacy of temporary trade barriers to protect "infant" industries and industries in decline. However, a clear set of ground rules would be established to avoid such restrictions becoming permanent.

Third, the current effort to treat the growth of financial services as simply another form of trade would be abandoned; there would no longer be pressures to force other countries to open their markets to large U.S. banks, brokerage firms, and insurance companies. In recognition of the sensitivity and difficulty of effective regulation of the financial sector, nations would have considerable freedom to regulate their financial sectors in ways that produce high-quality information and maximal coordination efficiencies.

Finally, there would be a restoration of restrictions on the free movement of capital across national boundaries. This would allow nations to restore a system of fixed exchange rates without the constant threat of speculative assaults on currency values. These moves would, in fact, help facilitate international trade because businesses would not have to contend with the present volatility and unpredictability of exchange rate changes.

Within this set of arrangements, there would still be vigorous international competition and profit opportunities for large international corporations. But the critical change is that governments would have much greater ability to steer their domestic economies and they would be able to pursue a broader range of adaptive reforms. A small-dose regime of free trade would open the way for creative reform efforts within nations.

Part Five

Constructing the Future

24 —— Beyond Stalemate

Where there is no vision, the people perish.

—Proverbs 29:18

It is enough that we can see the future as containing such imaginable possibilities. Openness and potential, without assurance of outcomes, are our substitutes for Yesterday's bright hopes for Progress and our consolations for Today's more knowing anxieties.

—Robert Heilbroner, 1995[1]

This book has argued that the Conventional Wisdom about the U.S. economy is fundamentally wrong. The current rush to balance the federal budget will not solve our deepest problems; it will only serve to intensify them. In fact, the Conventional Wisdom does not even correctly identify our most fundamental economic challenge—to find creative ways to adapt our institutions to our expanding capacity to produce.

But even if millions of citizens were suddenly to reject the Conventional Wisdom, the pursuit of new and more effective economic policies will continue to be blocked by the power that is wielded by domestic and global financial markets. Since the participants in those markets are likely to remain wedded to the Conventional Wisdom, their mistaken ideas will continue to dominate our politics. Even under the best of circumstances, it would take years to mount an effective challenge to the power entrenched in those markets.

But the probabilities of mounting such a challenge seem slight because of the absence of a persuasive and attractive vision of where our society should be headed. For close to a century and a half—from the 1840s to the end of the 1980s—the ideal of socialism—of a society without economic exploitation—inspired millions of ordinary people to fight both for immediate economic and political gains and for long-term structural reforms. The basic outlines of the reform agenda elaborated by New Deal liberalism in the U.S. were rooted in the socialist movement's strategic ideas about restraining and controlling a market economy.

But the socialist vision has lost its capacity to mobilize significant reform efforts. The collapse of Soviet-style Communism left too much uncertainty as to what "socialism" means for it to serve as an inspiration for social movements. To be sure, in many parts of the world, ordinary people have mobilized in large numbers to seek to block "economic reforms" that make individuals and families far more vulnerable to the market.[2] The most spectacular instance to date occurred in December of 1995 when a prolonged confrontation between striking workers and the state forced the French government to abandon a set of austerity proposals. Even so, such battles have been largely defensive; they have been waged to stop threatened cuts in public spending or to stop the contraction of employment. But these movements have rarely been able to suggest a positive vision of how the economy should be organized.

At the same time, the countervision to socialism—the neoliberal utopia of a society that gives unfettered scope to market forces—has also lost much of its power to persuade and to mobilize. This countervision—as articulated by Ronald Reagan and Margaret Thatcher—was extraordinarily effective as a critique of Socialist, Social Democratic, and New Deal liberal ideas. However, it has utterly failed to provide a persuasive positive vision of how society should be organized. When political leaders such as Thatcher and Gingrich attempt to legislate this neoliberal vision, their policies appear both mean-spirited and irrational.

In fact, one explanation for the continuing growth in the U.S. of the Christian Coalition and other far right political groupings is that they are a response to the moral bankruptcy of the neoliberal vision. While some of these groupings have been allied politically with Republican defenders of the free market, there are tensions between the two orientations. Many religious conservatives do not believe that a society can be organized simply around the individual pursuit of wealth and the invisible hand of the market. That is why the religious conservatives are explicit in their belief that governmental power must be used to enforce morality and to stamp out pornography, abortion, premarital sex, and other "immoral" behaviors. Such groupings are drawn instead to a more authoritarian vision of a theocratic state.

The same irony is also apparent on the global level. While some commentators anticipated that the conclusion of the long struggle between capitalism and socialism would usher in a new era of global harmony, the brief period since the end of the cold war has given rise to renewed sectarian violence by radical nationalist movements and escalating terrorism by various religious and political sects. As the great visions of socialism and free-market capitalism have lost their grip on the popular imagination, their place is being taken by local gurus and demagogues offering parochial and paranoid visions.

UNDERSTANDING
THE CURRENT IMPASSE

The lack of positive secular visions of the future has dire consequences for our politics, making it extremely difficult to mobilize popular energies for even relatively modest immediate reforms. For example, there is wide consensus in the U.S. that campaign contributions by special interests have been corrupting our politics. The classic case was the S&L debacle in which people who were literally looting such institutions were able to gain congressional support for "deregulation" through generous campaign donations.[3] But despite the flagrant abuses that are tolerated under current law, public support has not coalesced around any particular set of campaign finance reforms.

One reason for this public inaction is that broader visions of positive social change are necessary to make any specific reform proposals appear compelling. Even when there are significant abuses, nobody sees campaign finance reform as an end in itself; it is a step toward creating a better society. But in the absence of any shared vision, who is to say what would make this a better society. Our confusion on these questions is so great that some people are openly saying that the problem with politics in the U.S. is that there is not enough money in political campaigns. They say that the fastest way to eliminate corruption is to eliminate the present caps on individual and political action committee contributions. People who make such claims probably believe that a good society is one in which those with the most money have the most political influence. But unless the rest of us share a countervision of an egalitarian democracy, it is hard to counteract such claims.

This was very much the problem with Bill Clinton's health care reform package in 1994. Despite a consensus that the health care system was profoundly in need of reform, the absence of a broader positive vision of where the society should be heading made any concrete proposal extraordinarily vulnerable to criticism. Twenty or thirty years earlier, a reform proposal of similar complexity to the Clinton proposal would probably have fared better because the New Deal vision of using governmental power to restrain the operation of markets was still persuasive. But in 1994, the Clinton plan was vulnerable to parody as a fantastically complex Rube Goldberg contraption because people did not understand how managed competition in the health care sector was linked to a particular vision of a better future.

A society that cannot fix a broken health care system or a broken campaign finance system is certainly not going to be able to carry out dramatic reforms of its financial system that weaken the political power of financial markets. Those kinds of structural reforms in core institutions are likely to emerge only after a series of successful reform efforts in less weighty arenas. The old community organizing strategy is relevant here; one does not challenge city hall on the most important issues immediately. First, the community fights for a traffic light at a dangerous intersection, and then it mobilizes to clean up dangerous vacant lots. Only after a number of successes that have persuaded the citizens of their power does the movement challenge city hall to start providing the neighborhood with its fair share of city funds.

But without a shared vision of the future, the community will not even get to the first stage, and contesting for the fair share of city resources will never occur. This is our current situation in the U.S. Even though our politics and our economy is increasingly being strangled by an overgrown financial sector, the prospects of doing anything about it are remote since we cannot even collectively address less intractable problems. Since we do not have a shared vision of where we want to go, we are not even able to take the first small steps to get there, much less even think about the big steps.

This description of our political situation makes it easier to understand the pathologies of our recent politics. Since the path to meaningful reforms has been blocked, our politics have become preoccupied with the search for "quick fixes." Our current economic difficulties had their origins as far back as the 1960s, but the society lacked the political vision or will to address the problems at that point. The consequence was that the performance of the U.S. economy deteriorated during the 1970s. That deterioration generated enormous political anger and discontent. Hence, the inflation and severe recessions of the 1970s put Ronald Reagan into the White House because people wanted to believe his promises of quick and easy solutions. His "supply-side" tax cuts were supposed to cure all of our economic ills, but when combined with a military buildup, the results were budget deficits and a further weakening of the civilian economy. When the Reagan bubble burst, there was slow growth and mounting unemployment that fueled new eruptions of popular anger. That anger defeated George Bush in 1992, but it also swept the Republicans to congressional dominance in November 1994.

Yet, the Republican solutions outlined in the "Contract With America" are just another quick fix that will only make things worse. And in the wings, other politicians are already offering even further quick fixes that they hope will be irresistible to an angry electorate. After all, if moderate budget cuts do not solve our problems, why not try huge budget cuts? If medium-sized tax cuts do not work, why not try a flat tax that will dramatically reduce tax payments by high-income households?

At the same time, the fate of the Bush and Clinton presidencies has also made it clear that the old-style politics of trying to solve economic problems through centrist compromises also does not work. Bush's agreement in 1990 with congressional Democrats on a package of budget cuts and tax increases weakened him dramatically because he was seen by much of his political base as having reneged on his "no new taxes" pledge. And while Bill Clinton began his presidency seeking compromises with moderate Republicans on deficit reduction and health care reform, it turned out to be impossible to negotiate such deals.

IS THERE A WAY OUT?

It is easy to despair and to see politics in the U.S. remaining in this downward spiral for at least another generation. After all, we lack a compelling vision of the future that could give meaning and persuasiveness to immediate reforms. And without the ability to carry out immediate reforms, it seems utterly unrealistic even to contemplate major structural reforms. Moreover, in the current climate of stalemate and pessimism, any positive vision of the future is bound to seem utopian and out of touch with reality. At a time when this society is removing such fundamental entitlements as the provision of medical care and income to the poorest households, anybody who proposes an economic vision of a more egalitarian society is likely to be dismissed as an ivory-tower dreamer or worse.

Even so, finding a route out of the current impasse depends fundamentally on creating a shared vision of where we want to be going. History provides some insights into this process. Under the Absolute Monarchies of Europe in the seventeenth and eighteenth centuries, a variety of theorists began to articulate the liberal vision of self-governing democracies. At first, these visions could easily be dismissed as wildly impractical given the entrenched power of the ancien régime. But once the vision captured the popular imagination, it was the idea of continuing autocratic rule that became impractical.

Fortunately, our current task is nowhere near as difficult as that earlier "paradigm shift." The founders of the liberal tradition had to replace the slogans of hierarchy, authority, and tradition with the new slogans of liberty, equality, and fraternity. Our task is simply to imagine a different set of institutional structures through which those same Enlightenment values could be realized.[4] It is not a question of persuading people to overthrow their previous values, but rather to expand their conception of how society can be organized to give those values more weight.

The following chapters attempt to begin this task by outlining a "practical utopia"—a vision of how our society could be organized that would use our extraordinary productive power in ways that would increase equality, democracy, and liberty.

25 —— Toward a Shared Vision: A Practical Utopia

> *Should any causes of evil be irremovable by the new powers which men [sic] are about to acquire, they will know that they are necessary and unavoidable evils; and childish, unavailing complaints will cease to be made.*
>
> — Robert Owen, 1820[1]

P ractical utopia is an obvious oxymoron. "Utopia" literally means "not a place," and utopian visions are inherently impractical. Moreover, utopias promise solutions to all of society's most pressing problems, while being practical means recognizing that certain social problems are intractable. But for precisely these reasons, the concept of a practical utopia is extremely useful. It can serve as an antidote both to those totalistic utopian visions that have had such destructive consequences and to the paralyzing domination of the Conventional Wisdom.

TECHNOLOGICAL PROGRESS

It is the technological progress of the past two centuries that makes this utopian vision practical. That progress makes it possible to produce the basic goods and services with a labor force that represents a very small percentage of the total population. For example, the U.S. is able to produce vast quantities of agricultural goods for domestic and foreign consumption with only 1.8% of the population working on farms.[2] And the percentage of the population working as production workers in manufacturing has already dropped to less than 10% of the labor force. And such vital services as policing, food distribution, maintaining the telecommunications system, providing emergency health care, and collecting the garbage together account for only another 2% to 3% of all employees.

The fact that all of these critical tasks can be filled by less than 15% of the current labor force working at an average work year of 1,900 or 2,000 hours provides our society with an absolutely unprecedented degree of freedom in shaping our work arrangements. The cliché that one cannot structure an economy around people taking in each other's laundry is no longer valid. The cliché has been used to point out that many service-sector activities such as entertainment, social services, and a variety of retail businesses are basically luxuries that do not help a society produce the necessities on which life depends. But these employment figures show that it is now eminently practical to structure an economy around people taking in each other's laundry. As long as the relatively small percentage of employees who produce and distribute the really necessary goods and services attend to their work tasks, the rest of us can be preparing gourmet meals in restaurants, selling greeting cards, writing novels, providing social services, producing movies, staffing theme parks, and inventing new types of services. Since many of these tasks are far more compelling than doing laundry, we can call this a creative service economy.

But since this practical utopia is embedded within a world economy organized around small-dose free trade, there is an obvious limit to the practicality of the creative service sector. The domestic production of foods, manufactured goods, and internationally traded services has to keep up with international competitive pressures. In the worst-case scenario, foreign producers would become far more efficient than domestic producers at producing rice, cars, computer software, and dozens of other commodities, and those domestic producers would ultimately fail. Those of us who were producing creative services would then have no means to earn the foreign-exchange required to pay for the rice, cars, and computer software that were now exclusively produced abroad.

This scenario can be avoided, however, as long as many of the industries that are subject to foreign competition remain competitive and technologically dynamic. This technological dynamism is more likely if some of the people in service activities are engaged in scientific research, the training of employees, and other activities that contribute to continuing productivity gains in the sectors producing internationally traded commodities. In short, if something like 10% to 15% of the labor force is engaged in producing goods and services that are internationally traded and another 5% or 6% is engaged in activities that help those 10% to 15% achieve continuing productivity advances, that still leaves almost 80% of the labor force available for producing creative services either through the market, through the public sector, or through voluntary activity.[3]

These ratios provide unprecedented flexibility in organizing how work tasks are distributed. For example, it might be possible to maintain the dynamism of industries producing for international trade while cutting the average hours per worker in half. That would make it possible to involve as much as 30% of the labor force in the internationally oriented sector, but with much less working time per individual.

THE DYNAMIC FIRM CONSTRAINT

The key to this practical utopia is that the domestic economy has a core of internationally competitive firms that have the ability and the incentives to make continuous innovations in both product and process technologies. These firms have to be able to keep up with the best production practices on the planet. But the total employment in those firms might end up being relatively small compared to the total population and labor force. Most people would not work in these core firms.

But these firms have to be embedded in a supportive environment. It would not work, for example, if 90% of the jobs in the economy were similar to civil-service jobs that demanded minimal effort, while the last 10% of the jobs were extremely stressful jobs in internationally competitive firms. On the contrary, the same skills and orientation toward work that are valued in the internationally competitive firms have to be nurtured in other parts of the economy.

It is here that recent changes in long-established patterns of corporate bureaucracy become so important. Successful firms in the world market are no longer organized on a military-style chain of command with thousands of workers performing narrowly defined tasks. On the contrary, such firms increasingly depend on innovation, teamwork, and the ability of lower-level workers to take initiative.[4] Moreover, firms can now be world-class producers with labor forces that are relatively small compared to the giant industrial firms of the 1950s and 1960s. By taking advantage of advanced technologies and subcontracting relations with other producers, a firm with a few thousand employees or less might be able to produce a particular product line for both the domestic and the global markets.

These firms can best be nurtured in a society with a culture of "popular entrepreneurialism." The traditional model of entrepreneurialism is elitist and individualist; the entrepreneur is supposed to be a heroic individual with visionary ideas who deserves considerable deference. Popular entrepreneurialism, in contrast, rests on the idea that ordinary people working together have the capacity to innovate to provide goods and services that are needed by the community. Popular entrepreneurialism encourages the same values — taking initiative, teamwork, and creative problem solving — that these world-class firms need in their employees.

A culture that emphasized popular entrepreneurialism would encourage the growth of small businesses and employee cooperatives. This culture would also expect that both its nonprofit organizations and local governments continually find new ways to respond to perceived needs. After all, the motive behind entrepreneurial effort need not be the search for enrichment; it can just as well be the desire to solve social problems or to provide attractive employment opportunities. But a culture of popular entrepreneurialism will not emerge as a result of exhortation; it requires a network of financial institutions that are able and willing to finance and monitor a wide variety of initiatives.

With a culture of popular entrepreneurialism, there would not be any clear boundary between what occurs in the dynamic, globally-oriented firms and the larger economy. In both sectors, the emphasis would be on continuous innovation and problem solving. Developments in the computer industry provide powerful examples of this kind of porous boundary. The personal computer industry itself began from the explorations of young computer hobbyists who were driven more by the desire to build their own computers than any economic motivation. And it was the efforts of university-based scientists that created the infrastructure of the "information superhighway" — the Internet. In the future, local community groups might pioneer the development of new types of computer software that will ultimately be marketed by one of the dynamic internationally oriented firms. With that kind of porous boundary, it would not be difficult for individuals to move back and forth between these different types of employment.

SOLVING THE DISTRIBUTION PROBLEM

The main challenge in making this kind of economy work is to figure out the mechanisms for determining the income flows to the great bulk of people who are not employed by the internationally-oriented firms. Since only a very small segment of the population — perhaps just 15% of the labor force — is producing all of the cars, food, computers, and telephone services that the rest of us are consuming, the question is how do the rest of us — who either are not in the labor force or are engaged in creative services — get the income we need to buy cars, food, computers, and telephone services?

This is *not* the classic economic problem. The classic economic question is, how do we produce enough food, cars, and computers to meet people's needs? The answer to that classic question is, by doing everything we can to use resources as efficiently as possible — taking care to squeeze every ounce of waste out of the economy. It is in that fight against waste that limiting government expenditures loomed as such an urgent problem.

But when productivity has advanced to the point that just 15% of the labor force is producing all of the necessities, concentrating on the classic economic question produces crazy answers. Success in stamping out waste means that many of the other 85% of the labor force will not have the income that it needs to buy those commodities since the work it does is not completely necessary. As a result of minimizing waste, total employment and total purchasing power will contract. As a consequence, even the continued employment of the 15% will be jeopardized. Automobile workers, for example, will not be able to keep their jobs when nobody else can afford to buy a car.

In these circumstances, the classical problem is no longer relevant; it has been replaced by the distributional problem — how do we distribute income in a highly productive economy in a way that is consistent with continued dynamism in the internationally-oriented sector? There are basically only three options to provide income to those families or individuals who are outside of the internationally-oriented sector. First, they can rely on the market and attempt to sell services to the public directly. This category also includes symphony orchestras, private universities, and social-service agencies that are wholly or partially subsidized through charitable giving. Second, they can be employed by one or another branch of the government to provide goods or services. Third, they can rely on transfer payments, such as those provided to the retired, the disabled, and impoverished welfare recipients. Both the second and third choices rely heavily on generating revenues through the tax system.

The obvious limitation of relying only on the first distributional mechanism is that when only a small proportion of the total population is employed in the internationally oriented sector, it is extremely unlikely that the market alone will be able to generate sufficient employment for the rest of the population. For example, firms engaged in fierce international competition cannot afford to spend large sums of money on basic scientific research nor is it reasonable to expect charitable giving to fund such research. Not only would such a society slip behind in its research effort, but it would have to forego many of the jobs that could conceivably be created with a large research establishment. Without that and other sources of nonmarket employment growth, such a society would have high unemployment and weak demand, putting its internationally-oriented firms at a distinct disadvantage.

But relying primarily on the second and third mechanisms — the growth of state employment and state transfers also has serious drawbacks.[5] For one thing, it is extremely difficult for a government to combine deliberate employment creation with fostering a culture of popular entrepreneurialism. Establishing a government program to provide a certain service is difficult to reconcile with encouraging individuals and groups to take initiative in responding to community needs. For another, relying almost entirely on state redistribution of resources tends to produce fiscal crises because it is very difficult to match the pace of expansion of state spending with the growth of revenues.

The logical way of addressing the distributional problem is through a mixed strategy that combines the market, state employment, and state transfers in as flexible a manner as possible. In the mixed strategy, there would be three types of economic activities outside of the internationally oriented core — those that were self-supporting, those that were entirely funded by the state, and those that were receiving a partial subsidy from tax revenues. By keeping a tight rein on the size of the second category, the government would have more funds for subsidies, and it would be able to create many more jobs at any particular level of revenue. If, for example, the public sector had $100 billion in revenue, it could hire four million people at $25,000 each to do work that was fully funded by the state. Alternatively, if it hired only two million people to do work that was fully funded by the state, it could afford an average 50% subsidy for another four million jobs that were partially funded by revenues and contributions. In that case, the public sector would be supporting six million jobs. Or if the subsidy averaged only 25%, eight million partially subsidized jobs could be created for $50 billion, creating a total of ten million jobs.

The size of the subsidy could vary with assessments of the importance of the activity. For example, child care centers might be subsidized at a 50% rate, while theater companies might receive only a 20% subsidy. Moreover, this system would have the additional flexibility that organizations could make substantial use of volunteer or semivolunteer labor. A particular service, for example, might initially be provided with only one paid staff member and a group of volunteers, but as the service built a base in the community, more staff positions would open up. Similarly, another service that lost much of its support in the community would have to reduce its number of staff positions or consider closing down completely.

These subsidies in combination with the ethic of popular entrepreneurialism could help create the maximal supply of work opportunities outside of the internationally oriented sector of the economy. The goal is to assure that everyone has the opportunity for some kind of meaningful work, although for some, those opportunities might involve volunteer or semivolunteer activities. And the system of subsidies means that most of these jobs will be subject to a market constraint; if nobody really wants the services that are being produced, the jobs would disappear. But this market constraint is far less demanding than if all of these jobs had to be completely self-supporting.

What might all of this mean in a particular community? First, popular entrepreneurialism would encourage one group to start a new restaurant and another to open a small workshop to produce high-quality furniture. The local government in alliance with nonprofits might raise money to build new housing for lower income households. Another nonprofit could begin a local environmental watch and cleanup program, combining contributions and government subsidies to create jobs monitoring discharges and reclaiming a polluted area. Still another agency might launch an afterschool care program to provide child care, tutoring services, and recreation to unsupervised children. These various initiatives would be financed by local banks or other financial institutions; they would kill two birds with one stone. They create employment opportunities, but they also raise the standard of living of this community. In some cases, this might not be by increasing GDP, but rather by protecting the environment or simply improving the quality of community life.

BEYOND EMPLOYMENT

But the entire distributional problem cannot be solved through this subsidy mechanism alone. When only 15% of the labor force or 10% of the total population produces most necessities, even the most successful effort to stimulate the growth of service-sector jobs is unlikely to assure paid employment for everyone else who wants it. The problem could be eased by reducing the length of the average workweek and work year, but it is still likely that there will not be enough paying positions.

Moreover, in this kind of entrepreneurial economy, most jobs will not have a high level of job security. Technological change and shifts in demand will make the job market highly fluid.

In brief, for this practical utopia to work, society has to make certain that people who are not currently in the paid labor force have the economic means to consume a portion of society's output. This requires an extensive system of transfer payments to those who are not working. Without such transfers, there will simply not be enough demand to support the internationally competitive sector of the economy or the more locally oriented services. Further, this level of support needs to be generous enough that many people will be content—for significant periods—with voluntary activity or productive forms of consumption such as gaining additional education. Moreover, the level of support has to be high enough that people can easily tolerate the inevitable job disruptions.

It would be undesirable, of course, if large numbers of people were to take advantage of this generosity to become slackers or surfers; that would represent an unproductive form of adaptation. Such unproductive activity could be discouraged by shared disapproval of those who were unwilling to contribute to the common good.[6] But there would be no problem if people were to alternate periods of intense work or study with periods of a year or two of travel or volunteering for community agencies. That form of adaptation would be consistent with a continuing process of developing new skills and new capacities.

In a word, the logic of this practical utopia is precisely opposite from our current mentality. Now we worry that any form of benefits for able-bodied people will encourage slacking and draw energy away from the labor force. But in a society that is coming to terms with an expanding capacity to produce, there has to be an emphasis on persuading people to spend time outside of the labor force in productive activities such as raising children, volunteering, and developing new skills.

With appropriate government policies on taxes, subsidies, and transfers, this creative service economy could provide rising standards of living and meaningful work for most of its citizens. The key to the rising standard of living would be the steady growth in the quantity and quality of services for people to consume, since environmental constraints make it undesirable for people to consume an ever-growing quantity of manufactured goods. Better health care and education, more varied entertainment and travel options, and a broad range of community organizations and services would form the backbone of this improved quality of life.

At the same time, many people would have the opportunity to do work that was intrinsically meaningful. In both the internationally competitive sector and in the expanding service sector, most jobs would involve intellectual challenge and a feeling that one's efforts made a difference. Moreover, there would also be a large supply of nonpaying jobs that could make a very big difference for the recipients of services. Many people might choose to combine part-time paid work with extensive unpaid work to strike the right balance between income and interesting work.

Within this framework for organizing work and income, a society could adapt to changes in the global economy while also expanding both the equality of opportunity and the full empowerment of its citizens. Moreover, this practical utopia could be far more pluralist in its values than our current society. While the ability to make money would still be respected, there would be greater scope for respect and reward for those who devote themselves to serving others, to building communities, to cultivating the arts, and to pursuing spiritual knowledge.

26 —— Beyond the Economy: Other Dimensions of the Vision

> *The aim of political egalitarianism is a society free from domination.*
> *This is the lively hope named by the word* equality: *no more bowing and*
> *scraping, fawning and toadying; no more fearful trembling; no more*
> *high-and-mightiness; no more masters, no more slaves. It is not a hope*
> *for the elimination of differences; we don't all have to be the same or*
> *have the same amount of the same things.*
>
> —Michael Walzer, 1983[1]

This brief sketch of a highly productive economy with a small internationally-oriented core, a culture of popular entrepreneurialism, variable state subsidies for service-sector jobs, and transfers to those people outside of the labor force represents only the bare bones of a positive vision. It is only a first approximation to begin imagining an adaptive society in which continuing technological progress would be consistent with high standards of living. To put flesh on the skeleton requires discussions of equality, politics, and the global context.

HOW MUCH INEQUALITY?

Some might be tempted to fill out this sketch with ideas of an unequal society where managers and employees in the internationally-oriented core would be highly paid and most employees who were in the creative service sector would be poorly paid. In this two-tier vision, employment in the internationally-oriented sector would be relatively secure while employment elsewhere would be quite insecure.[2] But such a two-tier system would undermine the basic economic logic on which this vision is based.

First, the core idea is that the boundary between the internationally oriented sector and the rest of the economy would be easily crossed, so that employees in other parts of the economy would be developing similar skills and attitudes to those of employees in the internationally-oriented firms. But this could not happen if the two sectors had radically different pay scales. On the contrary, one would expect that skilled workers would earn relatively similar levels of compensation regardless of their location in the economy.

Second, since such a society's future adaptability depends upon the skills learned by young people, it would be completely irrational to have a large population in poverty whose children would be unlikely to take advantage of educational opportunities. "Writing off" some significant number of impoverished young people as impossible to educate makes no sense. The alternative is to pursue policies of inclusion that seek to provide real opportunities for all young people. But strategies of inclusion that simply provide some extra resources to children of the very poor are much less effective than strategies that seek to minimize the incidence of serious poverty. Minimizing serious poverty means using transfer programs to bring all households up to a level of economic well-being high enough to assure full integration into the society. And this, in turn, requires narrowing the gap between the richest households and the poorest.

Third, the idea of popular entrepreneurialism also points toward inclusionary policies that provide everybody with an opportunity to make a contribution. At present, the economic and racial divisions in the society mean that for many young people, crime is their only viable entrepreneurial opportunity. Criminal careers require very little start-up capital and can often be launched with only the social contacts acquired in one's own neighborhood. But is it farfetched to imagine that at least some of the leadership skills, the street smarts, and the energy that are currently invested in criminal activities could be redirected toward rebuilding impoverished communities and providing legitimate services? Again, if people in these communities had greater resources to start with *and* had access to financial institutions that could provide both credit and support, there could be a significant expansion in community enterprises.

This adaptive society would involve substantially less inequality than currently exists in the U.S. In the U.S. today, the CEOs of the 500 largest corporations average more thant $4 million per year in compensation, while full-time, full-year low-wage workers might be lucky to make $10,000 a year. This ratio of 400 to 1 in before-tax income is very high even by recent historical standards: the same ratio for 1960 was closer to 95 to 1.[3] The main justification for these extreme inequalities is that incentives are necessary to get extremely talented entrepreneurs and managers to work as hard as they can. But in Japan, for example, where the ratio between top and bottom is much smaller, there seems to be no problem in inducing hard work from those higher up in the management hierarchy.[4] And does anybody really believe that people like Ross Perot or Bill Gates would suddenly stop working if they were limited in the amount of income that they could earn in a given year? The obvious mechanism for reducing the gap between the income of the rich and the income of the poor is to reestablish high rates of taxation — 60% or higher on income above a certain level.[5] The likely response of the very rich would not be to work less, but rather to take less income out of the business firms that they operate.

But the most telling argument against these dramatic inequalities lies in the distinction between the old model of the heroic entrepreneur and the new model of popular entrepreneurialism. In that older model, a genius such as Henry Ford had a vision, and he directed hundreds of subordinates to carry out many of the relatively routine tasks that were required to implement that vision. But with contempoary entrepreneurs as exemplified by Bill Gates, the implementing tasks are anything but routine;

his firm's success has been built on the creativity of dozens of programmers and strategists. But the old model in which one person gets such a disproportionate share of the rewards threatens to undermine the collective nature of these contemporary entrepreneurial successes. The cult of personality built around a single leader is difficult to reconcile with the delicate task of building organizational cultures in which people learn to focus on the quality of an idea rather than on the status of the person who suggested it.

Finally, placing upper limits on what an individual could earn in any given year would also serve to discourage people from pursuing the "get rich quick" option of financial entrepreneurialism. This would also help redirect entrepreneurial activity into the production of goods and services rather than to the speculative sale and repurchase of assets. Limiting income inequalities is a good strategy for keeping the society's financial plant pruned.

But where should this upper limit on income inequality be placed? Making an intellectually defensible proposal requires more detailed analysis of patterns of income inequality across all of the developed market societies. But my intuition is that limiting after-tax income inequalities to the order of 20 or 25 to 1 would be both feasible and desirable. A full-time low-wage worker, for example, might get positive transfers that brought his or her annual income to $20,000, while individuals with annual incomes above $600,000 would enter a tax bracket where they would be required to pay 80% to 90% taxes on each additional dollar of income. At that intermediate level of inequality, there would be both the full inclusion of the poor and ample rewards for those who worked harder or more creatively.

THE ORGANIZATION OF POLITICS

This vision of an adaptive society requires political institutions that are closer to the ideal of democratic self-governance than are our current arrangements. In this adaptive society, continuous government steering would be necessary to accomplish two main goals. First, government has to help the internationally competitive sector remain dynamic and efficient. Second, government must also keep the relationship between the internationally competitive sector and the rest of the economy in balance to preserve high levels of employment and demand.[6] This latter goal would be accomplished by adjustments in the system of taxation and subsidization as well as shifts in public-sector spending. But in both cases, policies will have to be adjusted on an ongoing basis as circumstances change.

The best way to assure that this steering will be done effectively is through a system of competitive party politics that is rooted in an informed and active electorate. With a vigorous democratic politics and high rates of political participation, there is less chance that the flight crew will long remain on a misguided course based on obsolete metaphors or defunct economic thinking. Yet, to assure active political participation requires that people have a sense that their preferences can make a difference. Such a feeling is difficult to sustain when the democratic process is tilted in favor of the rich or corporate interests, or when popular preferences can easily be vetoed by the exercise of power in the financial markets.

To avoid these distortions of democracy requires a system of campaign finance that prevents higher-income households or large firms from exercising disproportionate influence over electoral outcomes.[7] But it is also important to curb the indirect power of large corporations. For example, when a firm that is a large employer threatens to close an entire factory if tighter pollution controls are enforced, it is using economic blackmail to frustrate the popular desire to clean the environment. One way to deal with this indirect power is to extend the sphere of democracy into the corporate sector. For example, if the firm's employees had a share of the votes on the corporation's board of directors, the more flagrant instances of blackmail could be avoided. Since the firm's employees might also benefit from greater efforts at pollution control, the firm could be pushed toward taking a more reasonable position with the regulatory authorities.

In this adaptive society, there would also be several obstacles to the undue exercise of power by participants in the financial markets. First, a small-dose system of international free trade would allow for fixed exchange rates as well as restriction on international capital flows. This would insulate the society from the danger that each political decision would be weighed for its impact on the value of the currency. Second, within the society there would be greater emphasis on direct lending by financial institutions as compared to impersonal markets. Since there would be competition in these financial markets, the likelihood is reduced that creditors could attempt to influence the polity by withholding credits.

These institutional arrangements would expand the scope of democratic decision-making. Citizens could make decisions on issues such as the actual amount of pollution that they wanted to tolerate, without the debate being distorted by the threats of powerful economic interests. But with this expansion in democratic politics would also come some dangers. The first is the threat of an overbearing government that would use its regulatory, tax, and subsidy policies to exert arbitrary power over individuals and to stifle initiatives by both individuals and firms. This is the familiar argument that the power of business interests in market societies is the only sure thing that keeps governments from taking these societies down "the road to serfdom."

But this argument has actually lost persuasiveness since the fall of communism in Eastern Europe. The successful revolt against those regimes shows that a mobilized citizenry can effectively challenge entrenched tyrannical regimes. This suggests that an active and involved citizenry should be able to block the consolidation of political power in the hands of the few and should be able to assure that both elected and appointed officials do not abuse their power.

The second danger is the possibility that citizens would abuse this expanded democracy by making political choices that would destroy the efficiency of the economy. The claim is that governments that face strong democratic pressures might push spending and taxation to counterproductive levels. Similarly, corporations that were required to give votes on their corporate boards to employees and other constituencies might lose sight of the necessity to make profits. A firm that was pressured through these more democratic arrangements into keeping a money-losing plant open might be forced into bankruptcy and have to close all of its plants.

But these arguments rest on the assumption that people are so foolish and shortsighted that they will abuse democracy to force firms and governments in directions that have disastrous economic consequences. It makes more sense to assume that democratic voters will be rational and pragmatic, especially on issues that determine their standards of living. If, for example, evidence accumulated that taxes had reached a level where they actually were discouraging people from taking economic initiative, it's very likely that citizens would agree to reduce those tax levels. Moreover, employees whose livelihoods depend on the survival of a corporation are unlikely to take actions that push their firms toward financial disaster.

THE GLOBAL CONTEXT

As suggested earlier, this adaptive society would be embedded in a world economy. But the central feature of the present world economy are the enormous differences in levels of income and well-being between citizens of the developed market societies and the majority of the world's population that lives in poverty in Asia, Africa, and Latin America. Any vision of the future that fails to address the issue of global poverty is of dubious value.

As suggested earlier, a small-dose regime of international free trade would provide a better environment for reducing global poverty than present arrangements. Poorer nations would be freer to establish temporary protections for infant industries, and they could use restrictions on capital mobility to protect themselves from capital flight. Moreover, the small-dose context would give governments considerably more freedom to pursue policies that could contribute to economic growth that benefitted the poor.

But it is critically important that there also be a real process of global redistribution from the rich nations to the poor. To be sure, the last fifty years have seen an elaborate development of "foreign aid" flows from developed to developing countries, but most of these flows have come with complicated strings.[8] Poor nations have been required to buy certain goods from donor nations and to conform to a set of rules that have served to perpetuate their poverty. For example, pressures from Western nations and international agencies have pushed many developing countries to dismantle capital controls. The outflow of funds as local elites seek the safety of deposits in Swiss banks more than offsets the benefits of aid.

What is needed are stable and dependable annual flows from rich to poor nations that are not tied to coercive requirements. These flows could be organized through international development banks that reloaned the funds to finance real investments by both public and private borrowers within developing nations. Experiences with microfinance in different parts of the developing world suggest that very small loans to the urban and rural poor can make a significant difference in people's well-being and productivity. If the resources were available to make such loans available to all who qualified in the developing world, the results could be signficant.[9]

Moreover, these real transfers to the developing nations would ultimately help the developed nations with their process of adaptation. If the developed nations, for example, were able to make $100 billion in real transfers to developing nations in a given year, the developing nations would be given the ability to import another $100 billion worth of goods and services each year. If the money were spent to purchase capital goods such as computers and machine tools, developing nations would be able to increase their own levels of the basic commodities that people need. At the same time, demand for the products of the most technologically dynamic firms in the developed nations would be that much stronger.

In short, there is a scenario in which the processes of adaptation in the developed nations and rising living standards in the developing nations reinforce each other.[10] At this moment in human history, the well-being of people in the developed nations does not require that people elsewhere live in misery and deprivation. To be sure, particular global corporations extract extra profits by raping the landscape of one or another tropical country or by paying workers in developing countries ridiculously low wages. But the standard of living of people in the developed nations now depends primarily upon the productiviness of our technologies rather than on the exploitation of people overseas. This creates an unprecedented opportunity for global cooperation.

27 —— Is This Vision Practical?

The political problem of [hu]mankind is to combine three things: Economic Efficiency, Social Justice, and Individual Liberty.

—J.M. Keynes, 1926

The question we confront is whether we can create conditions as supportive of liberty as those Tocqueville thought Americans, and perhaps other nations, could provide, and as conducive to equality as he believed American society to be at a historical moment that is irreversibly behind us.

—Robert Dahl, 1985[1]

The skeptical reader is likely to question the designation of this vision as a practical utopia. Even if the institutions described work, how can we possibly get from our present stalemate to an adaptive society with a reinvigorated democratic politics and an economy that is able to distribute the benefits of growing productivity to the entire population? The short answer was suggested earlier—when a compelling vision captures the imagination of millions of people, the impossible can become utterly practical. But there is also a longer answer.

THE INSTABILITY OF THE STATUS QUO

Our present society is built on an extremely unstable foundation. The increasingly integrated global financial system is incredibly vulnerable to a catastrophic meltdown. When the U.S. stock market crashed in 1987, the world's central bankers were terrified of a global financial collapse that would mean the failure of most of the world's largest banks.[2] At any given moment, banks in the U.S. owe hundreds of billions of dollars to banks in Western Europe and Japan and vice versa. The simultaneous failure of several key financial institutions would create a scenario of falling dominoes. Nobody knows how long it would take for the world economy to recover from such a crisis, but a prolonged period of catastrophically high unemployment would seem to be a certainty. It would be similar to the crisis in Mexico or Orange County being played out on a global scale.

It is difficult to understand why people would allow such a vulnerable system to continue without carrying out major reforms that would protect us all from the threat of a meltdown. Some people argue that since such a crisis has not yet occurred, then the system must be basically sound. But this is nothing more than whistling past the graveyard.

The best option would be one in which political leaders summon the political will to carry out major reforms of the international financial system before this financial catastrophe unfolds. But if that does not happen, the task will have to be faced after a financial crisis. Either way, at the moment when the global community is reevaluating its basic financial arrangements, the question of our vision of the future will be squarely on the agenda.

AN EMERGENT CONSENSUS

At that moment, the vision outlined here might have a chance because it is based on values that are deeply rooted in U.S. culture. Despite the intense polarization of our current politics, citizens of the U.S. are surprisingly united on a number of core values, in particular, the idea of the empowerment of the individual. Since the adaptive society envisioned here is built on the value of individual empowerment, it could have broad resonance.

With the end of the cold war, it is much easier to see how this concept of empowerment is shared by both Marxist critics of capitalism and "economic liberal"[3] defenders of the "free enterprise" system. Theorists in both of these traditions identify a single overarching evil that their preferred institutional arrangements are designed to eliminate. For Marxists, that evil is the economic oppression to which individuals are exposed in a market society characterized by the unequal distribution of economic resources. As Marx emphasized in his early writings, the pressures of economic need force people to do things that are against their very nature—poor women sell their bodies on the street while workers with craft skills are forced under threat of starvation to accept degraded factory jobs of mindless repetition. For economic liberals, the core evil is a powerful state that is able to exert arbitrary power over individuals and that prevents them from realizing their life-plans. Whether through excessive taxation or regulation, or through the use of police powers, these regimes will, at best, punish individual initiative, and, at worst, discourage it completely. This is the reason that conservatives prefer as little state intervention as possible. They believe that the greater the scope of state power, the greater the danger that the state will use its resources to coerce individuals.

Not surprisingly, given their common roots in the Enlightenment, these two traditions share an underlying conception of the good society as one in which individuals are empowered to live out their own life plans without external interference. The difference, of course, is that Marxists' efforts to reduce market coercion have historically strengthened state coercion, while the efforts of economic liberals to weaken state coercion have generally intensified market coercion.

The obvious question is why not try to design institutions that would reduce both economic coercion and political coercion to the lowest possible level? In other words, both of these traditions provide us with partial visions of the empowered individual—

the individual who is able to realize his or her life plans. Instead of choosing between the economic empowerment promised by Marxism and the political empowerment promised by economic liberalism, why not redefine empowerment to mean maximizing the individual's ability to realize goals with a minimum of frustration by either economic or political coercion.[4]

In short, the vision of an adaptive society is one that is based on this more complete view of empowerment. Significant inequalities in income and wealth would continue to exist, but there would also be systematic efforts to minimize the possibilities of economic coercion. The average person born into a poorer household would have educational opportunities similar to those of the average person born into wealth.[5] And those with higher levels of income and wealth would not be allowed to command disproportionate political power.[6] But minimizing economic coercion also means providing protections to all employees against arbitrary and unreasonable demands by their employers. Further, it also requires that employees at the lower end of the labor market be guaranteed sufficient income support so that they will not even be tempted to work under degrading and coercive conditions.[7]

At the same time, the possibilities of political coercion would be minimized by strengthening people's capacity for self-governance. The culture of popular entrepreneurialism and its supporting institutions would also diminish the chance that people would become helpless relative to governmental authorities. They would have significant resources with which to solve their own problems and to force government to be responsive to their needs.

This vision of popular empowerment fits perfectly with core American values. That old staple of political rhetoric — the "American Dream" upholds the idea that everyone, no matter how humble his or her origins, should have the opportunity to achieve and succeed. Moreover, hostility to unfairly entrenched privilege—whether political or economic—is an equally important theme in this culture. Hence, far more than the partial visions of the political left and the political right, the vision of the adaptive society might be able to reframe our increasingly sterile political debates.

THE DYNAMIC
OF DECENTRALIZATION

There is still another reason for believing that this vision could be practical. It has to do with organizational changes that are spreading rapidly in many workplaces in the U.S. and in other developed market societies. While these changes are profound, they have not yet had any obvious impact on U.S. political debates. But if history is any guide, these organizational changes will ultimately have profound political consequences.

Many large organizations are self-consciously reorganizing in ways that decentralize and disperse decision-making authority.[8] They are abandoning bureaucratic organization and trying something new. Bureaucracy provided a clearly delineated chain of command and individual jobs were defined by their fixed and exclusive jurisdiction over certain types of decisions.[9]

The movement away from bureaucracy is based on two insights. First, the hierarchical chain of command discourages initiative at the bottom—if people need permission from four or five levels of supervisors to implement a more effective procedure, they are likely to keep doing things the old way. Second, people at the higher levels of the organization simply do not have the concrete knowledge that is required to figure out the best way to do things. It is better for the people at the higher levels to establish organizational goals and allow people at lower levels to figure out the best means to acheive those goals.

This shift away from bureaucracy is not the fulfillment of some radical dream of workplace democracy. Top executives in firms that are going through this kind of decentralization are still the ones who call the shots on the big decisions — whether, for example, financing will be provided for the development of a new product or a new production line. They are still the ones who set the goals for the organization; decentralization is seen as a better means to achieve those goals. Moreover, even the decentralization of less important decisions often remains a contested and uneven process because high-level managers retain final authority.

Even so, it would be a mistake to see this shift as lacking any broader significance. Think of the difference between two societies. In the first, most employees — blue collar, white collar and middle managers — work in traditional bureaucracies in which they largely follow a pregiven script in carrying out virtually all of their work tasks. In the second, similar employees have been told that they must — in collaboration with their co-workers — redesign the scripts that they follow in carrying out their work tasks, and that they have to do this redesigning on an ongoing basis. Employees in the second society would be exercising a capacity for creativity and collective problem solving that was discouraged in the first society.

Moreover, these more decentralized workplaces teach people the importance of being experimental rather than being bound by some traditional prescriptions. If a new set of procedures or a new way of organizing the workflow is not an improvement, then it makes sense either to go back to the old ways or to try something else. One cannot be content with the status quo, and one should keep trying new ideas until something works better. This kind of experimentalism is oriented to acheiving results and it is inherently skeptical of ideological claims. It is very different from the search for "quick fixes" that has played such a large role in our politics.

This process of decentralization and debureaucratization occurring in many workplaces could help to make the vision of an adaptive society seem more practical to many people. The idea of a society based on empowered individuals is simply an extrapolation of these same processes of decentralization and increased organizational reliance on people's problem-solving capabilities. Of course, there is nothing automatic or inevitable about people making this connection. It is entirely possible that some people will learn to be pragmatic and experimental in their workplaces and still prefer quick fixes in the political arena. Yet, it is also possible that as people work in adaptive and flexible organizations, they might be drawn to a vision of a more adaptive society.

28 —— The Road Forward

"How does mass protest happen at all, then — to the extent that it does happen?

"The Populist revolt — the most elaborate example of mass insurgency we have in American history — provides an abundance of evidence that can be applied in answering this question. The sequential process of democratic movement-building will be seen to involve four stages: (1) the creation of an autonomous institution where new interpretations can materialize that run counter to those of prevailing authority — a development which, for the sake of simplicity, we may describe at 'the movement forming'; (2) the creation of a tactical means to attract masses of people — 'the movement recruiting'; (3) the achievement of a heretofore culturally unsanctioned level of social analysis — 'the movement educating'; and (4) the creation of an institutional means whereby the new ideas, shared now by the rank and file of the mass movement, can be expressed in an autonomous political way — 'the movement politicized.'"
— Lawrence Goodwyn, 1978[1]

For those who are persuaded by the attractiveness of the vision, the big question, then, is how do we move forward? Further, what would a strategy of change look like that would make this vision of an adaptive society a reality sometime in the twenty-first century? What kind of movement should we build? Which political candidates should we support? What slogans should we start printing for the bumper stickers?

These questions can only be answered effectively by people who decide that it is time to reshape and reform their society and who join together in movements to make changes. Those movements will have to figure out how to balance immediate demands with long-term struggles, and how to bring together different groups that have different priorities. All that I can offer here are some broad suggestions drawn from the history of earlier reform efforts.

But one other point follows from the earlier chapters. Effective social movements must contest the Conventional Wisdom — they have to challenge the prevailing terms in which economic and political issues are defined. This means articulating a narrative complete with its own countermetaphors. While any scribbler can challenge the dominant metaphors, it generally takes a movement to dislodge them. Hence, it is not enough for a movement to have logic or justice or even millions of people on its side; it has to be able to tell powerful stories about how the society has changed in the past and how it could change in the future. The development of a movement's rhetorical repertoire is central to all four of Goodwyn's stages of movement-building.

IMMEDIATE DEMANDS

Social movements have to begin with fights that can be won. This is the way that these movements gather supporters and strength so that they can wage the more difficult battles for structural reforms against entrenched power. But developing a set of specific demands to fight for raises complicated questions of coalition building and priorities. Environmentalists, women's groups, labor unions, AIDS activists, community groups of the urban poor, and hundreds of other constituencies all have their own lists of what is most important to fight for today. The task is not to replace those lists, but to persuade diverse constituencies that at the same time that they continue to fight for their own priorities, they need to fight together for political and economic reforms that could potentially benefit many different constitutencies by creating a different political playing field. These specific reforms could help many different groups become more effective in achieving their particular ends. Four different types of demands immediately come to mind.

1. Stop the Budget Cutting

The most urgent task is to challenge the mistaken belief that balancing the federal budget is good for society. As long as the proposed seven-year balanced-budget plan moves forward, the quality of life in the society will deteriorate and millions of people will have to struggle harder just to get by. And the possibility of moving forward to a more positive future will recede further into impracticality.

It is not necessary to defend every cent of existing spending priorities. There are billions of dollars of spending that should be shifted to other purposes. But it cannot be repeated often enough that there is nothing wrong with government borrowing as long as the borrowing is used to finance such productive types of spending as physical infrastructure, scientific research, and the development of the intellectual capacities of the future labor force. In a word, the arguments against government deficits have to be revealed as specious and hypocritical. For example, those who claim they want to protect our grandchildren from mountains of government debt usually do not have the future generation's welfare in mind. Some of these arguments are elaborated further in this book's conclusion.

2. Revitalize Democracy

Without a vigorous and effective democratic politics, all of our hopes for the future are likely to come to nothing. There are important and winnable reforms that would go a long way toward increasing political participation and reducing the distortion of politics by big money. The federal "Motor Voter" law that mandates states to register voters at motor vehicle and welfare offices has been an important first step, and its passage indicates that even in dismal times, reforms that extend democracy can be won. But further steps should be taken to reduce obstacles to political participation. One route might be to schedule national elections over two weekend days to provide voters with the maximal opportunity to get to the polls. Alternatively, Oregon's recent experiment with voting by mail might be the best route, although it would be sad to lose the civic ritual of going to a polling place on election day.

It is also urgent that something be done about our utterly inadequate sytem of campaign finance where people are able to buy elections by pumping millions into last-minute attack ads, and where elected officials spend a disproportionate amount of their time raising funds from special interest groups. It is urgent that we move to a system of public financing of House and Senate races that would effectively free elected officials from the current pressures for continuous fundraising from business interests. Such a step is extremely important in leveling the political playing field; challengers would be able to mount effective campaigns against incumbents even if they were not personally wealthy or closely linked to those who are. It is also important to close the present loopholes in campaign finance at the federal level that allow individual donors to contribute huge amounts of money for "party building" activities. Without closing these loopholes, the same election buying tactics will persist. These kinds of campaign finance reforms should also be carried out at the state and local levels so that those elections will not resemble auctions.

Another important step is to level the playing field when citizens come into conflict with powerful economic interests. For example, the tobacco companies have fought local antismoking initiatives with vast budgets, but the courts have consistently ruled that the corporate right to "free speech" makes it impossible to impose any restriction on the amount that firms spend on these campaigns. Such rulings conflict with the idea that democratic outcomes should depend on who has the best arguments, not on who can afford to make a bigger media buy.

3. Reducing Economic Inequality

Immediate steps need to be taken to halt the growing polarization of income in the society between rich and poor. If this polarization is allowed to continue, it will accelerate the processes of social decay and critically weaken the economy. Moreover, all other efforts at social reform will ultimately be overwhelmed by rising inequality. All the preaching to the poor about the need for morality, virtue, and discipline will come to nothing without reforms that allow the poor to gain more resources.

Here, again, the first step is to challenge the commonly held view that we cannot afford to have a more equitable distribution of income or that somehow economic prosperity depends upon the misery of the poor. It is much more true that we cannot afford the status quo; locking up ever larger numbers of minority young people is the fastest route to bankrupting our state governments. And if, for example, firms in Silicon Valley are forced by successful unionization campaigns by janitors to raise their pay by two or three dollars an hour, the impact on the international competitiveness of the U.S. computer industry will be totally insignificant.

Some of the steps necessary for reversing the pattern of growing income inequality are familiar. They include raising the minimum wage and tightening enforcement of existing labor laws to assure employer compliance with wage, hour, and working condition statutes.[2] A combination of changes in labor law that simplified the certification of unions and public support could also help spur more unionization drives by low-wage workers. It is also important to defend and expand the Earned Income Tax Credit, a federal program that provides income subsidies to low-income households. The fact that this program enjoyed bipartisan congressional support up until the 1995 budget battle is proof that redistributive reforms can be successful even when welfare bashing has become a popular political sport.

Finally, it is urgent that the arguments for a system of progressive taxation of income be restated with much greater political force. The notion that a tiny percentage of the population should be able to command a totally disproportionate share of the society's income is a threat to the very concept of a civilized society. The threat has been exemplified recently in the behavior of a number of billionaires who renounced their U.S. citizenship to become citizens of tax havens in the Caribbean. Through this strategem, they have been able to avoid millions of dollars of income tax.[3] What they were doing was completely reasonable within the prevailing conservative ideology; since they earned this money through the sweat of their brows, they should be able to wrest it away from the blood sucking state and enjoy themselves on the white sands of the Caribbean.

But no matter what line of work these billionaires were in, the fact is that they did not make all of this money simply from their own efforts; it was a product of the labor and hard work of thousands of others, and it depended on a physical and social infrastructure that has been painfully built up over hundreds of years. The idea of progressive taxation is that all of these contributors to income production need to be acknowledged and rewarded, even if a particular set of economic dealings has left one person holding huge amounts of income. Without a steeply progressive system of taxation that places some limits on the income that any one person can take home, society is bound to degenerate into kleptomania.

4. Grassroots Financial Reform

The last set of immediate demands are steps designed to begin moving toward popular entrepreneurialism and much more vigorous creation of new employment opportunities. The idea would be to expand significantly the availability of loans at reasonable interest rates to various categories of borrowers who have historically found it difficult to borrow. This would include small businesses, including the microenterprises of the poor, nonprofit groups, employee cooperatives, local governments that wanted to branch out into new areas, and various combinations of these groupings. In all cases, the lending would include careful screening and monitoring, but without the prejudices or arbitrary decision rules that have often been used by existing financial institutions.

This democratization of access to credit could occur both through shifting the priorities of existing financial institutions and through the creation of new institutions that specialize in lending to several categories of these nontraditional borrowers.[4] But the key thing is that this reform does not require any big increase in government spending; it is a matter of rechanneling funds that are already in the capital markets. For example, pension funds that have trillions of dollars of assets could be persuaded to diversify their portfolios by ultimately lending tens of billions of dollars to intermediaries who would reloan the funds to the ultimate borrowers. What is needed to facilitate this is a regulatory structure that provided some insurance for lenders and diminished the opportunities for fraud by both borrowers and lenders.[5]

There already exist many different small initiatives that are designed precisely to provide finance for a broad range of nontraditional activities, but the idea is to accelerate this process dramatically. If it worked, there would be several significant consequences. First, the range of activity for groups working at the local level could expand significantly. Nonprofit groups in alliance with local government, for example, could step up the pace of building low-income housing units for the poor. Carried out on a large scale, these initiatives could begin to put more people to work and assure that considerable amounts of new investment — including investments in "human capital" — occurred outside of the corporate economy. Finally, by making productive use of available savings, these initiatives would help protect the society from financial speculation.

All of these immediate demands fit well with the rhetoric of empowerment; they do not fit the standard caricature of New Deal programs that put too much power in the hands of bureaucrats in Washington. Moreover, in each of these domains, it is possible that significant gains can be made even in the few years left before the end of the century. If that were to happen, early in the next century, the movement could begin to address four structural reforms that would help dismantle the political power that is now concentrated in impersonal financial markets and would help empower the citizenry for the transition to an adaptive society.

STRUCTURAL REFORMS

1. International Financial Reform

The most urgent of the structural reforms is to change the ground rules of the international economy and shift to a small-dose free-trade regime. This reform is necessary both to save the world economy from a financial disaster and to break the antidemocratic power of the financial markets. While currency traders and speculators benefit enormously from the current system of financial integration and floating exchange rates, most people would be far better off with a return to the old regime of fixed exchange rates and capital controls. Such a regime would actually improve the prospects for expanding international trade because firms would face lower levels of uncertainty with less volatile exchange rates.

A return could be negotiated at another international conference such as the one that took place at Bretton Woods in 1944. The new agreement would include the restoration of a system of fixed exchange rates, so that most currencies would trade within a narrow range. Governments would retain the authority to change the value of their currency, but such changes would be infrequent. Part of this new agreement would also have to be a set of measures that placed substantial restrictions on the free movement of capital across national borders.

One measure would be a transaction tax on international currency exchange of about half of 1%. This has been proposed by economist James Tobin as a way to dampen speculative activity in the foreign-exchange markets.[6] Currently, $1.2 trillion change hands every day in global foreign-exchange transactions. Of this, less than 5% of the transactions are motivated by actual trade, travel, or investment; the overwhelming bulk of the transactions are carried out by exchange rate dealers who are trying to make profits on small shifts in rates. By forcing these traders to pay a .5% tax on each transaction, many trades would cease to be profitable, and the volume of transactions would drop sharply. With this drop in volume, there would be a corresponding drop in volatility. While tourists and trading firms would also have to pay the transaction tax, they would ultimately save money because they would face much less exchange rate risk.

But along with agreeing to this global transaction tax, the nations would also have to agree to help each other enforce a variety of routine and emergency controls on capital movements. The idea is that if any Brazilian citizen or firm moved capital to another country in violation of Brazil's capital controls, that other country would agree to return the funds to the Brazilian government. In short, the individual or the firm would face the complete loss of their funds if they were caught violating these restrictions.[7]

Different nations might place their routine capital controls at different levels. For example, citizens might be allowed to shift $10,000 abroad in any given year in one country and $100,000 in another. But all countries would be able to impose emergency controls that sharply limited what individuals and firms were allowed to do. Such emergency controls would be the key line of defense if a particular nation faced a major foreign-exchange crisis.

These routine controls could be structured so that they would not interfere with legitimate global transactions. Banks and other financial institutions would be allowed to extend credits to finance international trade, but they would be limited in their ability to shift capital simply for speculative purposes. Corporations would be encouraged to finance foreign investments abroad; when IBM wants to build a new plant in Germany or Japan, it would raise the needed capital on the local financial markets, and the same would be true of Toyota or Daimler-Benz. And as discussed earlier, these agreements would also provide a framework in which there would be a much more reliable flow of real resources from developed nations to developing nations.

It is not farfetched that such an international agreement could be reached. Every national government now suffers from diminished power because of the tyranny of international traders. A return to the old regime that I have described would restore to governments very significant power to make their national economies work more effectively. This is in the interest of political leaders who have suffered declining legitimacy as their ability to influence the economy has diminished.

2. *Domestic Financial Reform*

Parallel with these international financial reforms is the need for changes limiting the power exerted by financial markets within countries. Eliminating the threat to shift capital abroad would go a long way toward diminishing the power of domestic financial markets, but other steps are needed as well to limit the ability of financial markets to enforce the Conventional Wisdom on political leaders.

Within the U.S. economy, the introduction of transaction taxes on trades in stocks, bonds, and other instruments would play a constructive role in dampening volatility and shifting entrepreneurial energies away from buying and selling pieces of paper.[8] If put at the proper level, such a tax would not interfere with long-term investment calculations or the liquidity of the markets, but it would eliminate many trades that are driven by tiny profit differentials.

It is also necessary to reinvigorate the regulatory agencies that oversee financial institutions. All of the mistaken rhetoric about allowing the free market to work in finance has undermined the legitimacy of these agencies. But without ongoing and serious regulatory efforts, financial prudence goes out the window and we end up having to pay a huge price for the resulting financial disasters.

One further step is to create a series of publicly-oriented financial institutions that would compete directly against existing banks. These new institutions would be protected from direct political interference, and they would seek to bring new approaches to the financial marketplace. They would extend the grassroots financial reforms discussed earlier by attempting to reorient the whole financial system toward the long term, toward concern with the public interest, and toward the production of high-quality information. They would seek, in short, to demonstrate that one can make a decent rate of return even if one ignores the Conventional Wisdom.

For example, several of these new banks might specialize in efforts by nonprofit agencies and local governments to finance energy conservation and recycling initiatives. This would mean building up a staff that has considerable expertise in the full range of issues relevant to evaluating such projects. Over time, the expertise of the staff would deepen and the bank would be able to help agencies make major improvements in their proposals. No amount of exhortation or regulatory threats would get a commercial bank to invest in developing that kind of expertise. But when those commercial banks realize that this could be a money-making activity, then they will be far more likely to make comparable investments. In short, these new types of financial institutions are necessary to teach existing institutions what banks should be doing.

3. Democratizing the Corporation

The movement toward an adaptive society also requires that power in the large corporations will not be so concentrated in one person or in a handful of people. The trick is to do this without compromising the ability of these firms to respond quickly to the market. This can be done by reconfiguring ownership rights in the firm to make the board of directors more effective in monitoring the firm's top managers.[9] Ownership rights in the firm would be reconfigured by changing the way in which the firm's board of directors is chosen. Currently, the shareholders elect 100% of the members of the board of directors, but this arrangement fails to recognize that there are other extremely important stakeholders in the firm who have no representation on the board. By changing the laws governing incorporation, the voting rules could be shifted so that shareholders would elect only 35% of the board members. Employees would elect another 35% and various other constituencies—bondholders, suppliers, customers, and community representatives—would elect the other 30%. No single constituency would have a lock on the board; so that a process of negotiation and compromise would have to take place to create a working majority.

Simply by virtue of this change, the organization would be opened up to a greater level of democratic debate. In choosing a CEO and in devising a corporate strategy, there would be more pressure on board members to develop good arguments; no constituency could assume that it would automatically dominate. Moreover, since employees would need open political debate to choose their representatives to the board, there would be a significant expansion of debate within the firm over the relative merits of different strategies.[10] While the CEO would not be compelled to consult with employees other than those who were on the board, it seems likely that such consultations would expand significantly. And when the CEO met with the board to discuss issues of strategy and policy, he or she could not assume automatic agreement. The CEO would be forced like the British prime minister to develop good arguments.

This organizational change also helps to solve several other chronic problems of corporate governance. While the CEO, in theory, is hired by the corporate board that is constantly monitoring his or her performance, in practice, the top managers of a firm often become "entrenched." They gain effective control over the corporate board and nominate tame directors who are unlikely to interfere with their management of the firm. By electing the board from multiple constituencies, it would be much harder for top management to gain that kind of entrenched power, so the board would be more likely to fulfill its monitoring role. Moreover, the direct flow of information from employees to the board would increase the likelihood that any malfeasance by top managers would come to the board's attention.

Corporations also routinely underinvest in "human capital"—the skills and capacities of the labor force. Since employees can leave and take their newly acquired skills with them, management is usually tempted to spend additional investment dollars on hardware that cannot leave, instead of on people who can leave. But when this bias is carried too far, it can be destructive for the firm since workers with new skills are often needed to make various types of new hardware work effectively.

Since employees as a group have an interest in gaining new skills, the employee representatives on the board are likely to be a continuing lobby for additonal investments in human capital. To be sure, if the employee representatives cannot persuade other board members that these investments make good sense for the firm, they will not be made. But this new arrangement should reduce the existing bias against investments in employee skill.

Expanding the role of democracy inside the corporation should also have positive consequences for political democracy. It has been common, for example, for corporate chief executives to go to Washington to lobby against tax increases for high-income individuals. When they make these arguments, CEOs are not really speaking in the interests of their firm, but for themselves and other rich people. Under these new corporate governance arrangements, the testimony of the CEO might actually change. General Motors, for example, is actually likely to sell more cars when middle-income taxpayers get tax relief while taxes on the rich rise.

Finally, this expansion of democracy into the firm should reduce the oppressive power that large corporations can wield over the individual. For example, the private sector whistle-blower who reveals to government authorities some form of corporate corruption is usually fired. In rare cases, these individuals gain some vindication after long and costly legal battles. With this new structure of corporate governance, it is more likely that the board of directors would encourage whistle-blowers and would provide these individuals with protection against sanctions by their immediate supervisors.

4. A System of Income Guarantees

The last structural reform is necessary both to strengthen citizens in their relation to the state and to make the adaptive society's economy work. It is a more extensive set of income guarantees than what could be contemplated through expanding existing programs such as the Earned Income Tax Credit.

Instead of the current proliferation of transfer programs for different categories of people, there would be a negative income tax transfer that would provide all citizens with a subsistence level of income. While it is impossible to return to the Jeffersonian ideal of widespread ownership of productive property, a well-designed negative income tax could weaken the threat of state coercion through the guarantee to everyone of the right to a survival level of income.[11]

The income guarantee could also help spur an expansion of autonomous political activity. As long as most people are dependent on paid employment to secure a livelihood, relatively few people will devote large amounts of time to political activities unless they have funding from established interest groups or the government. Hence, at most times, relatively little political energy will be devoted to such activities as organizing impoverished communities, campaigns for evironmental justice, or even grassroots efforts to revitalize public schools. But if all citizens are guaranteed a subsistence income, there will be more people who choose—at least for a few years—the combination of voluntary poverty and full-time political work. Again, the income guarantee means that even those people choosing voluntary poverty will have a roof over their head and three meals a day.

The Negative Income Tax (NIT) would be integrated into the income tax system. Below a certain level of household income, individuals or families would receive a positive transfer from the government. The exact amount of the positive transfer would be determined in the same way as the determination of the annual tax obligation—by the individual filing an income tax return. But lower-income households would have the option to have "negative withholding"—their transfer from the government would come in monthly installments.

The amount of the transfer to which an individual is entitled would be determined by age, family status, and income. Children would be entitled to a transfer, but it would be a fraction of the adult transfer. Different tax systems are possible, but one typical arrangement would be to tax all income at a 50% rate until a household had income equal to twice the grant to which they were entitled.

The NIT can be structured so that it always pays for people to earn additional income. This contrasts with most welfare programs that place strict limits on how much income a household can earn before it loses eligibility. With Aid to Families with Dependent Children (AFDC) and similar programs, it is easy for an individual to face more than 100% tax on any additional income that he or she earns. With an NIT, this marginal tax could be kept at 50%. The NIT could also replace many existing programs that provide assistance to individuals or families that have suffered temporary or permanent reductions in their standard of living. The NIT would provide a universal protection against all of the contingencies that reduce income, and since its recipients would not be stigmatized, it could serve a higher percentage of those eligible than existing programs.

In a recent study, a colleague and I have estimated how much it would cost to establish such a NIT in the U.S. Drawing on data from the 1990 census, we calculated that a program that brought most households to within 90% of the poverty level could be financed with only about $80 billion of additional 1990 tax dollars.[12] The cost might be even less if one were to calculate administrative savings that would come from using the NIT in place of a variety of categorical programs with complex eligibility rules.

The NIT would also be a powerful tool to help society adapt continuously to changes in the employment structure. It would provide individuals with some security so they could upgrade their skills repeatedly during adulthood or afford to take entrepreneurial risks. Further, it would provide an important part of the subsidy mechanism by which the adaptive society would attempt to maximize the creation of employment outside of the internationally oriented sector. Moreover, since the level of the NIT grant could be adjusted upward as the society became richer, this mechanism could help assure that everybody moved up together.

Even if all four of these structural reforms were to be implemented, many pressing social and economic problems would continue to exist. People in the society would continue to have radically different views on a wide variety of questions. But these structural reforms would reshape the political and economic landscape in a way that enhanced the collective capacity to solve problems. Some of the major obstacles to effective self-government would be removed, while the opportunities to achieve greater equality and personal liberty would be expanded. This is the meaning of an adaptive society.

29 ——— Conclusion

Is the fulfillment of these ideas a visionary hope? Have they insufficient roots in the motives which govern the evolution of political society? Are the interests which they will thwart stronger and more obvious than those which they will serve?

—John Maynard Keynes, 1936[1]

This set of reform ideas is not meant to be exhaustive; there are many other changes that need to be discussed and debated. But these key reforms are designed to convey a sense of the extraordinary possibilities that lie before us if we could overcome the tyranny of the Conventional Wisdom. While these ideas are clearly radical in comparison to the terms of current debate, they echo themes of populist, progressive, and New Deal reformers of the past century. Moreover, they draw on the value of the empowered individual that is deeply rooted in U.S. political culture.

But the critical point is that any efforts to envision a better future and to develop strategies to get there will come to nothing if we allow the current processes of decay to proceed unchecked. And the major ally of the processes of decay is the ideology of budget balancing. Current plans to balance the federal budget over the next seven years will intensify all of our problems and prevent us from finding solutions. Our most urgent task is to stop this folly.

THE FOLLY OF BUDGET BALANCING

The frenzy to balance the federal budget is driven by the mistaken belief that a sustained round of belt-tightening will pave the way for renewed prosperity. But this will not happen. The inevitable reductions in federal investment spending will hurt our prospects for long-term growth, and the increased uncertainty for business will dampen overall rates of business investment. Budget cutting will inflict enormous hardships on millions as federal spending for welfare, health care, and education is cut, and those hardships are entirely unnecessary.

One of the powerful elements in the budget cutters' arsenal has been the telling anecdote. In any government program, there are always instances of waste or of undeserving recipients. Advocates of budget-cutting have skillfully used those anecdotes to generate support for large cuts. And there is a surface plausibility to the claim that large across-the-board cuts will force agencies to eliminate waste and target resources on only the most deserving recipients.

But for every instance of governmental waste, there are parallel anecdotes of corporations that have spent millions on luxurious residences for their top executives or that have wasted even more by incompetent monitoring of employees—as when a single bond trader has racked up billion-dollar losses. Yet, nobody thinks of proposing large across-the-board cuts in spending at these offending firms; the proposed solutions are usually for a gradual tightening of ethics rules or of reporting standards. Precisely the same types of measures are what is needed to reduce waste in government programs. Large across-the-board cuts are throwing the baby out with the bathwater; in the hope of getting rid of something undesirable, one sacrifices that which is most important.

The fantasy that large cuts will lead to increased efficiency in government agencies ignores the problem of generating high-quality information. The problems faced by government agencies in providing benefits are comparable to the problems faced by bankers in deciding how to allocate loan money. Deciding, for example, who meets the eligibility criteria for the federal food-stamp programs is similar to deciding who merits a loan. There are no simple and obvious rules of thumb that can always be relied on; the eligibility worker or loan officer has to make a complex determination. In both cases, the evaluator needs to look beyond the documents provided by the client in order to make sure that the case is not based on misrepresentation. And in both cases, there will be anomalous situations, such as people from an ethnic group with unusual family structures, that do not fit the standard criteria. Just as with the bank making loans, the government agency has to invest considerable resources in its staff if it wants to reduce its error rate in distributing the benefit.

But when a government program faces a 10% or 20% budget cut, there are powerful pressures on the agency to do the best that it can to minimize the impact of the cuts on recipients. The results are bound to be a more intense effort to economize on administrative costs, including the costs of generating high-quality information. As a consequence, not only do deserving recipients get fewer benefits, but the agency's ability to find undeserving recipients is likely to diminish.

Budget-cutting has a similar perverse dynamic in those situations where government agencies have been trying to reform the ways that services are delivered. Advocates of across-the-board cuts often suggest that since necessity is the mother of invention, budget cuts will force people to be more creative. But one only has to think of the instance of public-school reform to see how flawed this logic is.

In many large cities, there are exciting experiments in school reform based on creating smaller units in which teachers play a far more active role in shaping both curriculum and educational policy. Since these experiments challenge the traditional way of doing things, they are often unpopular with the central school bureaucracy. So what happens when funding levels are cut back? Do the school officials protect these fledgling experiments while cutting resources to traditional schools? On the contrary, the standard practice is to cut anything innovative and experimental.

In the case of urban-school reform, it might be that over the next few years the supply of private foundation funding will be large enough to protect these experiments, but the general point still stands. If you want to encourage government agencies to find innovative and creative ways to deliver services, across-the-board cuts are a sure route to disaster since the newest and least institutionalized programs are the ones that are most vulnerable to the budget axe.

SHRIVELING THE SAFETY NET

Budget balancers also claim that reducing government benefits will change behavior in positive directions that will strengthen the whole society. The belief is that by reducing welfare benefits through five-year limits, required work, and no allowances for additional children, the poor will be persuaded to stop having children out of wedlock. Larger copayments for health coverage will persuade people to avoid frivolous doctor visits and to invest more in preventive care. More generally, the reduced availability of government programs will make the U.S.-born poor behave more like the most admirable immigrants families — those families in which both parents work many hours in low-wage jobs, but succeed in saving enough to start a small business and finally gain a foothold in the middle class.

There is something deeply satisfying about this story line. Any parent who has disciplined a child has fantasized that someday the child will offer gratitude for having been straightened out. This is the logic behind the parental injunction: "This might seem harsh now, but it is for your own good." In the political arena, the story can be termed "forced penance." The recipients of this so-called benevolence might not even have realized that they were "lost," but once budget cutbacks have got their attention, they have no choice but to accept the penance that is their only route to salvation.

Once we strip away the powerful religious imagery, the reality is that most people who are made worse off through the denial of government aid end up being worse off. The claims that these reductions in benefits ultimately benefit those who are living in poverty are fraudulent. "Welfare reform" that reduces government spending for poor families means that there will be even larger numbers of children living in more devastating poverty. The requirement that most people will have to pay more out of pocket for their health care will mean a less healthy population and higher costs because of later diagnosis of serious illnesses. The denial of benefits will not miraculously transform poor people into the model immigrants of contemporary mythology.

There *are* recent immigrant groups that have achieved remarkable rates of social mobility and significant success in preparing their children for higher education. But when one looks closely at these communities, it becomes obvious that these families do not exist in isolation. They have drawn very heavily on extended family and community networks to help them care for their children, establish businesses, and provide financial protection against emergencies. The shared experience of recent arrival has produced in such communities extensive networks of mutual support.

For people who have been in the U.S. four, five, or six generations—regardless of race or ethnicity—the kinship and community ties are not as strong. We might wish it were otherwise, but wishing does not make it so. The chances that one of these impoverished families will find its way into the middle class through hard work and frugality are slim. Without the broader network of kinship and community support systems, one accident at the workplace, one family medical emergency, or one serious marital conflict can wipe out years of progress.

In fact, government social programs were established in the first place to provide such families with protection against these predictable disasters. So when those government programs are cut, the inevitable result is that a larger number of poor house-holds will be trapped in poverty. And all of the pious talk about family and community values will not suddenly provide these households with the community support that they need.

Moreover, these attacks on benefits for the poor are coming after years of deterioration in the wage rates at the low end of the labor market. The widening gap in wages between those at the bottom and those in the comfortable middle class makes it even harder for people to pull themselves up by their boot-straps. There is no way to put a pretty and benevolent face on dismantling programs that benefit the poor; the real conse-quence of cuts will be increased misery and diminished oppor-tunies for upward mobility.

THE PRIORITIES OF A GENERATION

There are many people who might be skeptical about these "for your own good" arguments, but who believe that we as a nation simply cannot afford to continue running these huge deficits year after year. Such people know that budget cutting will be painful and will hurt the poor most severely, but they see no choice but to break the habit of deficit spending. These peo-ple often invoke the language of generational equity; they worry that we are piling a mountain of debt on our children and grandchildren to finance our current consumption.

But burying our grandchildren under a mountain of debt is one of the most misleading metaphors ever invented. It works by focusing attention on government debt while completely ignoring the other side of the balance sheet — the assets that government spending creates. One example should suffice to demonstrate the illogic. Imagine two countries with similar geo-graphies. In the first country, the government has borrowed $10 billion to build a system of high-speed rail lines linking all of its major population centers. These rail lines allow for rapid movement of people and goods without the negative environmental effects of auto or air transport. In the second country, a preoccupation with budget balancing has meant that there is no government debt, but there are also no high-speed rail lines. In fact, the rail transport system has not been significantly improved in fifty years. In which country would you choose to have your grandchildren live? The weight of $10 billion in debt seems insignificant in comparison to the weight of a backward and environmentally wasteful transport system.

The real issue is not how much debt we are bequeathing to future generations, but what kind of a society and economy are we leaving them. Have we had the courage and foresight to leave them great cities with wonderful public spaces? Have we built a first-class educational system for our grandchildren and their children? Have we preserved the natural environment and protected them from the toxic legacies of nuclear and chemical wastes?

When we ask these questions, it becomes obvious that we have not been using our governmental revenues wisely. The long years of the cold war have done terrible things to our grandchildren's inheritance. The trillions of dollars that we have poured into various weapons systems could have been better spent on building those high-speed rail lines, those revitalized cities, and that first-class educational system. The U.S. has consistantly been cheating on outlays on the nation's infrastructure; our rates of such investment are only one-half to one-third of those of Japan and Germany. Moreover, the nuclear weapons programs have left us with mountains of contamination and many square miles of environmentally degraded territory. Many conventional military bases have been contaminated through careless use of various chemicals and ordinances.

These are problems not of the total supply of debt, but of our priorities. Will future generations be better off if we leave them less government debt, but we saddle them with various environmental time bombs that will cost hundreds of billions to disarm? Obviously not, since the burden of interest payments on the debt could be slight in comparison to the future cost of environmental rescue operations. In short, the concern with future generations dictates not that we spend less in the present, but that we focus our spending priorities on creating a strong and sustainable economy.

But the other central logical error in this budget-balancing rhetoric is the assumption that we will be better off by consuming less. After all, that is what austerity means—whether it comes in the form of reduced government spending or lower wages—it means that most people have to get along with less. This logic makes sense in impoverished rural communities where people sometimes have to choose between eating the corn now or saving it for next year's seed. In those circumstances, if people consume a little less now, everyone will be better off by assuring that there will be a harvest next year.

But this description does not fit a complex modern economy. There is no real equivalent of eating our seedcorn. A sudden fad of melting down machine tools and reselling them as lawn ornaments might create problems. And it is obviously deeply wasteful to take some of our most highly trained mathematicians and physicists and employ them on Wall Street to create better trading strategies for financial instruments. There is also a great danger of using natural resources in such a wasteful way that we endanger our future well-being. But there is basically no way that we can consume so much in the present that we will make our existing stock of machinery, factories, and offices less productive in the future.

When it comes to basic goods such as automobiles, foods, steel beams, machinery, and computers, our current capacity to produce vastly exceeds the purchasing power of domestic and foreign consumers. And if we pushed things by hiring workers for extra shifts and mobilizing unused capacity, we could produce an unbelievable glut of these commodities. This is one of the main reasons that we continue military production at such high levels despite the end of the cold war; we simply cannot think of ways to use that share of our productive capacity to make things that people really need.

In this situation of chronic excess capacity, what is the possible logic of austerity policies that make people get along with less? When we still pay farmers to reduce their plantings of certain crops, how can it make sense to force poor people to make do with less food? When unemployment among construction workers is high, how can it make sense to deny decent housing for low-income households? When industrial workers have to worry continually about layoffs because of slack demand, how can it help to force people to do without appliances or cars?

There is, of course, an argument that our civilization is far too materialistic and too environmentally wasteful, and that we would all be better off if we reduced our appetite for electronic gadgets, elaborately packaged goods, and closets full of seldomworn clothes. But the logic of this environmental critique is very different from the logic of austerity. Even the most ardent environmentalists have learned the important lesson that it is wrong to demand that the poor pay the price for the environmental excesses of the rich. If we want to reduce needless consumption, the initial focus should be on reducing the excess consumption of the rich. Austerity policies are a very poor instrument for cleaning the environment since they concentrate on reducing living standards at the bottom.

If, as a society, we decide that we want to reduce environmentally destructive consumption, there are very good policy tools for achieving that end. For example, it is possible to add externality taxes to products so that the consumer's costs include some share of the costs that the product imposes on society. Hence, with an elaborately packaged product, the consumer would have to pay part of the cost of disposing of the packaging materials. Such policies can work effectively to raise the environmental awareness of consumers.

The larger point still stands—we cannot eat our seedcorn. Our consumption sacrifices today will not make future generations better off. We do not need to tighten our belts collectively and balance the federal budget. Our real task is to assure that our government spending priorities are oriented toward the long term, so that they will help to create a strong and sustainable economy for future generations.

The battle over balancing the federal budget represents a test case of this society's ability to see its situation clearly. When the budget is seen through the pessimism of the Christian allegory and the distorted imagery of the vampire state, the results are budget cutting policies that will make millions of people worse off for no sound reason. The alternative is to recognize that many of our current problems derive from our failure to adapt our institutions to our economy's expanding productive capacity. Such adaptation is unlikely to occur if we persist in demonizing government. But if we have the courage to make structural reforms, we would be able to choose a far more effective flight crew for our Starship Enterprise that would help us exploit the treasure troves of currently unutilized resources. The result could be an improved standard of living, more equality, and a society of empowered individuals.

1. INTRODUCTION

1. John Maynard Keynes, *The General Theory of Employment, Interest, and Money* (New York: Harcourt, Brace & World, 1964, [1936]), p. 383; John Kenneth Galbraith, *The Affluent Society* (Boston: Houghton Mifflin, 1971, 2d ed.), p. 10.

2. Between 1990 and 1994, the federal deficit in the U.S. averaged 3.5% of GDP. The comparable figure for France was 3.1%, for the United Kingdom 4.8%, and for Italy 10%. Organization for Economic Cooperation and Development, *OECD Economic Outlook* 56 (December 1994), p. A64. The weight of the U.S. deficit is smaller when one combines federal, state, and local levels of government together, but reliable comparative data is hard to find.

3. Donald N. McCloskey, *The Rhetoric of Economics* (Madison: University of Wisconsin Press, 1985); McCloskey, *If You're So Smart: The Narratives of Economic Expertise* (Chicago: University of Chicago Press, 1990).

4. On the power of metaphors, see George Lakoff and Mark Johnson, *Metaphors We Live By* (Chicago: University of Chicago Press, 1980).

5. For a fascinating but very different account of the links between religious ideas and economic ideas, see Robert H. Nelson, *Reaching for Heaven on Earth: The Theological Meaning of Economics* (Lanham, Md.: Rowman & Littlefield, 1991).

6. In addition to the important work of Donald McCloskey, Philip Mirowski has made major contributions to the study of metaphors in economic thought. See *Against Mechanism: Protecting Economics From Science* (Totowa, N.J.: Rowman & Littlefield, 1988). Mirowski has argued that the discipline of economics shifted dramatically at the end of the nineteenth century away from biological metaphors and toward metaphors drawn from physics. Mirowski's argument is convincing, but the more easily understood biological images have continued to dominate the subterranean level of economic thinking that has shaped popular economic understandings and, to some degree, the discipline of economics itself.

7. The sociologist Ann Swidler has usefully suggested that each culture provides its members with a particular toolkit of ideas that individuals and groups employ to solve problems. In this sense, the metaphors are part of our culture's toolkit. See Ann Swidler, "Culture in Action," *American Sociological Review* 51 (1986): 273-86.

8. *The Affluent Society*, pp. 6-19.

2. THE SUBTERRANEAN UNDERPINNINGS OF THE CONVENTIONAL WISDOM

1. "Amazing Grace" lyrics are from Dan Fox, *Go In and Out the Window: An Illustrated Songbook for Young People*, (New York: Henry Holt, 1987), p. 11.

2. McCloskey, *If You're So Smart*, p. 12. Other authors use the term metanarrative similarly to this way of using the term allegory, but the basic idea is the same. For Margaret Somers, a certain metanarrative about citizenship has structured several

centuries worth of debates about the relationship between individuals and the state. See Margaret Somers, "Narrating/Mapping Anglo-American Citizenship Theory: The Place of Political Culture and the Public Sphere," *Sociological Theory*, forthcoming.

3. For the appearance of these allegories in art, see Adolf Katzenellenbogen, *Allegories of the Virtues and Vices in Medieval Art* (New York: Norton, 1964).

4. Max Weber, *The Protestant Ethic and the Spirit of Capitalism* (New York: Scribner's, 1958). This is, of course, an Old Testament story as well.

5. The centrality of this allegory to Methodism is discussed in E.P. Thomson, *The Making of the English Working Class* (New York: Pantheon Books, 1964), chap. 11.

6. "The chronic federal deficit is sapping our productivity at home and our ability to compete abroad. As a result, our standard of living has already begun to grow more slowly, and America's influence in world affairs has suffered. If we do nothing to correct the problem, both our standard of living and our global power will continue to weaken. Ultimately, the resulting decay will threaten our society's most fundamental values." Benjamin Friedman, *Day of Reckoning: The Consequences of American Economic Policy* (New York: Vintage, 1989), p. xiii.

7. The text was originally published in 1714. Bernard de Mandeville, *The Fable of the Bees: Or, Private Vices, Publick Benefits*, ed. F. B. Kaye (Oxford: Clarendon Press, 1924), p. 24; Adam Smith, *An Inquiry into the Nature and Causes of the Wealth of Nations* (Chicago: University of Chicago Press, 1976, [1776]), p. 18.

3. CAPITAL AS BLOOD: THE MACRO LEVEL

1. Cited in Michael Jackman, ed., *The Macmillan Book of Business and Economic Quotations* (New York: Macmillan, 1984), p. 11; Claude Menard, "The Machine and the Heart: An Essay on Analogies in Economic Reasoning," trans. from the previously published French version by Pamela Cook and Philip Mirowski, *Social Concept* 5, no. 1 (1989): 81-95. Nicholas-Francois Canard wrote *Principes d'economie politique*; *Congressional Record*, 1995, p. H4791 (accessed electronically). 104th Congress, 1st session, vol. 141, no. 77.

2. The blood metaphor was discussed in Fred Block, "Mirrors and Metaphors: The United States and Its Trade Rivals," *America at Century's End*, ed. Alan Wolfe (Berkeley: University of California Press, 1991), pp. 102-3.

3. William Harvey's work showing that blood circulated through the body was first published in 1628 (William Harvey, *The Circulation of the Blood and Other Writings*, tr. by Kenneth Franklin, London: Dent, 1963). Not surprisingly, many writers in the seventeeth, eighteenth, and nineteenth centuries elaborated the analogy between the circulation of blood and the circulation of money or capital. François Quesnay, the physiocratic economist, whose *Tableau Economique* was praised by both Adam Smith and Karl Marx, had spent much of his life as a surgeon and had been centrally involved in debates about blood circulation and the practice of bleeding. V. Foley, "An Origin of the Tableau Economique," *History of Political Economy* 5 (spring 1973): 121-50, has suggested Quesnay's theories of blood circulation influenced his economics. Timothy Alborn has recently written, "Coins and bank notes circulated during much of the early nineteenth century in more or less healthy doses, and contemporary observers seldom missed an opportunity to

compare the motion with the life-giving circulation going on in the human body." "Economic Man, Economic Machine: Images of Circulation in the Victorian Money Market," in *Natural Images in Economic Thought*, Mirowski, ed., pp. 173–96, 174.

4. Fred Block, *Postindustrial Possibilities: A Critique of Economic Discourse* (Berkeley: University of California Press, 1990), chap. 5.

5. *From Max Weber: Essays in Sociology*, ed. Hans Gerth and C. Wright Mills (New York: Oxford University Press, 1958), pp. 214-16. The classic statement on the advantages of post-bureaucratic forms of organization is Warren G. Bennis, "Beyond Bureaucracy," in Warren G. Bennis and Philip E. Slater, *The Temporary Society* (New York: Harper, 1968).

6. Maryann Keller, *Rude Awakening: The Rise, Fall, and Struggle for Recovery of General Motors* (New York: William Morris, 1989), chap. 10.

7. The tensions between organizational dynamics and technological processes are central to Shoshana Zuboff, *In the Age of the Smart Machine: The Future of Work and Power* (New York: Basic Books, 1988), and Robert J. Thomas, *What Machines Can't Do: Politics and Technology in the Industrial Enterprise* (Berkeley: University of California Press, 1994).

8. Keynes elaborated these arguments in *The General Theory*.

9. Chyuan-yuan Wu, "The Politics of Financial Development in Japan," Unpublished Ph.D. dissertation, University of Pennsylvania, 1992, pp. 112-13.

4 . CAPITAL AS BLOOD: THE MICRO LEVEL

1. *Congressional Record*, (1993), p. H3862 (accessed electronically), 104th Congress, 1st session, vol. 141, no. 14.

2. For example, firms that develop software use the same basic input—programmers, testers, and computer hardware. However, even bracketing its successes in shaping industry standards, Microsoft has been far more effective than its rivals in the efficient production of new software. For an account of the organizational practices that contribute to this higher productivity, see Michael A. Cusamano and Richard W. Selby, *Microsoft Secrets: How the World's Most Powerful Software Company Creates Technology, Shapes Markets, and Manages People* (New York: Free Press, 1995).

3. These arguments are made at greater length in Block, *Postindustrial Possibilities*.

4. The role of institutions in complementing the coordinating role of markets has been an important theme in both the recent economic and sociological literatures. For extensive references to both literatures, see Neil Smelser and Richard Swedberg, *The Handbook of Economic Sociology* (Princeton: Princeton University Press, 1994), especially chaps. 1, 3, 4, 18, and 28.

5 . THE STATE AS VAMPIRE

1. Charles Forman, *Some Queries and Observations Upon the Revolution in 1688* (London: Olive Payne, 1741), B2; *Congressional Record*, (1993), p. H3682 (accessed electronically), 103rd Congress, 1st session, vol. 139, no. 89; *Congressional Record*, (1995), p. S1260 (accessed electronically),104th Congress, 1st session, vol.141, no. 12.

2. In one recent strand of academic literature, states are referred to as predatory. See

Margaret Levi, *Of Rule and Revenue* (Berkeley: University of California Press, 1988), and James Buchanan, Robert Tollison, and Gordon Tullock, eds., *Toward a Theory of the Rent-Seeking Society* (College State: Texas A&M Press, 1980). But at least one recent book in this tradition goes a step further. See Jonathan H. Frimpong-Ansah, *The Vampire State in Africa: The Political Economy of Decline in Ghana* (London: James Currey, 1991). Ironically, the greatest popularizer of vampire imagery in the social sciences was probably Karl Marx who often used such imagery to describe the extraction of resources from the working class. For example, at the end of chapter 8 in *Capital* on the length of the working day, Marx describes the worker's realization "that in fact the creature sucking his blood will not loose its hold so long as there is a muscle, a nerve, a drop of blood to be exploited." *Capital* (London: J.M. Dent, 1930), 1: 310-11.

3. In recent months, this imagery has become increasingly explicit. Steve Forbes' stump speech in the 1996 Republican primaries uses the metaphor in reference to the IRS. "But Mr. Forbes continues to fairly mesmerize Iowa audiences with his single-theme denunciation of the Internal Revenue Code, an attack that always draws on the same Dracula specter that, word for word, he first raised at his campaign opening last year. 'Kill it, drive a stake through its heart, bury it and hope it never rises again to terrorize the American people!' he advises in his familiar peroration with his familiar unblinking smile of delight. He prescribes all but a clove of garlic, and inevitably audiences burst into applause at his imagery-filled message that a money-sucking 'monstrosity,' the graduated income tax, can be exterminated." Francis X. Clines, "Forbes? The Enemy Camp Turns Joyful," *New York Times*, 8 February 1996, p. A13.

4. This claim goes at least as far back as John Stuart Mill. "It would still remain true that in all the more advanced communities, the great majority of things are worse done by the intervention of government, than the individuals most interested in the matter would do them, or cause them to be done, if left to themselves." *Principles of Political Economy* (Oxford: Oxford University Press, 1994, [1848]), p. 331.

5. Significantly, some of the more articulate critics of the predatory nature of the central government in the U.S., such as Kevin Phillips, place much emphasis on the corrupting influence of lobbyists for private interests in Washington. While the power of this parallel government is deeply troubling, its existence is not an argument for shrinking the government, but for campaign finance reform. After all, other developed market societies appear to flourish without these legions of well-heeled lobbyists. See Phillips, *Arrogant Capital: Washington, Wall Street, and the Frustration of American Politics* (Boston: Little Brown, 1994), especially chap. 2.

6. Some of the best contemporary work is now asking these questions. See, particularly, Peter Evans' comparative discussion of the different abilities of government to guide industrial development in *Embedded Autonomy: States and Industrial Transformation* (Princeton: Princeton University Press, 1995).

7. John D. Donahue has recently reviewed the empirical studies on the relative efficiency of public and private provision of such services as garbage collection and public utilities. His conclusion is that public vs. private matters less than the amount of competition. Private monopolies tend to be less efficient than public monopolies, but private contracting tends to be more efficient than public provision. However, when public firms compete directly against private firms, they have

been able to match the efficiency of private firms. Donahue, *The Privatization Decision: Public Ends, Private Means* (New York: Basic Books, 1989). For a theoretical discussion of the relative advantages of public and private ownership, see Carl Shapiro and Robert D. Willig, "Economic Rationales for the Scope of Privatization," pp. 55-87 in Ezra N. Suleiman and John Waterbury, eds., *The Political Economy of Public Sector Reform and Privatization* (Boulder, Colo.: Westview Press, 1990).

8. Concern has been expressed recently in Romania for the reputation of the historical count on whom the Dracula legend has been based. "For Romanians, Dracula is a totally positive figure," says Christina Dinu, a 25-year-old computer programmer. "When he ruled, it was one of the most prosperous periods for Wallachia and he succeeded in completely getting rid of thieves." Carol Williams, "Romanians Feel Dracula Gets Bad Rap," *Los Angeles Times*, 25 October, 1994, p. A1.

9. See, for example, "Economic Crime Snowballs; What Can Be Done?" *The Current Digest of the Post-Soviet Press* vol. XLVI, no. 37 (October 12, 1994): 1-5.

10. This point has been made extensively by writers in the Critical Legal Studies movement. See Duncan Kennedy, "The Stakes of Law, or Hale and Foucault," in *Sexy Dressing Etc.* (Cambridge, Mass.: Harvard University Press, 1993), and Karl Klare, "Legal Theory and Democratic Reconstruction: Reflections on 1989," *University of British Columbia Law Review* 25, 1 (1991): 69-103.

11. Bob Ortega, "Retail Combat: Warehouse-Club War Leaves Few Standing," *Wall Street Journal*, 18 November 1993, p. A1.

6. SURVIVAL OF THE FITTEST
THROUGH MARKET COMPETITION:
THE FIRM

1. James E. Perella "Why American Business Works," *Vital Speeches of the Day* 57, (1990): 220; Milton Friedman, *Essays in Positive Economics* (Chicago: University of Chicago Press, 1953), p. 22.

2. Alexander Rosenberg, "Does Evolutionary Theory Give Inspiration to Economics?" *Natural Images in Economic Thought*, Philip Morowski, ed., (Cambridge: Cambridge University Press, 1994), pp. 384-407, 387 Stephen Jay Gould also writes, "We do not inhabit a perfected world where natural selection ruthlessly scrutinizes all organic structures and then molds them for optimal utility. Organisms inherit a body form and a style of embryonic development; these impose constraints upon future change and adaptation." *Hen's Teeth and Horse's Toes* (New York: Norton, 1983), p. 156.

3. See Gary Becker, *The Economics of Discrimination* (Chicago: University of Chicago Press, 1957).

4. Contributions to principal-agent theory include Armen Alchian and Harold Demsetz, "Production, Information Costs, and Economic Organization," *American Economic Review* 57 (1972): 777-795, and John Pratt and Richard Zeckhauser, *Principals and Agents* (Boston: Harvard Business School Press, 1986). Parallel arguments have been developed within the transaction cost literature. See Oliver Williamson, *Markets and Hierarchies, Analysis and Antitrust Implications* (New York: Free Press, 1975).

5. These arguments have been elaborated in the literature on "efficiency wages." George Akerlof and Janet Yellen, eds., *Efficiency Wage Models of the Labor Market* (New York: Cambridge University Press, 1986).

6. Harvey Leibenstein, *Inside the Firm: The Inefficiencies of Hierarchy* (Cambridge, Mass.: Harvard University Press, 1987).

7. James P. Womack, Daniel T. Jones, and Daniel Roos, *The Machine That Changed the World: The Story of Lean Production* (New York: Harper, 1991), pp. 93-98.

8. Harvey Leibenstein, *Beyond Economic Man: A New Foundation for Microeconomics* (Cambridge, Mass.: Harvard University Press, 1976).

9. Womack, Jones, and Roos, *The Machine that Changed the World*, p. 85.

10. Michael Porter, *Capital Choices: Changing the Way America Invests in Industry* (Washington: Council on Competitiveness, 1992), and Michael Jacobs, *Short-Term America: The Causes and Cures of Our Business Myopia* (Boston: Harvard University Business School Press, 1991).

11. One of the first to develop this argument in depth was John Zysman, *Governments, Markets, and Growth: Financial Systems and the Politics of Industrial Change* (Ithaca, N.Y.: Cornell University Press, 1983).

12. To be sure, the allocational efficiency of a stock market also depends on the rationality of investors. If, for example, they have very short time horizons, allocational efficiency will be reduced.

7. SURVIVAL OF THE FITTEST THROUGH MARKET COMPETITION: THE HUMAN SPECIES

1. Thomas Robert Malthus, *An Essay on the Principle of Population and a Summary View of the Principle of Population* (London: Penguin Books, 1985, [1798]), p. 101; *Congressional Record*, 1993, p. H6586, 103rd Congress, 1st session, vol. 139, no. 117.

2. Some of these arguments are traced in Benjamin Hunnicutt, *Work Without End: Abandoning Shorter Hours for the Right to Work* (Philadelphia, Pa.: Temple University Press, 1988), and Fred Block, "Technological Change and Employment: New Perspectives on an Old Controversy," *Economia & Lavoro* XVIII: 3 (1984): 3-21.

3. The Conventional Wisdom has been forcefully attacked by two recent books, Jeremy Rifkin, *The End of Work: The Decline of the Global Labor Force and the Dawn of the Post-Market Era* (New York: G.P. Putnams, 1995), and Stanley Aronowitz and William DiFazio, *The Jobless Future: Sci-Tech and the Dogma of Work* (Minneapolis, Minn.: University of Minnesota Press, 1994).

4. John Maynard Keynes, "Economic Possibilities for Our Grandchildren," (1930) in *Essays in Persuasion* (New York: Norton, 1963), p. 364.

5. Ibid. p. 366.

6. Ibid. p. 371.

7. See Juliet Schor, *The Overworked American: The Unexpected Decline of Leisure* (New York: Basic Books, 1991).

8. Block, "Technological Change and Employment."

9. While Schor argues that there has been little change in the time demands of housework, her data show a downward trend in housewives' weekly hours. *The*

Overworked American, pp. 86-88.

10. This was an important theme in the pioneering studies of Solomon Fabricant on productivity changes. Solomon Fabricant, *Employment in Manufacturing, 1899-1939* (New York: National Bureau of Economic Research, 1942).

11. "Economic Possibilities for Our Grandchildren," p. 366.

8. THE COUNTERNARRATIVE OF CONSCIOUS ADAPTATION

1. "Our Obsolete Market Mentality," reprinted in *Primitive, Archaic and Modern Economies: Essays of Karl Polanyi*, ed. George Dalton (Boston, MA: Beacon, 1971), p. 60; Franklin Delano Roosevelt, *Fireside Chats* (New York: Penguin Press, 1995), p. 31.

2. Barbara Ehrenreich, *Fear of Falling: The Inner Life of the Middle Class* (New York: Pantheon, 1989).

3. See Jeffrey Alexander's useful assessment of postmodernism in *Fin de Siecle Social Theory: Relativism, Reduction and the Problem of Reason* (London: Verso, 1995).

4. The view of Marxism as a secularized version of Christian doctrine is a familiar theme in the literature. See, especially, Robert C. Tucker, *Philosophy and Myth in Karl Marx* (Cambridge: Cambridge University Press, 1961).

5. Some caution is advisable here, since Marxism has resurrected itself several times after its obituaries had already been written.

6. This third position overlaps substantially with the tradition of philosophical pragmatism as exemplified by John Dewey. See Robert Westbrook, *John Dewey and American Democracy* (Ithaca, N.Y.: Cornell University Press, 1991).

7. Abraham H. Maslow, *Toward a Psychology of Being* (Princeton: Van Nostrand Company, 1962).

9. A FAMILY OF COUNTERMETAPHORS

1. Jose Ortega y Gasset, *The Dehumanization of Art*, cited in John Bartlett, *Familiar Quotations*, 16th ed. (Boston: Little, Brown, 1992), p. 653.

2. Recent, albeit still controversial, economic research even calls into question the claim that higher minimum wages reduce job creation. See David Card and Alan Krueger, *Myth and Measurement: The New Economics of the Minimum Wage* (Princeton: Princeton University Press, 1995).

3. This concept is elaborated in Block, *Postindustrial Possibilities*, pp. 175-77.

4. See Charles Sabel, "Bootstrapping Reform: Rebuilding Firms, the Welfare State, and Unions," *Politics & Society* 23:1 (March 1995): 5-48.

5. For a similar argument about the time-limited nature of any particular government policy, see Albert Hirschman, *A Propensity to Self-Subversion* (Cambridge, Mass.: Harvard University Press, 1995), pp. 148-49.

6. Past policies do create institutional and political legacies that diminish the choices available in the present. Hence, a new regime cannot choose a new policy direction as though the slate were completely blank. However, recent history provides numerous examples of new governments that have made sharp turns on key issues of economic policy.

10. THE LOGIC AND ILLOGIC OF AUSTERITY

1. Edmund Burke, "Letter to a Noble Lord," cited in Bartlett, *Familiar Quotations*, p. 332.

2. One common strategy for accomplishing austerity is to slow the domestic economy by pushing up interest rates. This tends to depress standards of living by increasing unemployment and slowing wage gains. Reductions in government spending can also have the same consequences. Note that while conservatives in the U.S. have been rhetorically opposed to tax increases, they have been extremely supportive of disguised tax increases that force consumers to pay more out of their own pockets for public higher education, health care, or other vital services. Usually, the burden of these disguised tax increases falls most heavily on poor and lower income households.

3. The calculation for 1947 is based on Gross National Product rather than GDP. The Clinton administration's fiscal year 1996 budget anticipated that federal spending would decline from 22% of GDP to 20.7% of GDP in 2000. The budget plan passed by the Republicans anticipated that federal spending in 2000 would be $126.8 billion less than proposed in the Clinton budget—or approximately 19.4% of GDP. To be sure, such projections of government spending and GDP growth are notoriously inaccurate, and it is even more difficult to anticipate trends in state and local spending. Data are from *Economic Report to the President, Budget of the U.S. Government 1996: Historical Tables*, and David Rogers and Christopher Georges, "Gingrich Says Clinton Must Move Right on Budget," *Wall Street Journal*, 21 November 1995, p. A2.

4. This kind of conversion is difficult to carry out, especially because defense firms are not used to the rigors of market competition, but it is not impossible. See Ann Markusen and Joel Yudken, *Dismantling the Cold War Economy* (New York: Basic Books, 1992).

5. Spending on non-defense physical infrastructure in the U.S. has been declining as a share of GDP since the late 1960s. Alicia H. Munnell, "An Assessment of Trends in and Economic Impacts of Infrastructure Investment," pp 21-54 in Organization for Economic Cooperation and Development, *Infrastructure Policies for the 1990s* (Paris: OECD, 1993). Similarly, total federal spending for physical capital, research and development, and education and training are estimated to be 1.9% of GDP in 1996 as compared to 2.8% in 1976. *Budget of the United States Government, Historical Tables, Fiscal Year 1996*, p. 122. Munnell also reports that in Japan, government physical capital outlays alone have been more than 6% of GDP through the 1970s and 1980s, and in West Germany, the rate fluctuated between 4% and 6% of GDP. In short, Japan was investing physical capital in the public sector at triple the U.S. rate while Germany was investing at least double the U.S. rate.

6. Michael Dertouzos, Richard K. Lester, and Robert M. Solow, *Made in America: Regaining the Competitive Edge* (Cambridge, Mass.: MIT Press, 1989), pp 264-66.

7. For a careful review of the inadequacies of existing levels of investments in education and training, see David. W. Hornbeck and Lester M. Salamon, eds., *Human Capital and America's Future* (Baltimore, Md.: Johns Hopkins University Press, 1991).

11. SELECTIVE MISMEASUREMENT

1. Cited in George Brockway, *Economists Can Be Bad for Your Health* (New York: Norton, 1995), p. 57.

2. I have made similar arguments in "Postindustrial Development and the Obsolescence of Economic Categories," in *Revising State Theory: Essays in Politics and Postindustrialism* (Philadelphia: Temple University Press, 1987), pp. 142-70, and in *Postindustrial Possibilities*.

3. The issue of quality comes up repeatedly in Dertouzos, Lester, and Solow, *Made in America: Regaining the Productive Edge* (Cambridge, Mass.: MIT Press, 1989).

4. Block, *Postindustrial Possibilities*, chap. 5.

5. Bruce R. Guile and James Brian Quinn, eds., *Technology in Services: Policies for Growth, Trade, and Employment* (Washington, D.C.: National Academy Press, 1988).

6. The neglect of costless quality changes in official price indexes is discussed by Zvi Griliches in "Comment," *The U.S. National Income and Product Accounts*, Murray F. Foss, ed. (Chicago: University of Chicago Press, 1983), pp 143-44; Dennis Fixler, "The Consumer Price Index, Underlying Concepts and Caveats," *Monthly Labor Review* 116, no. 12 (December 1993): 3-12; United States Congress, Senate Committee on Finance *Consumer Price Index*, 104th Congress, 1st session, March 13, April 6, and June 6, 1995.

7. The argument that our consumer price index (CPI) overstates the rate of inflation now appears to be moving from the margins of economic discourse to the political center. The Senate Finance Committee recently appointed a bipartisan panel of economists to examine whether the CPI overstates inflation. The panel, headed by Michael Boskin who chaired the Council of Economic Advisers in the Bush administration, provided a "best estimate" that the overstatement was about one point. Hence, when the CPI indicates inflation of 3%, the actual rate of inflation was only 2%. (Robert Hershey, Jr., "Panel Sees a Corrected Price Index as Deficit-Cutter," *New York Times*, 15 September 1995, p. A30). Congressional interest in this question is clearly driven by the pressures of balancing the federal budget. The Boskin panel suggested that correcting the bias in the CPI—including reducing cost-of-living adjustments for Social Security—would save $634 billion over the next ten years. This would greatly simplify the task of balancing the budget. Dean Baker, an economist at the Economic Policy Institute, has suggested that there might be ways in which the CPI understates inflation. However, his most telling argument is that if the CPI has been overstating inflation, then our economy has been performing better than we thought and there is far less reason to contemplate drastic budget cuts. Dean Baker, "The Inflated Case Against the CPI," *The American Prospect*, winter 1996, pp. 86-89.

12. WHY WELLBEING DOES NOT COUNT

1. Herman E. Daly and John B. Cobb, Jr., *For the Common Good: Redirecting the Economy Toward Community, the Environment, and a Sustainable Future* (Boston, MA: Beacon Press, 1989), p. 69; Marilyn Waring, *If Women Counted: A New Feminist Economics* (San Francisco: Harper Collins, 1988), p. 8.

2. This line of argument has been brilliantly elaborated by Tibor Scitovsky, *The Joyless Economy: An Inquiry Into Human Satisfaction and Consumer Dissatisfaction* (New York: Oxford University Press, 1976).

3. Christopher Jencks, Lauri Perman, and Lee Rainwater, "What Is a Good Job? A New Measure of Labor Market Success," *American Journal of Sociology* 93, no. 6 (May 1988): 1322-57.

4. Wallace C. Peterson, *Silent Depression: The Fate of the American Dream* (New York: W.W. Norton, 1994), p. 103. See also Frank Levy and Richard Murnane, "U.S. Earnings Levels and Earnings Inequality: A Review of Recent Trends and Proposed Explanations," *Journal of Economic Literature* XXX (Sept. 1992): 1333-81. On rising wealth inequality, see Edward N. Wolff, *Top Heavy: A Study of the Increasing Inequality of Wealth in America* (New York: The Twentieth Century Fund Press, 1995). Not only has inequality worsened in the U.S., but comparisons show that the gap between highly-paid workers and low-paid workers is greater in the U.S. than in fifteen other developed market economies. Keith Bradsher, "Widest Gap in Incomes? Research Points to U.S.," *New York Times*, 27 October 1995, p. D2.

5. Robert Reich, *The Work of Nations: Preparing Ourselves for 21st-century Capitalism* (New York: Knopf, 1991), chaps. 23-24.

13. WHAT WILL GETTING RID OF THE DEFICIT DO FOR US?

1. William Ford, "Looking Beyond the Current Recovery," *Vital Speeches of the Day*, 1983, vol. 49, no. 21, p. 656; Jacob Viner, "Inflation as a Remedy for Depression," cited in *A Dictionary of Economic Quotations*, Simon James, ed. (London: Croom Helm), pp. 90-91.

2. The breakdown of state and local government spending by function is in the *Economic Report to the President*, Table B-81. Data on federal infrastructure spending are in *Budget of the U.S. Government, Fiscal Year 1996: Historical Tables*, Table 9.1.

3. Similar arguments have been made by Robert Heilbroner and Peter Bernstein, *The Debt and the Deficit: False Alarms/Real Possibilities* (New York: W.W. Norton, 1989). See also Robert Eisner, *How Real Is the Federal Deficit?* (New York: Free Press, 1986).

4. Eisner, *How Real Is the Federal Deficit?*, chap. 12.

5. See, for example, David Calleo, *The Bankrupting of America: How the Federal Budget Is Impoverishing the Nation* (New York: William Morrow, 1992), and Friedman, *Day of Reckoning*.

6. See the analysis and works cited in Steven M. Fazzari, "Monetary Policy, Financial Structure, and Investment," pp. 35-63 in *Transforming the U.S. Financial System: Equity and Efficiency for the 21st Century*, eds. Gary Dymski, Gerald Epstein, and Robert Pollin, eds.(Armonk, N.Y.: M.E. Sharpe, 1993).

7. The effective federal tax rate on corporate profits fell from 36.3% in 1980 to 24.7% in 1992. Calculated from Tables B-79 and B-90 in *Economic Report to the President 1994*. Bond interest rates are reported in Table B-72 in the same source. Moreover, real interest rates on bonds also fell from 1982 to 1992.

8. See the sources cited in chapter 10, footnote 5. In an influential paper, David Alan Aschauer has shown the importance of public capital in productivity. See "Is Public Expenditure Productive?" *Journal of Monetary Economics* 23 (March 1989): 177-200.

9. Porter, *Capital Choices*; Louis Lowenstein, *Sense and Nonsense in Corporate Finance* (Reading, Mass.: Addison-Wesley, 1991), chap. 10.

10. Most observers also neglect the important role played by government debt in the financial system. If the opportunity to invest in government bonds did not exist, investors looking for safe returns would have no choice but to purchase far riskier private bonds. In short, the accumulated government debt plays a necessary and desirable role of providing a safe interest-earning asset.

14. THE ALLEGED SAVINGS DECLINE

1. Lawrence Summers and Chris Carroll, "Why is U.S. National Saving So Low?" *Brooking Papers on Economic Activity* 1987, no. 2: 607-35; *Congressional Record*, September 30, 1991, p. S 13958, 102nd Congress, 1st session, vol. 137, no 137; Keynes, *The General Theory*, p. 373.

2. These arguments are elaborated at length in B. Douglas Bernheim, *The Vanishing Nest Egg: Reflections on Saving in America* (New York: Priority Press Publications, 1991).

3. For critiques of the conventional saving story, see Fred Block and Robert Heilbroner, "The Myth of a Savings Shortage," *The American Prospect*, spring 1992, 101-06, and Fred Block, "Did Household Saving Really Decline in the Reagan Years?" *Review of Radical Political Economy*, 27, no. 4 (1995): 36-54. Several other observers have questioned the Conventional Wisdom on this issue. See Phillips, *Arrogant Capital*, pp. 128-37 and Robert J. Samuelson, "Whining About Boomers' Savings," *Washington Post National Weekly Edition*, 7-13 August 1995, p. 5.

4. On Japan, see William Tabb, *The Postwar Japanese System: Cultural Economy and Economic Transformation* (New York: Oxford University Press, 1995), pp. 102-11. For the U.S. Table B-26 in *Economic Report to the President* shows that gross business saving is often four times greater than personal saving.

5. Edward N. Wolff and Marcia Marley, "Long-Term Trends in U.S. Wealth Inequality: Methodological Issues and Results," pp. 765-839 in Helen Stone Tice, Robert E. Lipsey, eds., *The Measurement of Saving, Investment, and Wealth* (Chicago: University of Chicago Press, 1989).

6. Board of Governors of the Federal Reserve System, *Balance Sheets for the U.S. Economy 1945-94* (June 1995), Table B-100.

7. Despite the vast sums going into these pension plans, there are deep and serious problems with the private pension system. The Employee Retirement Income Security Act of 1974 was supposed to protect employee pension rights, but in this recent period of corporate restructuring, firms have found ways to escape from their pension obligations. Gordon Clark, *Pensions and Corporate Restructuring in American Industry: A Crisis of Regulation* (Baltimore, Md.: Johns Hopkins, 1993). Moreover, many companies have shifted from defined benefit to defined contribution plans that provide employees with a less secure future.

8. Tibor Scitovsky, "Why the U.S. Saving Rate Is Low — A Conflict Between the National Accountant's and the Individual Saver's Perceptions," pp. 125-34, in Jon S. Cohen and G.C. Harcourt, eds., *International Monetary Problems and Supply-Side Economics*, (London: Macmillan, 1986).
9. Block, "Did Household Saving Really Decline in the Reagan Years?"
10. Board of Governors, *Balance Sheets* (June 1995), Table R-100.
11. The data on wealth holding comes from the 1983 and 1989 Surveys of Consumer Finance, as reported by Arthur B. Kennickell and R. Louise Woodburn, "Estimation of Household Net Worth Using Model-Based and Design-Based Weights: Evidence From the 1989 Survey of Consumer Finances," unpublished technical paper available from the Board of Governors of the Federal Reserve Board, 1992. The estimates provided in this section are based on a re-analysis of this data that adjusts for inflation and changes in asset prices. These results are consistent with the analysis of the same data in Wolff, *Top Heavy*, pp. 10-13.

15. ALTERNATIVES TO AUSTERITY

1. Robert Heilbroner and Peter Bernstein, *The Debt and the Deficit*, p. 15.
2. This theme runs through much contemporary analysis of U.S. business. See, for example, Bennett Harrison, *Lean and Mean: The Changing Landscape of Corporate Power in the Age of Flexibility* (New York: Basic Books, 1994), and Eileen Applebaum and Rosemary Batt, *The New American Workplace: Transforming Work Systems in the U.S.* (Ithaca, N.Y.: ILR Press, 1994).
3. In 1989, the most efficient U.S. auto plants required less than nineteen hours of direct labor in automobile assembly. Womack, Jones, and Roos, *The Machine That Changed the World*, p. 85.
4. Even when one controls for intelligence, children from the poorest backgrounds are significantly less likely to go to college than children from wealthier backgrounds. William H. Sewell and Vimal P. Shah, "Socioeconomic Status, Intelligence, and the Attainment of Higher Education," pp. 197-215, in Jerome Karabel and A.H. Halsey, eds. *Power and Ideology in Education* (New York: Oxford University Press, 1977).
5. Bob Woodward, *The Agenda: Inside the Clinton White House* (New York: Simon and Schuster, 1994), pp 80-92.

16. FINANCE: GROWING LIKE A WEED

1. Joseph Stiglitz, *Whither Socialism?* (Cambridge, Mass.: MIT, 1994), p. 211; Kevin Phillips, *Arrogant Capital*, p. 100.
2. Sarah Lubman and John R. Emshwiller, "Hubris and Ambition in Orange County: Robert Citron's Story," *Wall Street Journal*, 18 January 1995, p. A8.
3. For an overview of the regulatory issues in constructing financial markets, see Jane W. D'Arista, *The Evolution of U.S. Finance,* vol. 2 (Armonk, N.Y.: M.E. Sharp, 1994).
4. Recent exceptions have occurred with high-tech entrepreneurs becoming multi-millionaires very quickly by selling shares in firms that promise to be the Microsoft of the next decade. But these are also cases of financial enrichment, since the wealth

flows in on the promise of future profits, not as a consequence of actual profits.

5. Giovanni Arrighi, *The Long Twentieth Century* (London: Verso, 1994). See also Phillips, *Arrogant Capital*.
6. Data are calculated from "Employment by Industry," *Statistical Abstract 1994*, p. 412, and *Historical Statistics of the U.S.: Colonial Times to 1970*, vol. 1, p. 137.
7. For an excellent analysis of these nonbank banks, see Jane W. D'Arista and Tom Schlesinger, "The Parallel Banking System," p. 157-99 in Gary Dymski, Gerald Epstein, and Robert Pollin, eds. *Transforming the U.S. Financial System: Equity and Efficiency for the 21st Century* (Armonk, N.Y.: ME Sharpe, 1993)
8. Michael Lewis, *Liar's Poker: Rising Through the Wreckage on Wall Street* (New York: Penguin, 1990), p. 24.

17. BAD INFORMATION DRIVES OUT GOOD

1. John Maynard Keynes, *The General Theory*, p. 155.
2. Recently, however, economists have developed analyses that recognize that economic actors usually have imperfect or inaccurate information and that the costs of improving one's information can be significant. This is the basis of much of the analysis in Stiglitz, *Whither Socialism?*
3. The key critique was developed in B. Greenwald and J.E. Stiglitz, "Informational Imperfections in Capital Markets and Macro-economic Fluctuations," *American Economic Review* 74 (1984): 194-99.
4. These arguments about bank monitoring draw heavily on Porter, *Capital Choices*, and Stiglitz, *Whither Socialism?*
5. This is discussed in the literature under the rubric of "signalling." Michael Spence, *Market Signalling: The Informational Structure of Hiring and Related Processes* (Cambridge, Mass.: Harvard University Press, 1974).
6. How firms deal with these pressures from shareholders is discussed by Michael Useem, *Executive Defense: Shareholder Power & Corporate Reorganization* (Cambridge, Mass.: Harvard University Press, 1993), especially, pp. 136-44.
7. Richard Florida and Martin Kenney, *The Breakthrough Illusion: Corporate America's Failure to Move from Innovation to Mass Production* (New York: Basic Books, 1990).

18. THE PROBLEM OF FINANCIAL DICTATORSHIP

1. Woodward, *The Agenda*, p. 84.
2. Keynes, *The General Theory*, p. 156.
3. Karen Pennar, "Why Investors Stampede," *Business Week*, 13 February 1995, pp. 84-85.
4. Robert E. Wood has analyzed this power with the concept of "strategic nonlending." "Foreign Aid and the Capitalist State in Underdeveloped Countries," *Politics & Society* 10, no. 1 (1980): 1-34.
5. The chronic reluctance of banks to lend to small businesses has led periodically to discussions of creating new government-sponsored enterprises to expand such credits in much the same way that government agencies have helped facilitate the expansion of housing and student loans. Andrew Taylor, "Lawmakers Seek

Way to Spur Small-Business Loans," *Congressional Quarterly Weekly Report* 51: 18 (May 1, 1993), pp. 1072-75.

6. *The Rating Game: Report of the Twentieth Century Fund Task Force on Municipal Bond Credit Ratings* (New York, Twentieth Century Fund, 1974).

7. Fazzari, "Monetary Policy, Financial Structure, and Investment."

19. WEEDS RUNNING WILD: SPECULATIVE FRENZIES

1. John Kenneth Galbraith, *The Culture of Contentment* (Boston, Houghton Mifflin, 1992), pp 163-64.

2. Some of the sociological literature on asset price booms is cited in Mark S. Mizruchi and Linda Brewster Stearns, "Money, Banking, and Financial Markets," pp. 313-41 in Smelser and Swedberg, eds., *The Handbook of Economic Sociology*. The classical work in economics is Charles P. Kindleberger, *Manias, Panics, and Crashes: A History of Financial Crises* (New York: Basic Books, 1978). On Japan's recent boom, see Douglas Stone and William T. Ziemba, "Land and Stock Prices in Japan," *Journal of Economic Perspectives* 7:3 (Summer 1993): 149-65.

3. The final cost of the S&L bailout changes over time as the government sells off assets from seized financial institutions. Paul Krugman estimated the cost in 1989 at $166 billion. Paul Krugman, *The Age of Diminished Expectations: U.S. Economic Policy in the 1990s* (Cambridge, Mass.: MIT Press, 1992), p. 138. Data on bank lending are from *Statistical Abstract 1994*, Table no. 781.

4. Robert E. Wood, *From Marshall Plan to Debt Crisis: Foreign Aid and Development Choices in the World Economy* (Berkeley: University of California Press, 1986). For the consequences of the debt crisis, see John Walton and David Seddon, *Free Markets and Food Riots: The Politics of Global Adjustment* (Oxford: Blackwell, 1994).

5. Steven K. Kaplan and Jeremy C. Stein, "The Evolution of Buyout Pricing and Financial Structure in the 1980s," *Quarterly Journal of Economics* 108, no. 2 (May 1993): 313-57.

20. GLOBAL OVERDOSING

1. Cited in Steve Dryden, *Trade Warriors: USTR and the American Crusade for Free Trade* (New York: Oxford University Press, 1995), p. 387.

2. There are some international banking havens that place almost no restrictions on the movement of goods and capital. While such havens have some of the trappings of national sovereignty, they are not "real" national entities.

3. On the contrary, the successes of the East Asian economies of Japan, South Korea, and Taiwan provide powerful evidence that the most dynamic economic growth can occur within quite elaborate regulatory structures. See Robert Wade, *Governing the Market: Economic Theory and the Role of Government in East Asian Industrialization* (Princeton: Princeton University Press, 1990); Evans, *Embedded Autonomy*.

4. One of the best accounts of U.S. efforts to pursue the large-dose version of free trade is in Robert Kuttner, *The End of Laissez-Faire: National Purpose and the*

Global Economy After the Cold War (New York: Knopf, 1991). For the theory behind the large-dose vision, see Milton and Rose Friedman, *Free to Choose* (New York: Avon Books, 1981), chap. 3.

5. David Vogel has recently argued on the basis of case studies that increased international economic integration can strengthen national regulatory policies such as consumer and environmental rules. Vogel, *Trading Up: Consumer and Environmental Regulation in a Global Economy* (Cambridge, Mass.: Harvard University Press, 1995). This line of argument is consistent with a small-dose version of free trade.

21. OVERSELLING THE CURE

1. Robert Kuttner, *The Economic Illusion: False Choices Between Prosperity and Social Justice* (Boston, Houghton-Mifflin, 1984), p 128.

2. From 1979 to 1988, there was no growth in West Germany's total civilian employed labor force. Growth did resume at the end of the 1980s. Organization for Economic Cooperation and Development, *Labour Force Statistics 1973-1993*, pp 222-23.

3. A United Nations study showed that U.S. trade with nine export-oriented developing countries followed this pattern in the period from 1973 to 1980 — U.S. job losses in labor-intensive industries more than offset job gains in capital-intensive industries. However, at that time, the study showed net job gains when U.S. trade with all developing countries was analyzed. United Nations Industrial Development Organization, *Industry and Development Global Report 1986* cited on pp. 182-84 in Ray Marshall, "Jobs: The Shifting Structure of Global Employment," pp. 167-94 in John W. Sewell and Stuart K. Tucker, eds., *Growth, Exports, and Jobs in a Changing World Economy* (New Brunswick, N.J.: Transaction Books, 1988). For a discussion of inequality in Japan, see John Bauer and Andrew Mason, "The Distribution of Income and Wealth in Japan" *Review of Income and Wealth* 38:4 (December 1992): 403–428. They report that high income Japanese face a marginal tax rate of 65%

22. UPPING THE DOSAGE:
FREE TRADE IN FINANCE

1. Committee for Economic Development, *Breaking New Ground in U.S. Trade Policy* (Boulder, Colo.: Westview Press, 1991); John M. Berry and Clay Chandler, "Trying to Cool the 'Hot Money' Game: There's Growing Fear That International Currency Traders Could Trigger a Crisis," *Washington Post National Weekly Edition*, 24-30 April 1995, pp. 20-21.

2. Robert Zevin, "Are World Financial Markets More Open? If So, Why and With What Effects," pp. 43-83, and Gerald A. Epstein and Juliet B. Schor, "Structural Determinants and Economic Effects of Capital Controls in OECD Countries," pp. 136-61 in eds., Tariq Banuri and Juliet B. Schor, *Financial Openness and National Autonomy: Opportunities and Constraints* (Oxford: Clarendon Press, 1992).

3. Craig Torres and David Wessel, "U.S. Considers Additional Aid for Mexico, Limits on Foreign Banks Could Be Loosened," *Wall Street Journal*, 29 December 1994, p. A3.

4. James Buchanan has even gone farther and argued that liberty requires that governments protect property holders from domestic inflation that might erode the value of their assets. James M. Buchanan, *Property as a Guarantor of Liberty* (Aldershot, England: Edward Elgar, 1993).

5. "Foreign Exchange Trades Grew 50% in Past 3 Years," *Wall Street Journal*, 24 October 1995, p. A19.

6. "Pound's Loss Had Winner," *New York Times*, 27 October 1992, p. D9.

7. R. Jeffery Smith and Clay Chandler, "Washington's Siesta: Was the Clinton Administration Snoozing While the Mexican Peso Went South?" *Washington Post National Weekly Edition*, 20-26 February 1995, pp. 8-9.

8. "Tokyo Shares Lose 1.1% in More Profit-Taking on Quake Theme," *Wall Street Journal*, 9 February 1995, p. C13.

9. An extensive literature has documented this declining effectiveness of government policies under an international regime of free-capital mobility. See, particularly, Fritz Scharpf, *Crisis and Choice in European Social Democracy* (Ithaca, NY: Cornell University Press, 1991); Eric Helleiner, *States and the Reemergence of Global Finance: From Bretton Woods to the 1990s* (Ithaca, N.Y.: Cornell University Press, 1994).

23. WEAKENING LOCAL ECONOMICS

1. Ronald I. McKinnon, "Flood of Dollars, Sunken Pesos," *New York Times*, 20 January 1995, op-ed column.

2. Bryan Sudweeks, *Equity Market Development in Developing Countries* (New York: Praeger, 1989).

3. Kindleberger, *Manias, Panics, and Crashes*, chap. 9.

4. The U.S. secretary of the treasury responded to the Mexican crisis by proposing the creation of an international superfund of $52 billion that would be able to serve as a lender of last resort when international financial panics occur. However, the political obstacles to Rubin's plan are formidable. "Robert Rubin's Uphhill Fight for No More Mexicos," *Business Week*, 23 October 1995, p. 57.

5. Paul Krugman, *Exchange Rate Instability* (Cambridge, Mass.: MIT Press, 1990).

24. BEYOND STALEMATE

1. Robert Heilbroner, *Visions of the Future: The Distant Past, Yesterday, Today, and Tomorrow* (New York: Oxford University Press, 1995), p. 119.

2. For some examples, see Walton and Seddon, *Free Markets and Food Riots*.

3. Stephen Pizzo, Mary Fricker, and Paul Muolo, *Inside Job: The Looting of America's Savings & Loans* (New York: Harper, 1991).

4. The revolutionary ideal of fraternity has to be reimagined to recognize the shared humanity of both men and women and people of all races and nationalities.

2 5 . T O W A R D A S H A R E D V I S I O N :
A P R A C T I C A L U T O P I A

1. Cited in Karl Polyani, *The Great Transformation: The Political and Economic Origins of Our Time* (Boston: Beacon, 1957, [1944]), p. 258B.
2. These figures are calculated on the basis of 1994 occupational statistics published in U.S. Department of Labor, *Employment and Earnings.*
3. It is difficult to estimate the percentage of the current labor force that is engaged in producing internationally traded commodities. In theory, virtually all manufactured goods could be imported, and with advances in global communications, much knowledge production and information-processing work could also be done abroad.
4. See the works cited in chap. 15, note 2.
5. This was — until recently — the strategy of northern European social democracies such as Sweden.
6. If such behavior became a real problem, stronger measures could be taken. Adults could be required to put in a certain number of hours of community service to qualify for their transfer payments.

2 6 . B E Y O N D T H E E C O N O M Y :
O T H E R D I M E N S I O N S O F T H E V I S I O N

1. Michael Walzer, *Spheres of Justice: A Defense of Plurality and Equality* (New York: Basic Books, 1983).
2. This inegalitarian vision is close to Robert Reich's description of the U.S. in *The Work of Nations.* He argues that the top 20% of U.S. employees are successful competing in the global market and drawing large salaries, while the bottom 80% experience stagnating or declining living standards because they lack world-class skills.
3. Calculated from data in "Executive Pay: The Party Ain't Over Yet," *Business Week* 26, April 1993, pp. 56-57.
4. For a discussion of inequality in Japan, see John Bauer and Andrew Mason, "The Distribution of Income and Wealth in Japan," *Review of Income and Wealth* 38:4 (December 1992): 403-28. They report that high-income Japanese face a marginal tax rate of 65%.
5. From World War II to 1964, the highest marginal tax rate in the U.S. was 91%. The 1981 Tax Reform lowered the marginal tax on unearned income from 70% to 50%. Kevin Phillips, *The Politics of Rich and Poor: Wealth and the American Electorate in the Reagan Aftermath* (New York: Harper, 1991), pp. 77-79.
6. Government has to respond to people's preferences as to whether increased output should be realized as more goods and services or as an increased supply of noncommodity outputs such as environmental preservation and voluntary leisure time.
7. For an excellent account of the distortion of current campaign finance as well as reform proposals, see Dan Clawson, Alan Neustadtl, and Denise Scott, *Money Talks: Corporate PACs and Political Influence* (New York: Basic Books, 1992).
8. Wood, *From Marshall Plan to Debt Crisis.*
9. Maria Otero and Elisabeth Rhyne, eds., *The New World of Microenterprise*

Finance: Building Healthy Financial Institutions for the Poor (West Hartford, Conn.: Kumarian Press, 1994).

10. This was the logic behind the Brandt Commission Report. Willy Brandt et al., *Common Crisis North-South: Cooperation for World Recovery* (Cambridge Mass.: MIT Press, 1983).

27. IS THIS VISION PRACTICAL?

1. John Maynard Keynes, "Liberalism and Labour," *Essays in Persuasion* (New York: Norton, 1963), p. 344; Robert Dahl, *A Preface to Economic Democracy* (Berkeley, University of California Press, 1985), p. 51.

2. Steven Solomon, *The Confidence Game: How Unelected Central Bankers Are Governing the Changed World Economy* (New York: Simon and Schuster, 1995).

3. In U.S. politics, "economic liberals" are conservatives who want to give the broadest scope to the market. They have historically been opposed by "political liberals" who believe that markets need to be regulated by governments.

4. Roberto Mangabeira Unger, *Social Theory: Its Situation and Its Task* (Cambridge: Cambridge University Press, 1987).

5. For a discussion of equality of opportunity that recognizes that society should only make adjustments for inequalities that are beyond the control of the individual, see John Roemer, "Equality and Responsibility," *Boston Review* April/May 1995, pp. 3-7.

6. The idea that inequalities in one sphere should not spill over into other spheres is elaborated in Walzer, *Spheres of Justice*.

7. The Supreme Court's unanimous recognition that employees have the right to be free of sexual coercion at the workplace can be seen as part of a historical process that redefines the employment relation moving away from a master-and-servant model in which the employer can demand anything of an employee that has not been previously defined as excessive.

   Defining what constitutes degrading and coercive work conditions is obviously a thorny problem. While it might be easy to get consensus that people should be protected from selling themselves into prostitution, agreement is less likely in the case of backbreaking farm labor at minimum wage with a tyrannical overseer who denies workers bathroom breaks. The solution is to recognize that such standards must change over time, and that what might have simply been considered ordinary hard work several generations ago is no longer acceptable.

8. The theory behind these changes has been discussed by Larry Hirschhorn, *Beyond Mechanization* (Cambridge, Mass.: MIT Press, 1984); Zuboff, *In the Age of the Smart Machine*. For descriptions of the process, see Sabel, "Bootstrapping Reform," and Eileen Applebaum and Rosemary Batt, *The New American Workplace*.

9. Social scientists have known for a long time that even highly bureaucratic organizations work in ways that diverge substantially from their organizational charts and written rules. But the shift away from bureaucratic work organization is completely different from this standard insight.

28. THE ROAD FORWARD

1. Lawrence Goodwyn, *The Populist Movement: A Short History of the Agrarian Revolt in America* (New York: Oxford University Press, 1978), pp. xvii-xviii.
2. Tightened regulation also means enforcing federal laws that prohibit employers from hiring foreigners who lack official status as legal immigrants. There is a fundamental conflict between effective legal regulation of workplaces and allowing large numbers of undocumented immigrants to enter the labor force.
3. For example, Laurie P. Cohen, "Kenneth Dart Forsakes U.S. for Belize," *Wall Street Journal,* 28 March 1994, p. C1.
4. Robert Pollin, "Public Credit Allocation Through the Federal Reserve: Why It Is Needed; How It Should Be Done," pp. 321-54 in Dymski, Epstein, and Pollin, eds., *Transforming the U.S. Financial System*; Fred Block, "Capitalism Without Class Power," *Politics & Society* 20, no. 3 (September 1992): 277-304.
5. The historic model is the Federal Housing Authority and the Veterans' Administration that provided sufficient protection so that private institutions were willing to take substantial risks in the area of mortgage lending.
6. James Tobin, "A Proposal for International Monetary Reform," *Eastern Economic Journal* 4 (July-October 1978): pp 153-59.
7. Such provisions for the return of illegal flight capital were included in early drafts of the plan for Bretton Woods. Fred Block, *The Origins of International Economic Disorder* (Berkeley: University of California Press, 1977), p. 45.
8. See the proposal by Robert Pollin and Dean Baker, "Taxing the Big Casino," *The Nation,* May 9, 1994, pp. 622-24.
9. This idea is elaborated at greater length in Block, "Capitalism Without Class Power."
10. Employees would need free-speech rights at the workplace and protection against arbitrary dismissal or demotion. The free-speech rights would also have to be qualified by the need for confidential treatment of certain types of information such as trade secrets. But there are mechanisms to balance these competing imperatives. University faculty, for example, have broad free-speech rights, but they are also subject to penalties for the failure to maintain confidentiality in personnel matters.
11. A negative income tax provides transfers to individuals whose income falls below a certain target level. For a review of recent debates on the topic, see Philippe Van Parijs, ed., *Arguing for Basic Income* (London: Verso, 1992).
12. In addition, the NIT would require that another $40 to $50 billion of tax burden be shifted to higher-income households. Fred Block and Jeff Manza, "Ending Welfare as We Know It: The Case for a Negative Income Tax" (paper presented at the American Sociological Association meetings, August 1995, Washington D.C.).

29. CONCLUSION

1. *The General Theory*, p. 383.